Contemporary Paganism

Contemporary Paganism: Minority Religions in a Majoritarian America

Carol Barner-Barry

First published in 2005 by
PALGRAVE MACMILLAN™
175 Fifth Avenue, New York, N.Y. 10010 and
Houndmills, Basingstoke, Hampshire, England RG21 6XS
Companies and representatives throughout the world.

PALGRAVE MACMILLAN is the global academic imprint of the Palgrave Macmillan division of St. Martin's Press, LLC and of Palgrave Macmillan Ltd. Macmillan® is a registered trademark in the United States, United Kingdom and other countries. Palgrave is a registered trademark in the European Union and other countries.

Library of Congress Cataloging-in-Publication Data

Barner-Barry, Carol, 1938–
    Contemporary paganism: minority religions in a majoritarian
    America / Carol Barner-Barry.
        p. cm.
    Includes bibliographical references and index.
    ISBN 1–4039–6441–6
        1. Neopaganism—United States. 2. Freedom of religion—
    United States. 3. United States—Religion. I. Title.

BF1573.B37 2005
323.44′2′0882994—dc22   2004057315

A catalogue record for this book is available from the British Library.

Design by Newgen Imaging Systems (P) Ltd., Chennai, India.

First edition: March 2005

10 9 8 7 6 5 4 3 2 1

Printed in the United States of America.

To SpiralHeart

Contents

Preface

The issue of Pagan religious rights was the original focus of this book. Over time, however, it became clear that the threats of discrimination and persecution that intimidated so many Pagans were not limited to them. Rather, all non-Christian religious groups in America shared these experiences in one way or another. This is not a book that is intended in any way to attack Christianity or Christians. It is about the relationship between a religious group that has historically and contemporaneously dominated the religious landscape in America and an emerging religion that has had, until recently, little visibility and is still subject to much misunderstanding. All religious groups include persons who are deeply threatened by religious differences and who do not hesitate to try to eliminate those differences by any means possible. It is one of the reasons the religion clauses were included in the First Amendment of the U.S. Constitution and one of the chief sources of turmoil and violence in the contemporary world.

The tradition of Christian religious dominance combined with the Christian proselytizing imperative has led some Christians to assert their privileged status in ways that are harmful to those who do not share their religious beliefs and practices. These Christians are in the minority. Overall, Christians have been relatively unaware and unconcerned about the religious minorities in their midst. When bad things happen to minority religious groups and individuals, however, Christians have often been in the forefront of efforts to try to ameliorate or remedy the situation.

It might be interesting to do a study of the psychological, political, and social characteristics that differentiate Christians who see this situation in a religiously ethnocentric, or even xenophobic, way from those who see religious differences as an expression of the freedom that America offers to all. This is not that book. Rather, it is intended to be a wakeup call to all those who value freedom of religion and see it as a core American principle. Minority religions are growing rapidly on American soil and an important part of the history of the twenty-first century will be the way in which they become a part of American society.

It is probably safe to say that the days of the "melting pot" are over and that the challenge now is to deal with the growing religious pluralism as what Diana Eck (2001, 56–69), drawing on the ideas of Horace Kallen, calls a "symphony of difference." She envisions something more like jazz than a symphony that is written before it is played. She points out that "in jazz the playing is the writing." Each player must attend closely to what the others are doing and bring all parts into a synchronization of differences. Applying this principle to minority religions she observes: "Learning to hear the musical lines of our neighbors, their individual and magnificent interpretations of the themes of America's common covenants, is the test of cultural pluralism. Our challenge today is whether it will be jazz or simply noise, whether it will be a symphony or cacophony, whether we can continue to play together through dissonant movements."

A host of persons have contributed to this book in one way or another. My first acknowledgment, however, should be to the adult religious education program of the Unitarian Universalist Congregation of Columbia. It inspired the group of women, Gaia Circle, with whom I first explored contemporary Paganism. Although two members are no longer alive and others have scattered, I owe a debt to each and every one of them. I also owe a substantial debt to the person who evaluated the first half of this manuscript for Palgrave Macmillan. Dennis Goldford made many valuable and incisive comments that broadened my focus to the wider implications of my research and changed the face of this book in very important ways.

During the years when I was working on this project, many people helped me in a number of ways, large and small. They include Marcos Bisticas-Cocoves, Cerridwen Connelly, Larry Cornett, Diane Conn Darling, William R. Eade, Richard Eicher, Sandy Fink, Selena Fox, Rev. Paige Getty, Flora Green, Abul Hassan, Margaret Held, Jerrie Hildebrand, Lady Ker of Dun Banatigh, Brent McKee, Andrea Marshall, Silvia Moritz, Dave Pollard, Rona Russell, Emma Sellers, Gay Sídhe, Cindi Simpson, Rev. Cynthia Snavely, Swansister, Geoffrey Vaughan, and Oberon G'Zell. They also include a number of people who prefer to remain anonymous.

A special mention is due to those hearty souls who were willing to read and comment on part or all of this manuscript. A special thanks is due to Marianne Goodrich, Cindy Hody, and John Machate.

Finally, I would like to thank all those who were willing to share their experiences. Although their identities have been protected, except when they appeared in the press or otherwise become public knowledge, their stories are valuable and, in some cases, their suffering great. They have my deepest respect and gratitude. In addition, I would like to acknowledge all the Pagans whom I have met and learned from over the years. They have immeasurably enriched both this book and my life.

As is the custom, I would like to absolve all persons mentioned above from any and all responsibility for what appears in this book. Any errors or misinterpretations are mine alone.

Introduction: Majorities, Minorities, and Religious Diversity

Majority rule is a value that is deeply embedded in American political culture. From the playground to Congress, when the need to make a choice arises and there are differences of opinion, Americans almost invariably resort to a vote. This is not just a casual practice. It represents a value that is profoundly ingrained in American political thought as the bedrock essence of democracy. But, where there are majorities there must also be minorities. The composition of most minorities tends to shift from situation to situation and from issue to issue. Also, in most cases, members of the minority have the option to decide to switch to the majority. Certain minorities, however, are more or less permanent. Either they are based on some immutable characteristic such as gender, or they are based on some deeply held belief or value that makes up a core aspect of a person's identity such as religion. In such cases, switching to the majority is not an option or it is an option that carries a very heavy psychological and social cost.

That minorities should have rights and protections is also a basic American political value. It is not, however, as entrenched in practice. Minority rights and protections are, to a very great extent, what the majority is willing to allow or, at least, to tolerate. This has varied greatly over time and from situation to situation. Historically, the rights and protections of relatively permanent minorities have been preserved or expanded more often by courts than by legislatures or executives. And, commonly, significant groups within the majority have met court expansions of minority rights or protections with consternation and resistance, fearing that they might disturb a status quo that favors their majority status. Often, only the fact that federal and some state judges have life appointments and, thus, are protected from direct accountability to the majority has permitted them to be responsive to the problems and needs of minorities, particularly those with relatively permanent minority status.

What a majority is willing to permit a minority to do (or not, as the case may be) depends greatly on the extent to which the majority is able to understand and empathize with the minority's problems or needs. The ability of a minority to prevail or, at least, to protect itself depends on a number of factors. First, the greater the size of a minority, the more likely it is to be a force that the majority must take seriously, particularly if the minority is well organized politically. The numbers that can be mobilized by a minority are not limited to the membership of the minority itself, but can also include members of the majority who, for whatever reason, are able to empathize with the minority and to support it at critical junctures in the political process.

Second, a minority is more able to protect itself from majority oppression if it is well organized and politically active in the community. Many actions that oppress minorities are not intended to do so, but are the result of indifference or a lack of understanding by the majority of the true characteristics of the minorities among them and the impact its decisions and actions can have on certain minorities. In some cases, lack of familiarity and understanding can lead to an unfounded fear of some minorities—a classic case of fear of the unknown. This is a direct result of the fact that in a majoritarian political culture, the members of the majority tend to be both uninformed and uninterested in minorities, unless something or someone forces them to take a serious look at who the members of the minority are and what unites them in their minority status. Thus, minorities need organizations and spokespersons to inform and persuade the members of the majority regarding the need for attention to the problems of the minority.

Perhaps most importantly, the minority must have a clear and well-conveyed message that imparts legitimacy or, at least, credibility when the minority presents itself to the majority. This means that it must have a message that members of the majority can understand and with which they can potentially sympathize. Its members must also appear to be "normal" in most salient respects. If they are too different or "weird," they are too easily dismissed, because the members of the majority simply cannot relate to them and this gives them an excuse not to take the minority seriously. In addition, obvious differences in behavior or dress can seem threatening. Finally, the demands of the minority must be such that they are likely to be perceived as menacing by significant subsets of the majority.

To date, the religious minority that has done the best job in interacting with the Christian majority in the United States is the Jews. Particularly since the Holocaust, Americans have been more sensitive to anti-Semitism than previously. And this is reinforced by organizations, such as the Anti-Defamation League, that are prepared to step in with appropriate publicity or political pressure when Jewish religious practices are threatened or actually harmed. More recently, American Muslims have devoted much energy to developing a network of organizations and activities that helps them to protect themselves and to exercise some leverage in the political process. In some ways, the events of September 11, 2001, have been a setback, but in other ways they have presented an opportunity to American Muslims to more clearly define themselves and their beliefs and practices while they could command an attentive audience. Finally, Native Americans have developed an effective information and advocacy network, but their situation is, in some critical ways, unique.

There are currently two basic types of non-Christian religious minorities in the United States. One is composed of followers of some of the world's most ancient and well-established religions that have recently established a rapidly growing presence in America. This can be traced primarily to the greater non-European immigration that followed the loosening of restrictions on immigration initiated by the Immigration and Nationality Act of 1965, as well as the adoption of Islam by many African Americans. Among these are the Sikhs, Muslims, Hindus, and Buddhists. The second type is composed of adherents to indigenous or "home-grown" religions. Some, such as Santeria, emerged in the United States fairly early in its history. Others emerged from the events of the 1960s and 1970s. While the latter includes a resurgence of Native American religious practices, most of the religious traditions that surfaced in the middle of the twentieth century have drawn on elements of what are believed to be ancient religions to create a host of sects that can be loosely grouped under the term "Pagan." Among these are Wicca, Asatru, and Druidism. Both types of religious minorities are growing rapidly and are, thus, impinging on what has been an almost exclusively Christian religious landscape in America.

While these religious minorities are very different from each other in a host of ways, they have in common the fact that they present a face of religion that is unfamiliar to most Americans who tend to equate "religion" with Christianity and, perhaps, Judaism. To these Americans, the practices of minority religions present a challenge of understanding. Their activities and concerns are so different from Christianity that many Americans, including government officials, find it difficult to take them seriously as religions and hesitate to accommodate them in a social and political system that is based on Christian norms. For those

Americans who are inclined toward ethnocentrism or xenophobia, they can engender considerable fear and hostility. This book uses one of these groups, American Pagans, as a case in point to illustrate the challenges faced by minority religions in the contemporary United States.

I first became aware of American Paganism in the late 1980s as a result of an adult religious education curriculum developed by the Unitarian Universalists. I found their ideas and practices fascinating and, with a group of friends, went on to explore Paganism more deeply. As I got to know more Pagans and participated in some of their activities and online discussions, I became aware of two factors that led to the research that has culminated in this book. First, most of the Pagans that I came to know were "in the broom closet." That is, they were afraid to identify openly as Pagans, except in situations that were private and Pagan, such as small group meetings or larger Pagan gatherings at remote locations. They feared discrimination or persecution. Second, I found that these fears were justified. Many people who chose to be open about their religious choices and practices paid a price.

Over the last decade, an increase in public knowledge about Paganism and some significant victories in court have helped to legitimate Paganism as a religion. Many people, however, are still reticent about their Paganism. It is easier to be open about a Pagan religious choice in urbanized areas, especially in the northeast, the middle Atlantic region, and the west coast. It is more difficult (though far from impossible) in rural areas, especially those with high concentrations of evangelical Christians. This geographic distinction is not absolute. I have known Pagans who have faced serious persecution in relatively urbanized areas of states such as New York or Massachusetts. Conversely, one Pagan of my acquaintance has thrived and been an influential member of a relatively small community in Iowa.

There have been many reasons why it is becoming easier to be open about being Pagan. One important reason is that Pagans have established a formidable presence on the worldwide web. This has made information about Paganism easily available to the curious. Second, media coverage, popular television shows, movies, and the phenomenon of the Harry Potter books have increased the number of people who are curious and open to more accurate information about Pagans, particularly about Witches and Wiccans. Also, Pagans have established a significant presence within Unitarian Universalism, creating the Covenant of Unitarian Universalist Pagans.

In addition, Pagans have used the internet to establish a network of groups that are organized to further Paganism and help Pagans who are experiencing significant problems attributable to their Paganism. On the one hand, there are groups that are organized to provide some coordination among Pagan leaders in order to enable them to speak out together on issues that affect Pagans. One of the most notable of these is the online group, Our Freedom. On the other hand, groups, such as the Lady Liberty League, are designed to provide resources and support to Pagans who face discrimination or persecution because of their religion. These groups (as well as individual Pagans) have also been able to tap into the resources of the American Civil Liberties Union.

A more recent development has been the organization of groups intended to call attention to Pagans in order to make the majority aware of Paganism and to educate them about it. Notable here is the active and growing Pagan Pride Project that organizes Pagan Pride days in cities and towns all over the United States. It makes available information about Paganism and collects charitable contributions, such as resources for local food banks and shelters, as well as money to be distributed to local, regional, and national charities. There are also fledgling Pagan professional organizations, such as the Pagan Bar Association, the [Police] Officers of Avalon, the Pagan Alliance of Nurses, the Pagan Teachers Association, and the Pagan Firefighter Association. The Military Pagan Network is one that has been around and active for a long time. Finally, Pagans have begun to establish community centers, such as Betwixt & Between in Dallas, Texas. It provides a meeting place for Pagans of all traditions, as well as a base for outreach activities and a vehicle through which Pagans can voice their concerns about events or activities that affect them. It also supports a range of community activities such as support groups and the Spiral Scouts.

Nevertheless, individual Pagans still suffer from incidents of discrimination or outright persecution. In this, their experience is similar to that of other minority religious groups, such as Muslims, Sikhs, Buddhists, and Hindus (Eck, 2001, 294–332). There are three major ways in which the religious majority has oppressed the religious minorities in this country. First, there are harmful actions that are taken through disinterest and lack of understanding. The damage these inflict ranges from giving offense and treating minority religious adherents like non-Americans to outright interference with their ability to practice their religions. Second, there are attempts to convert or force Christianity on people espousing minority religions. This is particularly a problem for parents who must deal with significant pressures that are put upon their children to convert to Christianity. Finally, there are outright and malicious attempts to try to drive minority religious people and their organizations from communities. Sometimes, the latter reach such an extreme that they can justifiably be called hate crimes.

This book attempts to call attention to what can happen to people who attempt to practice a minority religion in contemporary America. In spite of the Constitutional protections embodied within the First Amendment and in spite of a national pride in America's supposed religious freedom, it can be difficult or even dangerous to belong to a minority religion. The first chapter presents a historical context for understanding the legal and social role of religion in America. It also contains an introduction to the legal status of emerging and minority religions. Chapter 2 is intended for those who have little or no knowledge about contemporary American Paganism. Although it is impossible to do justice to contemporary American Paganism in the space of one chapter, it gives a brief introduction to those factors most important for understanding the information to be presented later in the book. In doing so, it places particular emphasis on Wicca and Witchcraft, because most of the illustrative incidents used in the book involve people who belong or are accused of belonging to this particular branch of Paganism. Chapter 3 traces the history of Christian political and social dominance in America, as well as the basic confusion and misunderstanding many Christians hold about Paganism and the nature of Pagan religious beliefs and worship.

Chapter 4 constitutes an introduction to Paganism as a religion, starting with a discussion of the legal definition of religion that has been established by the courts. This makes it clear that Paganism is definitely a religion. Subsequently, there is a discussion of the Pagan situation with regard to core religious concerns such as worship sites, ordination, clergy, and religious holidays. Chapter 5 focuses on the Christian proselytizing imperative and the ways in which it can affect Pagans, particularly children. Chapter 6 focuses on the types of persecution and discrimination to which many Pagans are subject. Within the context of the latter two chapters, chapter 7 explores Christian hegemony and privilege in the United States and its impact on those who are not Christian. Finally, chapter 8 returns to the theme of majority and minority status and how they affect the lives of those who are in the religious minority.

The dominant position of Christianity in the United States is secure for the foreseeable future. Its proportion in the population, however, is shrinking while the proportion of minority religions is growing. By most counts, there are well over 2,000 different religions in America, many of them non-Christian. As the population grows and its ethnic composition shifts, minority religions are likely to grow both in numbers and in the ability to play the game of American pluralistic politics. This will increasingly challenge the hegemony and privilege that Christians, particularly Protestants, have historically enjoyed. Much of the current discrimination and persecution being directed toward followers of minority religions has an air of insecurity and, at times, even desperation.

Americans, thus, are at a crossroads. The relations between the majority and minorities in our religious life can be treated as a win/lose situation engendering a considerable amount of strife—political and otherwise. Or, as Diana Eck (2001, 383) suggests, we can move toward a religious pluralism that accepts diversity and tries to create a positive and strong multireligious society.

CHAPTER 1
THE HISTORICAL AND LEGAL CONTEXT

The First Amendment to the Constitution of the United States begins with the assertion: "Congress shall make no law respecting an establishment of religion, or prohibiting the free exercise thereof." It is—at first glance—simple and straightforward. Since these words were written, however, the proper interpretation of this section of the First Amendment has been the subject of a debate that became particularly lively and contentious during the twentieth century and continues to be so into the twenty-first century. In addition, the Establishment Clause and the Free Exercise Clause seem to call for mutually incompatible outcomes in many concrete situations.

Although the idea of freedom of religion goes far back into the American colonial period, by today's standards its original meaning was very restricted. The primary notion was that there would be freedom of religion for the various Protestant sects that dominated American society during the colonial period and later (Berman, 1986; Duncan, 2003; Feldman, 1996; Newsom, 2001). Both Catholicism and Judaism were considered unacceptable in many parts of colonial society, but their adherents were able to worship openly in a few colonies where they were tolerated, if not exactly welcomed. Other less familiar (to Europeans) religions, such as those of the original native inhabitants or the imported Africans were not considered protected and their adherents were treated as fair game for the imposition of Christianity—by force, if necessary.

Thus, the idea of free exercise took on its meaning within a society that was highly homogeneous from a religious point of view. That the United States was a "Christian nation" was widely assumed and found its way (in various forms) into the law[1] (Green, 1999, 427–433; Feldman, 1996, 845). Gradually, Catholicism and Judaism became at least grudgingly accepted as having a legal right to exist, but religions outside of Judaism and Christianity were not always accorded even that much respect. Protestant Christianity remained dominant. The Establishment Clause was seen as a protection against domination of the government by any single Protestant sect. Other religions, such as Islam and Hinduism, because of their world status, were accepted as religions, but as their numbers grew during the late twentieth century, they were seldom welcomed and frequently their members and places of worship were attacked. The world "cult" came to be used for those religions that the speaker did not want to recognize as fully protected religions.

The United States, therefore, ended the twentieth century with a definition of religious freedom that clearly reflected a historical Christian homogeneity (Berman, 1986) that was pan-Protestant (Feldman, 1996). The First Amendment religion clauses, as well as the rest of the law, was interpreted within this context. For example, in 1984, Kent Greenawalt, Cardozo Professor of Jurisprudence at Columbia University School of Law, wrote an article entitled "Religion as a Concept in Constitutional Law." In it he stated: "My basic thesis is that for constitutional purposes, religion should be determined by the closeness of analogy in the relevant respects between the disputed instance and what is indisputably religion" (762). At that time, as now, in the United States the analogy would be with Christianity, regarded as America's "normal religion" (Ball, 1990; Duncan, 2003).

Perhaps more important in terms of day-to-day impact was the fact that all other laws involving religion were written and interpreted within the same context. Sometimes Christianity was even mandated by law. For example, until it was declared unconstitutional in 1971, the Maryland Annotated Code art. 27, sec. 20 read: "If any person, by writing or speaking, shall blaspheme or curse God, or shall write or utter any profane words of and concerning Saviour Jesus Christ, or of and concerning the Trinity, or any of the persons thereof, he shall on conviction be fined not more than one hundred dollars, or imprisoned not more than six months, or both fined and imprisoned as aforesaid, at the discretion of the court." By the advent of the twenty-first century, however, the United States had become the most religiously diverse country in the world (Eck, 2001) and was steadily growing more diverse. Nevertheless, its legal system still reflected its historical Christian homogeneity and its government reflected its pan-Protestant hegemony. Moreover, the Republican Party had formed a clear alliance with evangelical and fundamentalist Christianity and the administration of President Bush was strongly advocating legislation that would funnel governmental funds primarily to Christian charitable organizations and to Christian educational institutions.

This reflection of Christian homogeneity and hegemony is, as of this writing, still enshrined in the constitutions of some states. For example, the Texas Constitution's Bill of Rights (art. 1, sec. 4) permits a person to be "excluded from holding office" if that person does not "acknowledge the existence of a Supreme Being." Many other states have equivalent documents with similar language.[2] This not only formally excludes atheists and agnostics, but also most Buddhists and some Unitarian Universalists. If the section is interpreted literally, then followers of Hinduism, and Zoroastrianism could not hold office because they believe in more than one "supreme being" or deity (Robinson, 2000). At this point in time, it seems that these provisions are being treated as historical relics and not being enforced. As long as they are "on the books," however, it is uncertain what the future situation might be. Also, for members of affected minority religions, they hold considerable exclusionary symbolic significance.

Before turning to a consideration of the implications of this situation for minority religious groups, it is necessary to take a closer look at the history and development of the idea of religious freedom in the United States.

Free Exercise as a Legal Concept

The legal term "free exercise" can be traced back to colonial Maryland. In 1648, Lord Baltimore commanded the governor and councilors of Maryland to respect the "free exercise" of religion by Christians. This was a marketing decision. He was attempting to make Maryland more attractive as a refuge for people who felt threatened by the contemporary limitations on religious freedom in other colonies. Subsequently, the Maryland legislature enacted a statute that included the first free exercise clause in America: "noe person . . . professing to believe in Jesus Christ, shall henceforth bee any waies troubled . . . for . . . his or her religion nor in the free exercise thereof . . . nor in any way [be] compelled to the beliefe or exercise of any other Religion against his or her consent" (as quoted in McConnell, 1990b, 1425).

Maryland was one of a small number of colonies[3] that were havens for people who were religiously persecuted in Europe or in other colonies. The wording of Maryland's free exercise provision, however, made it clear that the goal was protection of dissenting Christian sects. In fact, more precisely, Maryland's major focus was on protecting its Roman Catholics who continued to be marginalized elsewhere by the de facto establishment of a cultural Protestant Christianity (Thiemann,

1998, 290) Jews did not fare as well and persons embracing other faiths were not even contemplated.

Thus, from the start, the protection of free exercise was primarily a safeguard for minority Christian sects against dominant Christian sects. While the federal government never had an established denomination, many of the states retained their established denominations well into the nineteenth century. The rationale was that the Establishment Clause of the United States Constitution limited only the federal government (Gray, 1998a, 518–519). In fact, at the time the Constitution was written the impetus toward religious freedom that shaped the First Amendment was an outgrowth of an evangelistic reaction against the established sects in many of the former colonies and the fear of discrimination (Furth, 1998, 594–595). Establishment was also seen by many as a way for state governments to limit and control religious enthusiasm and initiative, especially through the use of state financial support.

Although 1834 marked the end of all state-level established denominations, this did not stop the debate about the proper relationship between religion and government that continues to the present. During the eighteenth century, the dispute was framed differently from the contemporary debate. Argument revolved around what role religion should play in helping the government to maintain a well-ordered society. Contemporary concern about religion using the government for its own ends was still in the future. What McConnell (1990b, 1442), calls the "paradox of the religious freedom debates of the late eighteenth century" was "that one side employed essentially secular arguments based on the needs of civil society for the support of religion, while the other side employed essentially religious arguments based on the primacy of duties to God over duties to the state in support of disestablishment and free exercise." The main focus was on competing Christian sects. Other religious paths were perceived primarily as "non-Christian." And in the case of Native Americans, their "non-Christian" status was seen as a problem to be remedied by the federal government.

It is clear that when the founding fathers wrote the First Amendment they did not consider the free exercise rights of Buddhists, Hindus, Animists, Native Americans, or any of many other nondominant religions. This is not surprising given the religious context within which they were acting. They were attempting to address problems that overwhelmingly originated in the differences among the ways in which various sects practiced Christianity. The small number of Jews and atheists did not pose comparable problems and—with the significant exception of the Native American population—there were few Americans who practiced other religions.

To date, First Amendment free exercise jurisprudence has reflected much the same historical demographic—focusing primarily on the rights of Christians who were "different," like the Jehovah's Witnesses, as well as Jews and persons asserting rights based on conscience rather than any particular church dogma. Those with beliefs that fell outside this narrow focus were not a significant part of the legal debate until almost 200 years after the passage of the First Amendment. In both the colonies and the United States, religious freedom and toleration was seen as a way of handling differences among Christian sects. Jews were clearly second-class citizens and the traditional religious beliefs and practices of Native Americans and African Americans were scorned and suppressed. The Native American experience furnishes a useful guide to both Free Exercise and Establishment Clause interpretation relevant to the protection they afford for nondominant religious beliefs and practices.

The Native American Experience

The idea of America as a Christian preserve began in the fifteenth and sixteenth centuries "when the seafaring nations of Christendom (now Europe) began to 'discover' indigenous nations and their lands" (Newcomb, 1993, 309). The underlying theory was that the agents of a Christian monarch could locate and take possession of any lands not already claimed by another Christian monarch. Thus was born the right of discovery: "discovery dissolved the territorial sovereignty of non-Christian peoples, thereby rendering their lands subject to Christian invasion, conquest, and possession" (312). Under this early Doctrine of Christian Discovery, the United States formally found the Indian nations without freedom or independence. It did, however, make treaties with them. Given that treaties are usually formal agreements between or among sovereign states, such treaty making had a certain disingenuousness.

Chief Justice John Marshall took care of this logical problem, acting with the authoritativeness that he brought to many other uncertain areas of early American law. In an 1823 landmark decision, *Johnson v. McIntosh* (21 U.S. 543), he asserted that the Native Americans had exchanged their unlimited independence for the gifts of civilization and Christianity (which were assumed to be intertwined). For Chief Justice Marshall "discovery gave title to the government by whose subjects, or by whose authority, it was made, against all other European governments, which title might be consummated by possession." Therefore, "[t]he exclusion of all other Europeans, necessarily gave to the nations making the discovery the sole right of acquiring the soil from the natives, and establishing settlements upon it" (21 U.S. 543, 573). The indigenous people, thus, could only make treaties with the initial discovering Christian state. A title of occupancy could be conveyed, but not title to the land itself, because the land already belonged to the discovering state.[4]

When the United States was created, it initially confined its activities primarily to gaining possession of Native American land. By the middle of the nineteenth century, this had largely been accomplished. While Christian missionary activities had taken place during the period of conquest, it became a more express government policy in the latter half of the nineteenth century when the federal government financially underwrote the activities of Christian missionaries and used representatives of Protestant sects as government agents on many reservations. "The agents assumed that the government had the authority to suppress specific religious practices of its Native American wards, *because their practices were not Christian*" (Dussias, 1997, 794, emphasis added). In the 1908 case, *Quick Bear v. Leupp* (210 U.S. 50), the Supreme Court interpreted Indian religious freedom as the freedom to choose among Christian denominations, not—by implication—to choose traditional Native American religious practices. Neither the Free Exercise Clause nor the Establishment Clause was seen as a barrier to these governmentally sponsored Christian proselytizing activities. It was not until 1934 that the Commissioner of Indian Affairs "issued orders aimed at ensuring Native American religious liberty and curtailing missionary activity at Indian schools" (Dussias, 1997, 805).

Subsequently, the Native Americans were free to practice their ancestral religions, if they still remembered them and with significant limitations. Repeatedly, during the twentieth century, the courts handed down decisions that permitted obstacles to the free exercise by Native Americans of their ancestral religions—sometimes to the point of making traditional religious practices impossible. Thus, since the founding, the pattern has been one of an overwhelmingly Christian judiciary demonstrating its inability to appreciate or care about the suppression of practices that were radically different from the religious practices to which they were accustomed (Bannon, 1997).[5] This has left the way open for those administering the law to ignore the rights of adherents of minority religions and perhaps even to take measures intended to suppress their religious activities or to force them to move in the direction of a more "Christian" way of life.

For example, one of the hallmarks of Christianity is the building of structures wherein worship and associated activities take place. A church can, in principle, be built in an almost unlimited variety of locations. Although there are some traditionally sacred sites, such as the place in Israel where Jesus is believed to have been born, most Christian worship sites have become holy ground by virtue of the enclosures for worship built upon them. Occasionally, congregations have reason to sell a church, usually to build a new one elsewhere. The site of the former structure is not perceived as forever sacred. The land may be converted to any of a wide range of secular purposes and religious worship continues unhindered at the new location. American judges are accustomed to the portability of sites of religious worship and, thus, find it difficult to appreciate the site-specific nature of much traditional Indian religious life.

Many pieces of land are inextricably intertwined with the traditional religious practices of Native Americans. "Areas of sacred geography are often related to tribal creation stories and other historical events of religious significance. They may also be areas where sacred plants or other natural materials are available, or sites with special geographical features, or burial sites, or places where structures, carvings, or paintings made by tribal ancestors . . . are located." There can be no alternative places of worship and to move religious practice away from these traditional sacred sites is unthinkable. "The required ceremonies must be performed at certain sites to be effective" (Trope, 1993, 376). Native Americans, however, have waged a largely fruitless battle in the courts to try to save such lands from development (Rosenberg, 1985; Boyles, 1991). One of these cases made it all the way to the Supreme Court and can be used to illustrate the problem.

The 1988 Supreme Court decision in *Lyng v. Northwest Indian Cemetery Protective Association* (485 U.S. 439), affirmed the government's right to build a road through Indian sacred land, causing what the dissenters[6] characterized as a "cruelly surreal result . . . governmental action that will virtually destroy a religion is nevertheless deemed not to 'burden' that religion" (485 U.S. 439, 471). Both the district and circuit courts had ruled in favor of the Native Americans on the ground that the road to be built was not of great enough importance to justify its negative impact on the sacred sites at issue. The Supreme Court majority, however, saw it as a matter of the property rights of the federal government. This demonstrates a seemingly unbridgeable cultural gap: "that of the dominant western culture, viewing land in terms of ownership and use, and that of native American Indian tribes, wherein concepts of private property are often completely alien" (Boyles, 1991, 1147). Justice O'Connor, writing for the majority, conceded the seriousness of the road's impact:

> The Indians use this area, as they have used it for a very long time, to conduct a wide variety of specific rituals that aim to accomplish their religious goals. According to their beliefs, the rituals would not be efficacious if conducted at other sites . . . and too much disturbance of the area's natural state would clearly render any meaningful continuation of traditional practices impossible." (485 U.S. 439, 451)

Nonetheless, the Supreme Court, asserting the primacy of property rights and development, reversed the decision of the lower court that had prevented the government from building the road and precluded timber harvesting in the areas of the sacred sites.

The judges and government officials who do not see the value in preserving sacred sites were raised in a culture heavily influenced by the Biblical injunction: "And God blessed them, and God said to them, 'Be fruitful and multiply, and fill the earth *and subdue it; and have dominion over the fish of the sea and over the birds of the air and over every living thing that moves upon the earth*' " (Gen. 1: 28, emphasis added). Thus, "[t]he goals and needs of those who want to 'develop' land are more readily incorporated into governmental land management policies and decision-making than are the religious beliefs of Native Americans affected by that development" (Trope, 1993, 376). The same may be said of the judges who review these decisions (Worthen, 2000).

This problem is not limited to governmental and judicial decisions affecting sacred sites. It covers a whole host of situations in which government officials have made decisions preventing or significantly limiting Native American religious practices. Those harmed can only appeal these decisions to a judiciary that finds their beliefs and practices largely incomprehensible because they are so different from those of the judges (Dussias, 1997). This leads to the second major problem faced by religious groups embracing a worldview different from that of Christians. Under the rationale used in the *Lyng* decision and found in many other interpretations of the Free Exercise Clause, these minority religions not only face uncomprehending, unsympathetic government officials and judges, they also lack the political power to protect themselves through the political process because—for now and into the foreseeable future—they lack the numbers and resources necessary to give them an effective voice in the American vote-counting, money-oriented political process. In this, many contemporary minority religions are not as well situated as the Native Americans who have a large number of non-Indian sympathizers and who, thus, have—on occasion—been able to prevail in the political process.

Native Americans were to play an important role subsequently when the Supreme Court used a case involving the Native American Church to make a significant change in the way that it interpreted the Free Exercise Clause. Prior to 1990, the court had interpreted the Free Exercise Clause using a test set down in the 1963 case, *Sherbert v. Verner* (374 U.S. 398). This case involved a member of the Seventh Day Adventist church. This denomination requires its members to do no work between sundown on Friday and sundown on Saturday. Sherbert refused to work on Saturdays and was fired. Unable to find a job in which she would not be forced to work on her Sabbath, she filed for unemployment benefits and was declared ineligible because her religious preference was deemed an insufficient reason for her refusal of available jobs.

In this case, the Supreme Court established what came to be known as the "*Sherbert* test." This test had two prongs. First, a court had to determine whether a given governmental act substantially burdened the free exercise of the party's religion. If it did, the court would then have to ascertain whether there was some compelling state interest that justified such an infringement of this First Amendment right. While this protection seems to be reasonably substantial, in practice it was often more apparent than real, because the courts using the *Sherbert* test seldom found a law unconstitutional as a violation of the Free Exercise Clause (Freeman, 2001, 46–47). As David B. Salmons (1995, 1244, 1247–1248) puts it: [R]eligious minorities almost always lost." There was, however, the hope that the next time the courts would be more understanding about unfamiliar minority religious practices. *Employment Division v. Smith* dashed this hope.

In 1990, the Supreme Court in *Employment Division v. Smith* (110 S. Ct. 1595) upheld state action that denied two members of the Native American Church unemployment compensation in a situation where their sacramental use of peyote[7] had resulted in dismissal from their jobs. Justice Scalia, writing for a majority of five justices, abandoned the 1963 *Sherbert* test. He found the *Sherbert* test unacceptable because it required judges to "weigh the social importance of all laws against the centrality of all religious beliefs" (110 S. Ct. 1595, 1606). The *Smith* case established the test of facial neutrality as the authoritative interpretation of the Free Exercise Clause. Facial neutrality means that the Free Exercise Clause cannot be used to relieve an individual from the obligation to comply with a law of general applicability that is religion-neutral on its face even if that law proscribes or requires activity contrary to his or her religious convictions. Put more simply, it means that the appearance of religious neutrality is controlling; actual neutrality is not required. Justice Scalia understood that the Court was making free exercise highly dependent on a religious community's ability to exercise leverage in the political process to protect itself against laws that might interfere with its religious practice: "It may fairly be said that leaving accommodation to the political process will place at a relative disadvantage those religious practices that are not widely engaged in." He termed it an "unavoidable consequence of democratic government" (110 S. Ct. 1595, 1606). This interpretation clearly favors Christianity, particularly the sects of Christianity that are large and politically active.

That First Amendment protection for minority religions is a function of their ability to influence the legislative process is a relatively new idea—at least in Constitutional doctrine. It has been around for a long time in practice. Certainly, previous Supreme Courts had a different view of the role of the Bill of Rights. For example, in 1943, in *West Virginia Board of Education v. Barnette* (319 U.S. 624, 638) the Court upheld the right of public school students to refuse for religious reasons to salute the flag. The majority opinion, written by Justice Jackson expressed a different opinion about the relationship between majority rule and the First Amendment:

> The very purpose of a Bill of Rights was to withdraw certain subjects from the vicissitudes of political controversy, to place them beyond the reach of majorities and officials and to establish them as legal principles to be applied by the courts. One's right to life, liberty, and property, to free speech, a free press, freedom of worship and assembly and other fundamental rights may not be submitted to vote; they depend on the outcome of no elections.

In the *Smith* case, Justice O'Connor, while concurring in the result, wrote a strong defense of the *Sherbert* test and against the theory that facially neutral laws could not raise free exercise concerns: "A State that makes criminal an individual's religiously motivated conduct burdens that individual's free exercise of religion in the severest manner possible. . . . I would have thought it beyond argument that such laws implicate free exercise concerns" (110 S. Ct. 1595, 1610). She also called attention to the fact that the "history of our free exercise doctrine amply demonstrates the harsh impact majoritarian rule has had on unpopular or emerging religious groups. . . ." (110 S. Ct. 1595, 1613). In concurring with the majority's result, Justice O'Connor used the *Sherbert* test and found the interest of Oregon in criminalizing the use of peyote compelling enough to trump the burden it placed on the Native Americans' religious practice.

The dissenters essentially agreed with Justice O'Connor's defense of the *Sherbert* test and her concerns about the impact of facially neutral laws. In addition, they concluded that "Oregon's interest in enforcing its drug laws against religious use of peyote is not sufficiently compelling to outweigh respondent's right to the free exercise of their religion" (110 S. Ct. 1595, 1622). Seemingly, the Oregon legislature agreed with the dissenters, since it subsequently changed the relevant drug laws to permit the sacramental use of peyote. Even before the *Smith* case, Oregon had a policy of not enforcing its drug law with regard to peyote use. In fact, in 1990, the year the *Smith* case was decided, 23 states and the federal government exempted the religious use of peyote from their drug laws. Subsequently, Congress also amended the American Indian Religious Freedom Act to protect the sacramental use of peyote in all 50 states. In fact, the federal government licensed its production and importation (McConnell, 1990a, 1109,1113; *The Washington Post*, April 23, 2003).

The decision in *Smith* was severely criticized in the legal community. Critics divided on whether or not the *Sherbert* test should have been abandoned, but few defended the way in which the *Smith* decision was reasoned. For example, William Marshall writing to defend the establishment of a neutrality test was careful to disassociate himself from Justice Scalia's reasoning in the majority opinion: "The *Smith* opinion itself, however, cannot be readily defended. The decision, as written, is neither persuasive nor well crafted. It exhibits only a shallow understanding of free exercise jurisprudence and its use of precedent borders on fiction. The opinion is also a paradigmatic example of judicial overreaching." He went on to state that the "holding extends beyond the facts of the case, the lower court's decision on the issue, and even the briefs of the parties. In fact, it appears that the Court framed the free exercise issue in virtually the broadest terms possible in order to allow it to reach its landmark result" (Marshall, 1991, 308–309). These are harsh words indeed from a basically supportive commentator.

The *Sherbert* Test in the Post-*Smith* Era

Congress expressed its disapproval of the Supreme Court's *Smith* decision by enacting the Religious Freedom Restoration Act of 1993 (RFRA), which reestablished the elements of the *Sherbert* test for the interpretation of the Free Exercise Clause as it was applied to the states by incorporation into the Fourteenth Amendment. This law was, however, struck down by the Supreme Court as unconstitutional in 1997 in *Borne v. Flores* (117 S. Ct. 2157). The Court held that Congress had trespassed on the Supreme Court's power to interpret the Fourteenth Amendment of the Constitution. This left the *Smith* interpretation of the Free Exercise Clause intact as the law of the land—at least with regard to state court cases presenting a Fourteenth Amendment free exercise issue. Several circuit courts have held that RFRA is constitutional when applied to non-Fourteenth amendment cases involving federal entities, such as federal prisons and federal territories, as well as federal bankruptcy laws. They have held that RFRA was constitutional as applied in the "federal realm," because Congress has Article I power to legislate for the "federal realm." Thus, these courts reason, in such cases RFRA is not an interpretation of the Fourteenth Amendment, but rather a Congressional command that should be considered a part of federal law.

In response to *Borne v. Flores*, several states passed religious freedom restoration acts (Gildin, 2000). In some states they were vetoed by the governor, but many remain. Whether they can stand up to constitutional scrutiny is a matter of dispute among legal scholars, although their adherents claim that they can, if properly drafted (Gildin, 2000). On September 2, 2004, the Supreme Court of Florida decided a landmark state RFRA case, *Warner v. City of Boca Raton* (2004 Fla. LEXIS 1449). The case had been sent to it with two queries by the U.S. Court of Appeals for the Eleventh Circuit. Neither of the questions posed by the Eleventh Circuit dealt with the constitutionality under the U.S. Constitution of the Florida Religious Freedom Restoration Act (FRFRA). The first, and most interesting for purposes of this discussion was: "Does the Florida Religious Freedom Restoration Act broaden, and to what extent does it broaden the definition of that constitutes religiously motivated conduct protected by law beyond the conduct considered protected by the decisions of the United States Supreme Court?" (2004 Fla. LEXIS 1449, 9) The second dealt with its applicability to the Boca Raton situation.

Initially, it should be noted that the wording of the FRERA specifically declared the intent of the legislature to establish the *Sherbert* test as the controlling interpretation of the Free Exercise Clause found in the Florida Constitution's Declaration of Rights. Citing a 1992 Florida case, *Traylor v. State* (596 So. 2d 957) the court stated: "In interpreting the scope of constitutional rights, this Court has stated that in any state issue, the federal constitution represents the 'floor' for basic freedoms, and the state constitution represents the 'ceiling' " (2004 Fla. LEXIS 1449, 18). Its conclusion was that "The FRFRA expands the scope of religious protection beyond the conduct considered protected by cases from the United States Supreme Court . . . [and] under the Act, any law, even a neutral law of general applicability, is subject to the strict scrutiny standard where the law substantially burdens the free exercise of religion" (2004 Fla. LEXIS 1449, 35). Thus, it would seem—initially, at least—that state-level RFRAs can withstand judicial scrutiny. This is, however, only an early and inconclusive example.

A further issue, however, is whether the protection of religious freedom should be left to legislative bodies. For example, Ira Lupu (1999, 577) argues that the difficulties of drafting such legislation are "insurmountable" and that the activity of politically influential religious interest groups distorts the laws in favor of their preferences and needs. Even if the legislative process was to be negotiated successfully, he is pessimistic about the future of such laws: "The dangers associated with religious liberty legislation do not end after initial enactment. Such legislation creates statutory authority for courts to develop a body of law designed to limit government in its interaction with religiously motivated actors and institutions." Subsequently, the state legislatures can "ultimately 'microlegislate' by overturning particular exemptions or exemption refusals by the courts." He concludes that "[F]irst and inevitably, unpopular religions are those most vulnerable to legislative undoing of their judicial victories" (584).

Lupu emphasizes the potential weirdness (that is, to those whose cultural heritage is Christian) of it all: "Architects of religious liberty unprepared to defend strange and unpopular practices will constantly find themselves accused of cowardice and hypocrisy, and they may well deserve such appellations." His advice to legislators? "[J]ust say no" (593). Others do see state legislatures as the solution (e.g. Volokh, 1999). Daniel O. Conkle (1999, 495), however, while his "first preference would be for the Supreme Court to overrule *Smith* and to develop a vigorous interpretation of the Free Exercise Clause—an interpretation that would protect religious liberty throughout the nation"—does see some virtue in using the states as laboratories for experimentation in defining religious liberty in new and creative ways.

Another arena in which the *Sherbert* test seems at least potentially alive and well is in the supreme courts of the states (Crane, 1998). State constitutions commonly have language that parallels the free exercise clause of the U.S. Constitution. In some, the language is identical, but in others, it is unique to the particular state. In either case, however, the highest court of the state is the authority with reference to the interpretation of such clauses. Several state supreme courts have chosen to use this power to reinstate the *Sherbert* test in some form.[8] Others, notably Tennessee, have gone along with the *Smith* test. Thus, protection for minority religions from facially neutral laws that negatively impact them can vary according to the state's highest court's interpretation of the state constitution and in a majority of the states this issue is still open, because it has not been directly addressed by the state's highest court. The overall picture at the state level is one of uncertainty and confusion (Friedelbaum, 2000).

What remains of Free Exercise Clause protection? As discussed below, the First Amendment still protects religions from legislation that unambiguously targets a particular religion. In addition, Justice Scalia's majority opinion in *Smith* seemed to create what has come to be called a "hybrid" exception to the strict facial neutrality norm. Thus, "as an initial matter, the plaintiff must still prove that a particular state action has caused a burden to a sincerely held religious conviction *and at least one other constitutional right*" (Esser, 1998, 215, emphasis added). In an assessment of this hybrid, Esser came to the conclusion that the cases, so far, were "being decided based solely upon the strength or weakness of the 'other' constitutional provision without reference to the Free Exercise Clause" (242). Thus, under the current Supreme Court jurisprudence, the U.S. Constitution's Free Exercise Clause would seem to have little bark and virtually no bite—at least with regard to state laws.

All of this has led some to conclude that the Free Exercise Clause has become—for the most part—redundant (e.g. Conkle, 2001; Gedicks, 2000; Tushnet, 2001). The general argument is that there are other constitutional doctrines that now give as much and more protection to religious people. For the most part, this protection is thought to emanate from the free speech clause of the First Amendment. The argument is that most religious acts can be viewed as forms of protected speech. Religious speech, for example, is protected by the non-discrimination requirement. Correspondingly, most religious activity can be seen as symbolic speech. Religious activity that cannot be seen as some sort of protected speech can usually be seen as protected association, particularly under the emerging right of expressive association. All of these theories remain to be tested in the court system, however, and this leaves minority religions in a state of uncertainty with regard to their legal rights and the extent to which the courts will be a recourse when their religious practices are threatened by laws that are facially neutral.

The Legal Status of Emerging and Minority Religions

Currently, persons who practice emerging or minority religions can be assured of little protection under the Free Exercise Clause, unless the law harming them has clearly and unequivocally targeted their particular religion. This principle was established in the 1993 case, *Church of the Lukumi Babalu Aye, Inc. v. City of Hialeah* (508 U.S. 520). This case involved the Santeria religious practice of sacrificing animals at some rituals. When a group of followers of Santeria began the process of building a religious worship center in Hialeah, the city council held an emergency public session and passed a group of resolutions and ordinances the effect of which was to prevent the ritual killing of animals—with certain exceptions that limited the effect of the law to Santeria and exempted, for example, kosher butchering (Karst, 1994, 342). When the Supreme Court perused the record, it found that the city's assertions that the laws were of general applicability (i.e. facially neutral) unsupportable: "The record in this case compels the conclusion that suppression of the central element of the Santeria worship service was the object of the ordinances" (508 U.S. 520, 534). The Court then found that laws clearly and unambiguously targeting a particular and identifiable religion are unconstitutional under the Free Exercise Clause.

But, as the eminent constitutional scholar, Douglas Laycock, has pointed out "the obvious forms of persecution are not the ones a contemporary American majority is likely to use." The sheer number of government statutes and regulations create "ample opportunity for facially neutral religious oppression. Such oppressive laws may be enacted through hostility, sheer indifference, or ignorance of minority faiths." But, with the neutrality test the court has provided "a legal framework for persecution, and persecutions will result" (Laycock, 1990, 4). This is particularly likely when taken in conjunction with current political pressures to interpret the Free Exercise Clause in such a way as to give Christians wide latitude in expressing their religious beliefs in governmental settings.

Arguments about the scope and nature of religious freedom are abundant in the scholarly legal literature. For example, Michael J. Perry (1997, 34; 1998) argues that a governmental policy choice would violate the Establishment Clause only if there was no plausible secular purpose. Thus, under Perry's interpretation, it can be posited that posting the Ten Commandments in courtrooms can be theoretically secularized as an expression of legal heritage. Ignored are many potentially uncomfortable considerations. For example, posting the Ten Commandments clearly favors Christianity—unless the Jewish version is posted, which is not usually the case. Furthermore, given the fact that there are at least five different versions of the Ten Commandments any posting favors a particular denomination. And, whatever the version, the first three to four commandments concern themselves entirely with a person's obligations to the Judeo-Christian God.

In his review of Perry's book, *Religion in Politics*, Kevin Metz has observed (1998, 272): "Perry advocates a greater role for religious ideas in policymaking, arguing that the Free Exercise and Establishment Clauses require the judiciary to accept a very deferential stance toward laws justified by religious arguments." He acknowledges that "Perry continues to have a healthy regard for nonestablishment as a principle," but points out that Perry's "permissive attitude toward the role of religion in legislation and judicial review fundamentally underprotects the democratic value of nonestablishment, transforming the shield of free exercise into a sword for privileging the majority's religious views." Metz's basic argument is that minority religions are coerced in two ways. First, they have no protection against having the majority's religious values (and perhaps even theology) forced upon them. Second, their tax monies and, perhaps, even the government itself are aiding the majority's religion.

Also, according to Metz: "In addition to these tangible harms, one can argue that a deeper injury is inflicted in both types of cases when the majority communicates through the government the message that the minority is not part of mainstream society" (274). He points out that "any plausible secular purpose can validate a law even though the actual purpose was religious. This signals something like rational basis review where governmental actors imagine some reason, however weak, to base a decision on a secular foundation." Thus, when the Court defers to majority-approved legislation, the benefits flow to "those religious people able to muster majorities, not to those permanently relegated to minority status or even disinterested in political action." In other words, "those able to command majorities get the protection of the Court, while those too weak to have a voice in the democratic process do not" (Metz, 1998, 275; Gordon, 1997, 90–91).

In 2001, Diana L. Eck of Harvard's Pluralism Project published a book called *A New Religious America*. The subtitle was *How a "Christian Country" Has Become the World's Most Religiously Diverse Nation*. In it, she discusses how the passage of the Immigration and Nationality Act of 1965 signaled the beginning of the end of America's dominant white Protestant culture. Because it removed all the major impediments to immigration that had previously kept immigrants from certain parts of the world, notably the Asian-Pacific region, to a mere trickle, it began an enormous change in the religious makeup of the population of the United States. As it entered the twenty-first century, the United States was becoming a very different religious place. The seventh edition of J. Gordon Melton's *Encyclopedia of American Religion* (2003) lists 2,630 U.S. and Canadian faith groups (*The Associated Press*, January 31, 2003). This move toward greater religious diversity via the immigration of adherents following non-Christian religions was supplemented by the rise of emerging religious movements during the 1960s and 1970s. Many grew out of an increased interest in alternative spirituality that accompanied the political and social upheavals of that period. Some have disappeared while others have flourished and are growing steadily. One of the latter, contemporary Paganism, is the case study used in this book.

From the point of view of the legal system, Stephen Stein (2000, 41) notes, the religious diversity present in the contemporary United States is "bewildering." He adds: "Since 1970, religious change has accelerated in America, producing a situation in which existing conceptual models [for defining what is "religion"] have seemed increasingly inadequate" (50). He then calls for a "careful reassessment of certain longstanding assumptions about religion in America" (57). This reassessment should, according to Stein be focused on a set of changes in the way Americans perceive their religious life. First, traditional denominational categories increasingly fail to capture many peoples' primary religious identity. Second, many Americans distinguish between religion and spirituality, often embracing the latter and rejecting the former. Third, monotheism and Judeo-Christian values no longer enjoy the degree of numerical dominance they once did. Fourth, the idea that religion can or should be a unifying force in society no longer reflects contemporary reality. Finally, "the possible matters of contestation regarding religion in the future are likely to become more and more complex and less and less related to the historical concerns that informed" the writers of the First Amendment. Stein concludes: " 'Free Exercise' is a glorious principle; it is a wild thing in practice!" (60).

For persons who have a non-Christian religious commitment, the First Amendment, as currently interpreted by the Supreme Court, affords little protection from laws that discriminate or even persecute, provided the circumstances of the laws' passage and their words appear to be neutral with regard to religion (Mykkeltvedt, 1991, 631; Sanchez, 1994, 61–62). They can only claim protection from the courts when a law expressly targets their religion. With the current limitations placed on the scope of the Religious Freedom Restoration Act and with the new, restrictive interpretation of the Free Exercise Clause in *Employment Division v. Smith*, the legal system has effectively removed itself as a practical recourse for adherents of minority religions that are too small and politically weak to protect themselves in the legislative process.

The idea of neutrality will only work well when all religions in the United States adopt a stance of mutual respect and deference. This will be difficult, if not impossible to achieve, when some of the most numerous and politically powerful religious groups have proselytizing at the core of their religious missions. At present, the idea of the religious neutrality of political actors is far from being achieved in practice and may ultimately prove to be overwhelmingly difficult to achieve. Given the growing diversity of religious practices and the growing intrusiveness into the privacy of both persons and institutions that has been exacerbated by the terrorism threat, it may be impossible to achieve. Also, the current situation privileges politically powerful Christian persons and institutions that are invested in maintaining Christian hegemony.

In the meantime, most Christian sects are reasonably well understood as religions by politicians and, in a pinch, they can muster enough economic and electoral support to protect their own interests. This situation is currently combined with a rise in religiously motivated political agendas and activity by evangelical Christian groups that wish to use the law to impose their religious values on all Americans. As Stephen M. Feldman (1996, 873) notes: "[I]n a hegemonically Christian society, such as America, 'neutrality' equals Christianity." For him, the current situation amounts to the "de facto establishment of Christianity" (1997, 267).

Facially neutral laws, no matter how much damage they do to an adherent's ability to worship freely and to have their religiously motivated values respected (Note 1987a, 610; Note, 1987b, 1637–1739), are virtually untouchable under the current interpretation of the free exercise clause. Whether the free speech clause or other constitutional doctrines will give them adequate protection remains to be seen. As more and more Americans worship in ways that are difficult for the Christian majority to sympathize with (or even understand) the probability that facially neutral laws will impinge on their freedom of religious exercise will grow and this may lead, in turn, to a growth in religiously based resentments and divisiveness.

This book is an effort to study a group of people who have chosen a religious path that is very different from Christianity and one that has historically been associated with condemnation and persecution. Contemporary Pagans are part of a rapidly growing cluster of religions that began to emerge in their contemporary forms in the mid-twentieth century. Many adherents of Paganism claim to be resurrecting belief systems that were crushed by the Catholic Church before and during the Inquisition. Others are consciously creating essentially new religious traditions. The average American thinks of these religions, particularly Witchcraft, in terms of the meanings given such labels by Christians who were trying to convert entire populations and to justify torturing, hanging, or burning people they claimed were dangerous to Christians.

Pagans have been chosen for study because they represent an extreme example of the kinds of situations that will continue to arise as more and more Americans practice religions that their fellow citizens do not understand and may even fear. As Catherine Cookson has said of Wiccans (1997, 746), adherents of all contemporary Pagan traditions "represent a litmus test for the state of religious freedom and tolerance in America: they are non-Christian outsiders whose normative practices are within the bounds of the law." She adds that "it is quite clear that any religious discrimination and hatred directed at them arises purely from disagreements with their theology and a misunderstanding of their practices, and not because they are normatively lawless or disruptive to the peace and good order of society."

If the Free Exercise Clause is to have any significant meaning as a protection for religious worship in the twenty-first century, people whose religion is poorly understood by their neighbors and communities must have the ability to practice it and feel safe. At present, many Pagans feel constrained to hide their religious beliefs, worship, and chosen affiliations and to remain in the "broom closet" because they fear for the safety of themselves and their families. Just the words "witch" or "pagan" create misunderstanding, and many who condemn and threaten them do not pause to ask what Pagans believe or how Pagans worship. Rather they assume that it is true that, for example, Witches do terrible things, such as sacrificing babies and worshipping Satan. If confronted by the fact that neither of these assumptions is a true description of the beliefs and practices of those who follow established contemporary Witchcraft traditions, they often refuse to listen or to be diverted from their path of confrontation and condemnation.

This is in part because the very words Pagans use in identifying themselves and their beliefs and practices evoke historical religious choices that have been feared and despised by the Christian majority. Thus, Paganism, particularly Witchcraft, is highly vulnerable to misunderstanding and persecution. The fact that it is organizationally diffuse and has a large number of solitary practitioners makes it difficult for Pagans to raise public awareness of their true beliefs and practices. In a 1985 article, discussing the legal position of minorities and their need for protection, Bruce A. Ackerman considers four distinct characteristics of minorities. Without going into his whole scheme, it is significant to note that the type of minority that he concludes is most vulnerable is the "diffuse and anonymous" minority, because "it is these groups that both political science and American history indicate are systematically disadvantaged in a pluralist democracy" (Ackerman, 1985, 724). An "anonymous" minority is one that is difficult to identify. In Ackerman's article, he contrasts homosexuals and blacks. It is impossible for most blacks to "pass" as white. It is, however, quite possible for homosexuals to mask their homosexuality and "blend into" the heterosexual majority, if they choose. In this same sense, Pagans tend to be an "anonymous" religious minority, since they can easily hide their true religious identity.

For Ackerman, a minority is diffuse when its members are scattered throughout the larger society, with little or no intra-group interaction. This, again, is true of Pagans who tend to practice their religion as solitaries or in small groups. Chances to meet other Pagans and interact with the larger Pagan community in an ongoing basis are limited. That, in turn, makes it difficult for Pagans to create solidarity and encourage organized political action on behalf of Paganism as a religion. The problem of isolation for Pagan groups and individuals has been mitigated somewhat by the periodic Pagan festivals held in various locations throughout the United States, as well as Internet groups and a few widely read Pagan journals. This is, however, no substitute for ongoing face-to-face relationships or a generally accepted umbrella organization that can give a single voice to Paganism. Currently, the most significant vehicle for Pagan interaction and cooperation is the Internet. It has facilitated the sharing of ideas and the organization of inter-group cooperative organizations, such as the Pagan Educational Network, the Lady Liberty League and the Earth Religions Assistance Network. In addition, a group has formed to organize annual Pagan Pride days throughout the United States.

Because contemporary Paganism is poorly understood by most Americans, it is assumed that the readers of this book need some introduction to the history and religious beliefs of contemporary Pagans.[9] Therefore, chapter 2 briefly introduces the reader to a few of the core beliefs of contemporary Pagans and indicates some of the reasons why many fear persecution in the present based on their beliefs about the persecutions of the past. In subsequent chapters, these fears are also traced to instances of discrimination and persecution that are very much in the present.

CHAPTER 2
THE EMERGING PAGAN MOVEMENT IN AMERICA

Throughout the world during most of recorded time, religion and ideas about the sacred have permeated social life. Ancient artifacts and myths indicate that our distant ancestors' concept of the sacred affected public, as well as private, life. Human societies have, to a greater or lesser extent, been regulated with an eye to whether the actions of both individuals and social institutions are consistent with whatever is considered sacred by the dominant religion's theology. Something as basic as the prevailing perception of the nature of the deity (or deities) can profoundly affect public policy making, as well as individual conduct (Berger, 1985; Gimbutas, 1982; Goodrich, 1990).

Although particular religious beliefs might seem important with reference to specific policy alternatives, such as whether to permit legal abortions, much more important is the basic orientation of the theology. What people believe about deities, human nature and their relationship to the rest of the natural world limits the options for the societal policies that can even be considered, let alone adopted. For example, if you believe that a deity presides over the earth from "above" and gives humans the duty of controlling and exploiting the earth primarily for human welfare, it is much easier to adopt public policies that damage or destroy parts of the earth and its nonhuman living creatures. If, on the other hand, the deity is explicitly nature or the earth itself, policy makers are constrained to approach it more respectfully, since they are proposing to alter something that is inherently sacred.

Correspondingly, if you believe people to be innately sinful and to need saving at all costs and if you believe that salvation means to go to heaven (somewhere off of the earth), then the earth is of temporary concern. The eternal sacred transcends the earth and the concerns of the earth's inhabitants. If, on the other hand, people are thought to reincarnate again and again on the earth, those who live in the present have a much more personal stake in what their policies will do to future generations.

This can profoundly affect public policy making, as well as individual conduct (Berger, 1985; Gimbutas, 1982; Goodrich, 1990).

Most contemporary Pagans[1] concern themselves little or not at all with explicitly political ideas or activism.[2] They are much more preoccupied with ritual and the personal practices of their tradition. Most, however, have some fear or uneasiness regarding the potential for the political and legal order to be used against them. They look back to the times when witches (or alleged witches) were tortured and executed in the name of Christianity and they wonder if what they call "The Burning Times" could return. They know that the names they call themselves, such as Pagan, Witch, Wiccan, or Druid, might be considered (at best) eccentric or (at worst) threatening by others. They fear for the safety of themselves, their families, and their fellow Pagans. Many choose to keep their religious beliefs secret—to stay in "the broom closet" (Chapin-Bishop, 1993, 35–37). Others are open about their beliefs in some situations and secretive in others.

During recent years, there has been a trend toward being more "out." At the forefront of this trend has been a small group of Pagan leaders who, recognizing the advantages of educating the general public about Paganism, have become more and more willing to make themselves available to the media, to hold seasonal rituals that are open to the public and to write books and articles explaining more fully the nature and basic characteristics of Paganism. There has also been more scholarly research about Pagans, including historical and anthropological studies involving surveys, interviews, and the observation of worship practices. The average Pagan, however, is still hesitant to be completely candid about his or her religious preference and many remain completely "in the broom closet."

Before going on to the types of situations in which contemporary Pagans have reason to feel threatened, it is important to understand something about them and their religious beliefs. The first thing that must be said is that Pagans tend to be highly individualistic and independent people. They know that they have chosen an unusual, potentially dangerous, religious path. It is not the way of conformity. In fact, they tend to be proudly and adamantly nonconformist, resisting anything they consider undue influence from inside, as well as outside, the Pagan movement. The metaphor often used when the discussion turns to getting Pagans organized behind any leader or cause (not to mention any dogma) is that of herding cats.

This means that generalizing about Pagan beliefs and practices is not as easy as it would be for a centrally organized religion with an official leadership and theology, such as Roman Catholicism.[3] There are a myriad of groups practicing Paganism in America today and each has its own beliefs and traditions, many of them quite eclectic. Also, an unknown number of Pagans choose (for many reasons) to worship alone and, thus, assume complete control over their beliefs and practices. Despite this anarchic situation, however, it is possible to make some very broad generalizations that indicate some of the most basic ways in which most contemporary Pagans differ from the dominant Christian religion in the United States.

What follows, however, does not do justice to the wide variety of pagan beliefs and practices. To do this would be to write a whole book or more on that topic alone. There is an emphasis on Wicca and related eclectic practices, because it is Witchcraft and similar Pagan sects that are the most widespread and that have aroused the most hostility among certain Christians. Although some, such as Asatru, are briefly mentioned, others, such as Hellenic, are not. This choice was dictated by the need to give context to what follows and that primarily concerns Wiccans and persons who are thought to be Wiccan.

Widely Shared Core Beliefs

At the center of most contemporary Pagan systems of belief is some concept of the Goddess as central or primary to all that is considered sacred. And, the Goddess is or is closely associated with the earth or with the totality of nature. Often she takes on three aspects, most commonly those of maiden, mother, and crone (or wise old woman). Many Pagans also associate these aspects with the waxing, full, and waning moons. Such images are meant to evoke the cycle of life and its procreative imperative. The maiden and the waxing moon are associated with birth and youth; the mother and the full moon are associated with maturity and nurturance; and, finally, the crone and waning moon are associated with old age (usually connoting wisdom) and death.

The idea of the Goddess may also include some concept of a female (i.e. generative) primal force: creator of the universe, of the earth, of life. In this context, there may be specific reference to ancient goddesses who were associated with the creation of the universe, such as Tiamat or Isis. Sometimes, there is simply a formless primordial Mother. The common thread seems to be a focus on the natural world. The Goddess, on some level, presides over the entire natural world. Thus, Astarte, a Middle Eastern goddess of nature might be revered as She who creates, preserves, and destroys, disposing of the old and generating the new. At the same time, the Goddess's more specific forms may be associated with particular parts of the natural world. An example would be Nimue, the Celtic moon goddess.

The concept of the Goddess as deity is not a mere feminist device aimed at asserting the value of the feminine in the face of the patriarchal Christian traditions into which most contemporary Pagans were born. Although it does that, it does much more. Primarily, it places, at the center of religious consciousness earthly life, procreation and the passing of the phases of life, as well as the changing of the seasons. This is not the idea of the sacredness of human life and procreation that energizes the "right to life" movement. It is more broad and subtle. The central value is not some absolute "right to life" for human beings, but the celebration of life in all of its diversity—human and nonhuman.

Pagans accept the necessity and inevitability of death as part of the natural cycle. In addition, most acknowledge the need to terminate life "prematurely" when circumstances warrant, but hold that every such act needs to be considered on its own merits. Thus, Pagans can be found among the ranks of those who are both "pro choice" and "pro life" with regard to the abortion issue. The point is that all life is sacred and that no life, human or nonhuman, should be terminated lightly or without adequate justification. Even parts of the natural world, which would normally be regarded as nonliving—such as mountains, rivers, or rocks—are often considered to be alive on some level.

Indeed, when a British chemist, James Lovelock, advanced the idea that the earth is an organism that is self-regulating, he called it the Gaia Hypothesis (Lovelock, 1979, 1987, 1988). This directly relates the earth to the Goddess, since Gaia (also spelled Gaea) is the ancient Greek goddess of the earth. This terminology has been picked up by some people in the academic world who are writing about environmental issues (e.g. Miller, 1991). It has also been used by some in the Pagan community who refer to members of that community as Gaians (or Gaeans) (see G'Zell, 1990, 2). In fact, Otter G'Zell,[4] a founder of the Church of All Worlds, advanced a similar concept in 1970, before Lovelock's first published reference to the Gaia Hypothesis (G'Zell, 1988b, 4–7, 26).

The centrality of the Goddess, however, does not necessarily equal monotheism. While acknowledging the central role of the Goddess, most contemporary Pagans work with a number of sacred, spiritual beings, including a corresponding God or any one of a variety of more specific ancient pagan gods and goddesses derived from a host of traditions. Some also work with "spirits of the land," faeries, and other types of spiritual beings. Currently, there is an attempt in several contemporary

Pagan traditions, to place more emphasis on the idea of the God in tandem with the Goddess (e.g. Circle of the Winter Moon, 1996, inside front cover; Avery, 1999, 37–38).

Thus, the Goddess and God can be evoked either in specific forms (such as Astarte or Odin) or as a symbol representing all of nature on earth and, often, even the wider cosmos. An example of the latter can be found in Janet and Stewart Farrar's version of the Wiccan opening ritual where the High Priestess, speaking as the Goddess, says: "For I am the soul of nature, who gives life to the universe. From me all things proceed, and unto me all things must return. . . ." (Farrar and Farrar, 1984, 43; also Starhawk, 1989, 90–91).

Within this general framework, most Pagans focus on the earth as the most personally relevant locus of the divine. Many regard their beliefs as a revival, or reemergence of an ancient nature-religion. This is perceived as "the most ancient of religions, in which the earth was worshiped as a woman under different names and guises throughout the inhabited world" (Luhrmann, 1989, 45). This view, however, is controversial. There are those, notably Aidan A. Kelly (1991), who claim to have demonstrated by historical research that modern Witchcraft, is a twentieth-century invention. The scholar, Ronald Hutton, in his 1999 book, *The Triumph of the Moon: A History of Modern Pagan Witchcraft*, weighs the evidence carefully and concludes that contemporary Witchcraft is probably a twentieth-century phenomenon that draws on esoteric traditions dating back farther, but not to some ancient religion (also see Orion, 1995). He does, however, leave open the possibility that some who claim to practice a religion handed down through their families may actually be practicing a very old Pagan religion.

So, the Goddess is nature, but for most Pagans She is immediately and primarily the earth. Thus, the Druids of Ár nDráiocht Féin (ADF), refer to "our Holy Mother Earth" (New Member's Guide, 1990). The deification of the earth means that everything that is part of the earth—both living and nonliving—is sacred. The Goddess is not transcendent, as God is in the Christian tradition. Rather, She is immanent equally in a person, a bird, a tree, a stream, or a stone. Therefore, sacredness characterizes all humans, all other animals, all plants, and all earth components usually thought of as nonliving. The corollary of this is that when humans do anything to alter the natural order, we are manipulating, or trying to change, something sacred. This is not interpreted as an injunction to mandate a "hands off" policy toward the natural world or a return to a primitive hunter–gatherer lifestyle. As housewives, professors, programmers, and plumbers, contemporary Pagans would find this impossible.

Rather they hold that any attempt to modify the natural world should be undertaken: (1) with a sense of reverence for the subject of change; (2) with a clear concept of the need for a change; and (3) with a view toward both the short-term and long-term impact of the change contemplated. This approach is seen to be in express opposition to the Jewish and Christian idea of a deity who is separate from the world and who commands humans to rule over or subjugate the rest of the natural world (Gen. 1: 26–29).

If one is going to modify or destroy something sacred (i.e. a part of the natural world), it must be established that there is a clear necessity to do so. For example, killing animals for food is acceptable; predator–prey relationships are part of the natural order. To kill animals for sport or to make luxury garments, however, raises serious spiritual questions for many (but not all) Pagans. Often cited is a Native American practice of explaining to a freshly killed animal the necessity to take its meat and skin for food and clothing, then asking its forgiveness for the act of killing it. Important in this connection is the need to explain, which presumes that, before the act is committed, the hunter must be sure that there is a persuasive explanation. This makes it harder to interfere with the natural pattern. It cannot be done thoughtlessly or frivolously.

In fact, Pagans tend to assume that humans interfere with the natural order at their peril. As contemporary ecological problems demonstrate, the negative consequences of disrupting natural processes can be devastating. Pagans are very aware that if the natural world and its processes are regarded as sacred, humans will be more hesitant to manipulate them without giving deep thought to the consequences. Such a value system can make people more inclined to limit the amount of interference to that which is absolutely necessary. During much of the past, including the twentieth century, decisions to modify or manipulate the natural world and natural processes have traditionally been made on economic grounds with little or no attention paid to the ecological consequences. There has been a widespread conviction that any ecological damage that turns out to be a problem can be righted by some future technological "fix."

Most contemporary Pagans would agree with James Eggert when he reminds his fellow economists that they must broaden their approach, to "incorporate ecological thinking and ecological values with market thinking and values" in order to "protect the standard of living of the other organisms with whom we share the planet" (*The Washington Post*, August 4, 1991). While Eggert urges the use of "grandchild impact statements," however, many Pagans would probably call attention to the

Native American injunction to consider the impact of our actions on the seventh generation following our own.

Thus, the concept of the Goddess forms a link between the spiritual and the political. When the deity is seen as transcendent, above the world, the world assumes secondary importance. A spirituality that is focused on heaven, hell, and where one "goes" after death can encourage an instrumental, short-sighted approach to what is happening in the here and now. This is particularly true if there is no explicit connection between such decisions and one's fate in the hereafter. When the connection is made with regard to a particular public policy issue, however, its potential for mobilization can be considerable, as demonstrated by the Roman Catholic and Protestant fundamentalist organization of opposition to abortion.

If the deity's charge to the human race is to rule and subjugate the earth and everything on it, there is spiritual justification and permission to regard humans as, somehow, outside of nature and, thus to ignore the ecological effects of policies designed to make life better for humans—at least in the short run. Most Pagans explicitly reject this. Thus, new members of ADF are told: "In keeping with our reverence for and worship of the Earth Mother, we advocate and practice ecological and environmental research, education, and activism" (New Member's Guide, 1990, 4). On a practical level, recycling garbage can be a religious act.

Men and Women in Paganism

Many of the most visible figures in the Pagan movement have been and are men. This raises the question of why men should be drawn to a nontraditional religious movement that is based on largely feminine imagery when Jewish and Christian religious traditions give primacy to male images and most contemporary Pagans were raised as Jews or Christians. The idea that the centrality of the Goddess means that Paganism is a women's movement is explicitly refuted by Otter G'Zell: "As a man and a devout worshiper and priest of the Goddess for over 20 years, and as a founder and thealogian of a major Goddess-oriented religion, I must take umbrage at this attitude. No, the Goddess is not only for women!" Acknowledging that Paganism is, to a large extent, a reaction against the problems created by "millennia of male supremacy" he asserts the importance of teaching males "to love their Mother" so that there can be a "true healing of the Earth" (G'Zell, 1991, 2).

Historically, men were in the forefront of the contemporary Pagan movement. For example, Gerald Gardner (1884–1964) pioneered the twentieth-century revival of Witchcraft. He founded what is now known as the Gardnerian tradition, considered by many to be the dominant tradition in contemporary Wicca[5] (Guiley, 1989). He claimed to have learned Witchcraft from a group of hereditary English Witches, the New Forest coven. However, much of what he published in his most important books, *Witchcraft Today* (1954) and *The Meaning of Witchcraft* (1959), is thought by some to have been invented by him (based on older esoteric practices and with the collaboration of Doreen Valiente) rather than passed down to him as an ancient tradition (Kelly, 1991; Hutton, 1999; Rowan, 1987, 80).[6] For others the historical record may be of relatively little importance. For example, Otter G'Zell thinks: "We may forge a mythological continuity to account for how we have gotten from there to here, but we need not be overconcerned about its 'factuality' " (G'Zell, 1989, 20)

Raymond Buckland is generally (but not universally) credited as one of the major influences bringing Gardnerian Witchcraft to the United States (Guiley, 1989, 40; Orion, 1995, 61). Born in England, he became interested in magic and the occult at an early age. He met Gardner in the early 1960s and was initiated into Gardnerian Witchcraft in Scotland. Later, in the United States, he decided that Gardnerian Witchcraft did not meet his spiritual needs and founded his own version of Witchcraft. His ideas were disseminated by a series of books that he published during the 1970s and 1980s, culminating in *Buckland's Complete Book of Witchcraft* (1986). As a result of his writings, he became a highly influential and visible figure in the twentieth century Pagan movement until the mid-1980s when he decided to play a less public role.

In addition, men founded many of the other major and minor traditions in the contemporary Pagan movement.[7] In fact, during the 1960s and early 1970s a majority of Pagan organizations[8] had predominantly male leadership. Otter G'Zell attributes this to the fact that contemporary feminist leaders were preoccupied with achieving political goals and were not interested in devoting time and energy to spiritual pursuits (G'Zell, 1991, 2). Starhawk asserts that most feminists were hostile toward spirituality, because they identified it "with either patriarchal control or apolitical escapism" (1989, 3). With the subsequent rise of feminist spirituality (especially during the 1980s and early 1990s), the relationship between the dominant religious belief systems and the secular status of women received more attention. Once women had embraced a feminist perspective on spirituality, movement toward some form of Goddess worship came quite naturally for many of them.[9] In turn, this has fostered the rise to prominence of many women who first became involved in Paganism when its leadership was dominated by males. Although there are no reliable figures on the Pagan movement as a whole,[10] fragmentary evidence indicates that contemporary Pagans are as likely to be men as women, though women probably predominate.[11]

At this point, it is necessary to return to the question of why men would desert religious traditions in which the central figure is male for a religion in which the central figure is female. The reasons include both a desire to move away from patriarchal traditions that are seen as harmful to men, as well as women, and a desire to move toward a belief system with a male imagery more attractive to many men. This male imagery revolves around a number of god images, including the Horned God,[12] as well as the many other male gods the modern world has inherited from various ancient religious traditions. For example, John Rowan (1987, 1991) sees the Horned God as the most satisfactory spiritual way for males to respond to nature and the human condition. Rowan defines patriarchy as "a form of hierarchy, arranged . . . such that each level is allowed to exploit all the levels below it without criticism." God is at the top, followed by men, women, children, animals, plants and, on the bottom, earth. He sees patriarchy as harmful to all, because "the intellect and the dominating, controlling, aggressive tendencies within each individual are given sway. This results in a society dominated by violence, exploitation, a reverence for the scientific and a systematic rape of nature for man's benefit" (1991, 4).

Thus, although patriarchy gives power and privilege to a man, it also "entraps him in a rigid role which is hard to escape from." Rowan suggests an alternative relationship between males and the rest of the world, a relationship that asserts a critical role for the feminine: "Imagine a stone circle with a tall stone in the center, an image of the healthy relationship of male with female. The female circle forms the matrix or context in which the male pillar can be filled with power. As long as that male power is contained within the circle, it is safe and usable, but if it tries to be self-sufficient, it comes to grief." He then adds that: "All power is first of all female power, and the God can only act by relating to her and being with her. But this God is male without a doubt—there is no question about his masculinity, which goes to the very depths of his being" (1991, 4–5).

This is similar to the imagery found in what is probably the most influential book in the twentieth century development of the American Pagan movement, *The Spiral Dance*, by Starhawk to whom Rowan acknowledges his debt. She writes: "The Goddess is the Encircler, the Ground of Being; the God is That-Which-Is-Brought-Forth, her mirror image, her other pole. She is the earth; He is the grain. She is the all-encompassing sky; He is the sun, her fireball. She is the Wheel; He is the Traveler. His is the sacrifice of life to death that life may go on. She is the Mother and Destroyer; He is all that is born and destroyed" (Starhawk, 1989, 109).

In most of contemporary Wicca, the God is the consort of the Goddess and represents the masculine principle within the deity. He is associated with the sun, green growing things, and the hunt. He is ritually reborn every Yule (winter solstice), couples with the Goddess at Beltane (May 1) to bring fertility to the world and dies to be reborn at the next winter solstice. Starhawk (1989, 109) describes him thus: "The Horned God represents powerful, positive male qualities that derive from deeper sources than the stereotypes and the violence and emotional crippling of men in our society." In her opinion, "if man had been created in the Horned God's image, he would be free to be wild without being cruel, angry without being violent, sexual without being coercive, spiritual without being unsexed, and able to truly love." Thus, the God becomes a powerful and positive symbol to which men can relate within the context of a religion that assigns a primary place to a female figure, the Goddess.

Depending on the Pagan tradition, the God plays a greater or lesser role. In some feminist traditions, he plays almost no role at all. This can implicitly exclude males or relegate them to a clearly subordinate status. For example, some (but not all) feminist traditions have, in the past, explicitly excluded men—most notably the tradition led by Zsuzsanna Budapest (Adler, 1986, 121–122) Even Budapest, however, has modified her position in recent years: "So things are not as bleak as they used to be. There are natural allies to the Dianic Women" (Budapest, 1989, 179). These natural allies are gay men and non-homophobic heterosexual men. They are accepted, but they play a distinctly secondary role. Their main function is to help women to create a circle (i.e. a sacred place for worship) and then to leave and guard the circle against hostile men.

At the other extreme are the Norse traditions that center on male gods, most prominently Odin, as well as more traditional masculine imagery. It is a segment of the Pagan movement that stresses courage, the martial arts and warrior virtues. Some groups have espoused extreme right-wing and even Nazi ideas, but the overwhelming majority repudiate Nazism[13] (Adler, 1986, 273–282). The central problem for mainstream Norse Pagans is that Hitler used many Norse symbols. Norse Pagans tend to make a point of using these same symbols, because they think the symbols need to be reclaimed for their proper and more traditional religious use.[14] Unfortunately, when they do use these symbols, they tend to attract some people who assume that they are being used the same way that the Nazis used them. Many groups screen potential new members for such misconceptions. Mainstream Norse Paganism can be a means of exploring and expressing pride in Scandinavian or Germanic ancestral roots. But there are those for whom the issue of heritage is irrelevant; they are simply attracted by Norse beliefs, rituals, and activities.

Since there is a definite tendency in Norse Paganism to place the male deities in the primary position, this would, seemingly, make it one of the more attractive Pagan traditions for males. In the words of Alice Rhoades (as quoted in Adler, 1986, 281): "It's true the most visible gods are Odin and Thor, and they have warrior values. They are very macho gods—so they appeal to men and more men join the group and people say it's a male religion." But it also attracts many females who can see in it deities—and even a Goddess—that they admire. Another Norse Pagan, Thalia Treeshadow, sees women as having a definite place: "We do not put any race or sex above any other. Including the idea that Norse is mostly masculine. It's true that Norse culture was often warlike and many masculine ideas of strength are battle related, but women in these cultures were often very strong willed, much like the Huntress Goddess." She adds that "[S]ome women rode to battle in men's garb, most women ran the house and estates. . . . Many times in the sagas, if men did not avenge a wrong, the women got disgusted and took matters into their own hands" (as quoted in 5 #2 *Free Spirit Rising*, 1990, 5). So, in this tradition, female concepts of the sacred are present, but less central, and they tend to be revered for their more traditionally masculine traits.

Thus, there are many ways in which men occupy an important place in contemporary Paganism. There are reasons for men to be attracted to Goddess religions and find imagery and symbols, as well as beliefs and activities, which are congenial. Although there is still some tendency to exclude or subordinate men in the more feminist groups, this is not a mainstream position. And, at the very foundation, the twentieth century Pagan movement began at the impetus of primarily male founders.

One of the reasons why Paganism, in its various forms, can accommodate as much diversity as it does is because of the wealth of images from which founders of new traditions or members of eclectic groups can choose. The Goddess has multiple aspects and these aspects take on their own names and characteristics, usually related to ancient ideas about the sacred in the many parts of the ancient Pagan world. The same is true of the God. In fact, followers of Pagan traditions frequently find goddesses or gods with characteristics particularly relevant to their lives and center their worship on these. In this usage, the gods and goddesses can become archetypical figures or they can be specifically conceived and utilized for their archetypical values (Woolger and Woolger, 1989). There is even a trend to invent new gods and goddesses with characteristics more appropriate to the modern, technological world. For example, Stormcrow (1991) advocates the God, Ah-To San or, alternatively, OTTO as a patron for automobile mechanics. Also, there is the goddess, Squat or, alternatively, Asphaltia, who helps harried urban dwellers find parking places.

The Pagan Mythical Basis

The myths underlying any body of religious thought are important, because they specify and dramatize what the thinkers choose to regard as true about the past, present, or future. They are stories that are understood by people's cognitive, analytical thought, along with an element of drama that triggers the affective or emotional processes. Myths give people an identifiable past, present, and future that they regard as true in some sense, ranging from the literal to the metaphorical. They also attach an emotional valence to particular versions of the past, present, or future. It does not matter whether myths are true in the scholarly or scientific sense, though some believers may assert that they are. If people believe them to be true and if they act upon that belief, then the myth becomes true in the sense that it affects what happens in the real world (Nimmo and Combs, 1980). Correspondingly, if people have a strong emotional investment in myths, they are more apt to act on their messages than they might otherwise, and when they do, it is more likely that they will act on them with passion.

Furthermore, there is a sense in which any version of the past or future can never be regarded as absolutely true. Certainly, our ideas of the future are only more or less accurate probability statements (the accuracy to be determined subsequently). More subtly, our ideas of the past are also probability statements. They are always filtered through the intervening time, as well as by the methods and minds of the people instrumental in passing any ideas or "facts" down to the present. Thus, our ideas of the past are unavoidably anchored in present reality. We can only talk about the past in the present, and any version of the past is colored by that reality (Mead, 1959).

The mythical foundation of much of contemporary Paganism depends on a definite interpretation of history. This interpretation uses the myths and artifacts we have inherited from the past to generate a version of history that legitimizes a Pagan claim to have returned to past spiritual and political values that were good and were tragically destroyed. Whether this interpretation of history is scientifically valid or not is controversial. But, it fills its function as a mythical foundation for the resurgence of what are, to a greater or lesser extent, claimed to be reconstructions or new interpretations of ancient religious ideas and practices. Thus, they are myths according to the definition of that term by Nimmo and Combs: "A credible, dramatic, socially constructed representation of perceived realities that people accept as permanent, fixed knowledge of reality while forgetting (if they were ever aware of it) its tentative, imaginative, created, and perhaps fictional qualities" (1980, 16; see also Tudor, 1972, 17).

There is great diversity in the myths espoused by contemporary Pagans. There are, however, three overarching, historically oriented myths that seem pervasive in the Pagan community and that form much of the basis for Pagan reactions to instances of persecution, as well as their fear of future persecution. The first is the myth of the world as it is thought to have been before the advent of patriarchy and patriarchal religions. Starhawk calls these "the mother-times" (1987, 32). The second is the myth about how Christianity spread, particularly in Europe, and the way in which the pre-Christian native religions were suppressed and their symbols and deities destroyed or incorporated into Christianity. Finally, there is the myth about the burning times. This deals with the purposes, actions, and effects of the Inquisition in Europe. Briefly, it holds that the major purpose of the Inquisition was to eliminate those who held power and status in local communities (primarily women: the midwives, herbalists, and wise women) by accusing them of witchcraft and burning them. Thus, the Christian church fathers were able to consolidate their patriarchal power over society.[15] Each of these needs to be considered in more detail with reference to the role it plays in the mythology of contemporary Paganism and in the propensity of contemporary Pagans to fear persecution.

The Mother Times
The myth of pre-patriarchal times is that of a lost Eden. It is about prehistory, a time before written records. Geographically, it centers on the Middle East and Europe. Religiously, it is concerned with the worship of the Goddess as the divine generative force in creation; women were revered because of their ability to bear children. Socially, it posits

communities that were matrilineal and, some would assert, also matriar-chal. Politically, it assumes structures of rule in which females held high posts and were either more important than men or equal to them. Riane Eisler's book, *The Chalice and the Blade*, is one of the most influential treatments of the Mother Times theme.

According to this myth, in early human hunting and gathering groups women were considered to be making a vital contribution to society because their gathering of plant foods was central to the subsistence of the group—hunting being a much less reliable source of food—and because of the fact that they bore and nurtured children. During this period and the subsequent early period of the transition to an agricul-tural way of life, society was essentially peaceful and cooperative. As agriculture became more and more important, however, the small, scat-tered settlements that had characterized the early agricultural period began to coalesce into larger cities. At the same time, religious worship became more centralized, as small shrines in or near homes gave way to larger centralized temples with a professional priesthood. An elite arose around the priestly caste.

Initially, religious, social, and political leadership was exercised relatively equally by both men and women. With the trend toward centralization, however, the predominance of female deities and priestesses began to give way to male deities and increasingly powerful priests. Gradually, women were excluded from both religious and secular leadership posi-tions as warfare became more common and men assumed the leadership roles having to do with warfare. The growth of warfare was a response to nomadic invasions from the north and east and led to an increasingly stratified social order. As warfare became chronic, more and more of the elements of the social and political order were adjusted to meet the needs of war. This eventually led to the transition to patriarchy and the rise of religions based on male gods. In the polytheistic variation, the female goddesses became subordinate to the male gods. In the monothe-istic variation, one transcendent male god became the supreme divinity. In either case, such a religious framework was used to support a patriarchal social and political order that has persisted to the present.

This Pagan myth derives from two major sources. One was an attempt by people interested in Paganism to rediscover the roots of Witchcraft. Their efforts took place in the first half of the twentieth cen-tury. They were heavily influenced by the writings of Margaret Murray. The other is the more recent growth of a feminist revisionist interpretation of history and is based on the work of such writers as Merlin Stone and Marija Gimbutas. Unlike Murray's work, which predates most of the modern Pagan movement, the feminist revision of history came to prominence after several of the more lasting Pagan groups were founded.[16] The relevant work of feminist historians, however, was discovered and used by many who were already involved with Paganism. Others discovered it as they began to take an interest in Paganism. This was particularly true of many of the women who came to Paganism via feminism.

Margaret A. Murray was a British historian and anthropologist who taught at University College in London and did archeological excavations in many places, especially Egypt. She published three books on Witchcraft. The first was *The Witch-Cult in Western Europe* (1921) in which she traced the roots of Medieval and Renaissance Witchcraft to Goddess-oriented fertility religions in the Paleolithic Era. This idea did not originate with Murray, but can be traced at least as far back as Sir James Frazer who discussed the prehistoric roots of Witchcraft in his work, *The Golden Bough* (1890). Murray's interpretations have been very controversial. Most are considered questionable or downright wrong by both historians and Pagans. (Hutton, 1999, 194–201). Her work contributed to the mythic foundation of contemporary Paganism, however, when Gerald Gardner utilized her theories in his book *Witchcraft Today* (1954). In addition, he asked Murray to write the introduction to this book.

The first of the feminist revisionist historians to have a major influence in the Pagan community was Merlin Stone who wrote a book called *When God Was a Woman* (1976). In it, she quoted Murray's work with respect and without criticism. Although she specifically states that she does not support a return or revival of the ancient Goddess religion, she expresses the hope that "a contemporary consciousness of the once-widespread veneration of the female deity as the wise Creatress of the Universe and all life and civilization may be used to cut through the many oppressive and falsely founded patriarchal images, stereotypes, customs and laws that were developed as direct reactions to Goddess worship by the leaders of the later male-worshiping religions" (Stone, 1976, xxv). Then she invites women to use her book as part of a "search to find out who we really are" and invites men to become aware of the historical and political origins of contemporary sexual stereotypes (xxv–xxvi).

Although Stone claims to be giving an accurate account of history, *When God Was a Woman* is not a dry historical tome. The dramatic quality found in the title is also found in the text. For example, in the first paragraph she writes: "In the beginning, people prayed to the Creatress of Life, the Mistress of Heaven. At the very dawn of religion, God was a woman. Do you remember?" (1). Thus, her work presents a set of facts embedded in accessible, even theatrical, prose. These factors lend themselves to the use of her work for mythic purposes by many contemporary Pagans.

Marija Gimbutas' work is far more scholarly in tone and substance. Based on extensive fieldwork, her research gave a more solid, though not uncontroversial, academic basis to the Mother Times myth. In the preface to a new edition of her book, *The Goddesses and Gods of Old Europe: Myths and Cult Images*, she summarized her interpretation of the historical record. Using the term "Old Europe" to designate the pre-Indo European culture in Europe, she asserts that this culture was "matrifocal and probably matrilinear, agricultural and sedentary, egalitarian and peaceful." Then she contrasts it with the "proto-Indo-European culture which was patriarchal, stratified, pastoral, mobile, and war-oriented" and was "superimposed on all Europe, except the southern and eastern fringes" by warriors from the Russian steppe between 4500 and 2500 b.c.e." This historical shift, in turn, led to the replacement of the Great Goddess in her many aspects, by the male gods of the Indo-Europeans (Gimbutas, 1982, 9). Other authors, such as Riane Eisler, used her work extensively and translated it into a less scholarly, more dramatic and didactic message. This, in turn, bridged the gap between the work of an academic and the growing Pagan movement.

Although there is a dramatic and didactic quality to the works of authors such as Merlin Stone and Riane Eisler, they claimed to be presenting a verifiable version of history based on a defensible interpretation of authentic historical artifacts and other evidence. This is also, to a greater or lesser extent, true of other feminist writers, such as Pamela Berger, Elinor Gadon, and Norma Lorre Goodrich. What many Pagan writers have done is to select from and embellish such accounts of history and use them in mythical ways.

Perhaps the most overtly mythologized retelling of this story is that of Zsuzsanna Budapest. For example, in the section of her book that deals most explicitly with this myth, the opening sentence is: "Come with me to the Temple, close your eyes, and then open them again. I will show you images of the Goddesses created before us by Goddess-worshiping people. We are not the first, nor the last" (Budapest, 1989, 278). This signals the kind of dramatic account of history that is the hallmark of myth. She then goes on to define as unimportant the historical accuracy of the tale she is about to tell while, at the same time, emphasizing its usefulness to the sympathetic reader: "I will not attempt to convince you of the authenticity of what you see. You must trust your own eyes and common sense, and learn to look. It is important to see these images without being distracted by what they are called, classified, or thought to be by archeologists. Archeologists are not witches who yearn to see the Goddess" (278). Here she is clearly telling the reader to believe in this account—to suspend any skeptical sense or demand for proof—and experience the story about to be told as both historical reality and relevant to the present.

As Budapest's version of these times unfolds, it is clear that it is necessary to take it on faith, since much of what she asserts as reality is, in fact, incapable of proof. For example, this is her account of the transition from matriarchy to patriarchy: "In matrilineal society, superior males were chosen as mates by matriarchal women. Men not selected as mates were unable to gain any of the status, property, wealth or recognition associated with a woman's family. These males banded together outside the communities. Soon they found that if they had their 'own' women to breed like cattle, they could produce their own people and become more powerful." She then illustrates this with the story of the rape of the Sabine women, which she readily acknowledges is mythological: "While the Sabine men were away, patriarchal soldiers marched into town, raping all the women and impregnating most of them. The 'logic' of it was that if each man impregnated at least one woman, who then bore a child, the original males would double their numbers. It was a small step from there to possessing women, breeding them like livestock and keeping them pregnant as much as possible" (1989, 295).

This then led to a patriarchal, war-oriented social order: "Soon the patriarchs had their armies . . . Within a fifty-year period, patriarchs produced entire armies and continued to escalate such degenerate activities as ransacking cities, raping and murdering women and female children." Budapest then goes on to assert that "this sort of thing happened all over the world at about the same time" (294–295). Note how she blithely ignores the distinction between myth and reality. Since her purpose is not to write scholarly and verifiable accounts of history, but instead to inspire via the creation of new myths, this distinction is unimportant.

Although it is possible that the events recounted could have taken place, it is highly unlikely that this is a precise account. And, it is even more unlikely that it is an accurate account of events that happened "all over the world at about the same time." This is, however, irrelevant, since the purpose of this account is to create a certain frame of mind, not to add to the scholarly accumulation of knowledge about history. Finally, it should be noted that Budapest defines herself as addressing a primarily female audience, one that is feminist and sympathetic to lesbianism, if not actually lesbian. Thus, she clearly labels these Goddess-worshiping societies matriarchal, while less militantly feminist Pagan writers emphasize their matrilineal and egalitarian qualities. She also tends to equate the terms "virgin" and "lesbian," in referring to the status and practices of Goddess priestesses (282). On the whole, her interpretation of this myth is likely to be the least attractive to males, particularly heterosexual males. This does not, however, detract from its importance to some segments of the Pagan community, particularly to feminists and lesbians.

Another major contributor to this myth is Starhawk who was initially influenced by Budapest (Starhawk, 1989, 3). Unlike Budapest, however, Starhawk addresses her version of the myth to both men and women without particular emphasis on distinctions based on sexual orientation. In fact, she repeatedly underlines the acceptability of any sexual preference while proclaiming the centrality of the erotic. Although she deals with this myth in her first book, *The Spiral Dance* (1979), her most complete version is in the later book, *Truth or Dare* (1987).

Starhawk is very frank about the historical uncertainties of the story she is telling. For example, at the beginning of her discussion of history, she states: "Scholars, including some feminists, argue about whether such times existed" (Starhawk, 1987, 32). Also, she asserts specifics that cannot be verified, but she is careful about doing so and sticks closely to the writings of academic historians. In the end, however, she gives a dramatic account of the story and clearly intends to appeal to her readers' emotions, as well as their minds: "It is a tragic story that names our condition as one of loss, that gives us a vehicle through which we can feel our pain, grieve, rage, heal, and fight. Without the story, we don't know what's wrong with us" (32–33). Also, the drama is heightened by the poetry and story-telling she weaves into her account of history.

While it is difficult to ascertain how literally such accounts of ancient history are taken by all Pagans, most of the leading Pagan writers who deal with the Mother Times myth seem to be aware of its mythic quality and to understand that historical accuracy—while desirable—is less important than psychological impact. The main function of this myth is to legitimize Goddess religions by showing that they are not solely a contemporary invention, but a tradition that can be traced back to the dawn of time. Thus, Pagans are enabled to lay claim to a legacy that predates modern patriarchal religions. The goal is to attempt to move back toward this early Eden-like state via the practice of Pagan traditions, such as contemporary Witchcraft.

The Christian Conversion

This myth bridges the other two. It is similar to the Mother Times myth in that it posits a time in which Paganism was the dominant religion, followed by a conquest of Pagan lands. In this myth, however, the conquest imposed a specific religious tradition, Christianity. The Pagan lands are those of the western part of Europe. The conquerors are, first, the Roman legions and, second, the Christian missionaries who accompanied or followed them. During this period many of the gods and goddesses, as well as Pagan rituals and holy places, were converted into Christian saints, rituals, and shrines. The horned gods such as Pan and Cernunnos, were associated with Satan (Berger, 1985). Some Pagans and Pagan groups have devoted considerable energy to an attempt to recover—generally through scholarship—as much as possible of these lost traditions. This myth is also a bridge to the myth of the burning times in that it sets the stage for the tale of the suppression of Witchcraft—which is perceived as the most persistent and widespread survivor of these ancient traditions.

One of the most widely read variations on this myth appears in fictionalized form in Marian Zimmer Bradley's *The Mists of Avalon* (1982), which is a favorite among many Pagans. This novel tells the legend of King Arthur from a new point of view, that of Morgan, Arthur's half sister, who is usually portrayed as a sinister figure. In Bradley's version, Morgaine (as her name is spelled in the book) is portrayed as a complex but basically good character, who is a priestess of the ancient and magical Goddess religion of Britain. Throughout the book, the forces and values of the old, tolerant Pagan religion struggle to maintain themselves against the onslaught of an intolerant and imperialistic Christianity. Finally, Christianity prevails and Avalon, the center of the old religion, becomes disorganized, gives way to the growing strength of Christianity and slips further and further away into the mists.

The point of the Christian conversion myth is that it develops a series of principles about the relationship between Pagans and Christians. First, Pagans are seen as tolerant of other religious traditions, while Christians are seen as intolerant. Second, Pagans do not proselytize, while Christians proselytize vigorously and persistently. Third, Pagans are basically peaceful, using violence only in defense and then reluctantly; Christians have no compunctions about using violence to convert or punish non-Christians. Finally, while the Pagans see the virtue of having many gods and goddesses and ways of worshipping them, Christians are implacably determined to stamp out any worship that is not their own monotheism.

Thus, the conversion of Europe to Christianity is seen as an imperialistic takeover, backed by force or the threat of force. The indigenous, pre-Christian religions are seen as going "under ground" preserved in small enclaves and in local "Christian" customs and saints. The organized political and religious forces of Rome impose their way on a scattered and disorganized local population that is forced to bow to superior power. Older ways of worship, however, persist in enclaves in the countryside. Also, older traditions are kept alive and passed down in families, particularly significant among the "old ways" are herbal healing and the "women's' mystery" of childbirth.

The Burning Times

This refers to a period in European (and American) history that lasted from approximately the mid-fifteenth to the early eighteenth centuries. It is seen as a time of intense witch hunting and executions—usually by fire, sometimes by hanging. Just to be called a witch was enough, no proof of evil deeds was necessary. Jean Bodin, a sixteenth-century demonologist, made this clear: "Even if the witch has never killed or done evil to man, or beast, or fruits, and even if he has always cured bewitched people, or driven away tempests, it is because he has renounced God and treated with Satan that he deserves to be burned alive. . . . Even if there is no more than the obligation to the Devil, having denied God, this deserves the most cruel death that can be imagined" (as quoted in Guiley, 1989, 43). Many people were caught up in this frenzy—most of whom, it is now thought, were probably not witches in the sense that the church authorities were using the term. In the Pagan mythology, a disproportionate number were herbalists and midwives who were using skills passed down to them from ancient times. Many Pagans also believe that it was a way for the church to eliminate any remaining pockets of opposing political power, as well as a way to make room for a male-dominated modern medical profession.

Pagans often express the fear of a return to "the burning times." In the view of many, some sort of return to the widespread, socially sanctioned persecution of Witches and other Pagans is possible (Stead, 1991). Thus, they view with apprehension the influence of the radical religious right in the Republican Party and on certain political leaders of both parties at the local, state, and national level. During a court battle in which the leaders of the Church of Iron Oak in Florida went to court to try to protect their right to worship at a private residence, money was needed for legal expenses. One of the ways in which this money was raised was by the sale of t-shirts bearing the slogan: "Never Again the Burning."

There is a tendency for educated people to dismiss the power of myth. This does not mean that they do not have their own mythologies; it simply means that they are not conscious of their myths, mistaking them for other types of information, commonly either pure fabrication or absolute historical truth. Historically, the various interpretations of the Christian Bible have ranged along this continuum. And, it is important to remember that all lasting myths contain more than a small element of truth. This is what gives them their verisimilitude. Myths are the stories we carry in our minds that help us to know who we are and how we fit into the world. They speak of our past, present, and future. They are usually based on the most fundamental truths of human existence, but express those truths as stories that can be regarded as anything from metaphor to literal fact. It is because myths speak deep truths that they have their power.

There is much discussion both inside and outside the Pagan community regarding the historical accuracy of the three stories presented above (e.g. Gibbons, 1999). This book is not about whether or not they are true. It is sufficient to note that they are the stories that—to a greater or lesser extent—inform views of the historical past that pervade the Pagan community. And, as Joseph Campbell stated, "When the story is in your mind, then you see its relevance to something happening in your own life. It gives you perspective on what's happening to you" (1988, 4). Thus, when Pagans are threatened or harassed because of their religious beliefs, they are acutely aware that people like them have been punished, tortured, and even killed for their beliefs in the past. This is reinforced when the person doing the harassing and making the threats claims to do it on behalf of Christianity. Most Christians would never be involved in this sort of activity, even if they had some reservations about Paganism. But, because of the power of the Pagan mythology, the few who are involved have the power to instill fear in both the object of their attention and many others who feel similarly vulnerable.

Pagan Identity

Identity is the internal, subjective, psychological, and normative self-portrait that each person has regarding their essential nature as human beings, their self-concept. It "encompasses notions of self and of the groups in which the self is embedded or feels identified with." This implies a self-definition that "differentiates oneself from, or at least compares oneself to, groups believed to be different from one's own." Thus, a person's identity "includes the I, the we, and the not-we" (Sigel, 2001, 112).

It "focuses on the meanings comprising the self as an object, gives structure and content to self-concept, and anchors the self to social systems" (Gecas, 1982, 4).

Social identity has at least four important aspects (Brewer, 2001, 117–119). First, it can be seen from the perspective of the self. It is about the person's "sense of self and the meaning that is derived from that identity." From this perspective, the social groups with which one identifies influence the individual in ways that are salient to the self with respect to the person's personality and value system. Historically, religious choice was been inherited at birth and remained immutable until death. In the contemporary world, however, religion-by-choice, as opposed to religion-by-inheritance has become more and more common (Giddens, 1991). Today, in the United States it is almost commonplace for people to have made a religious choice that is different from their inherited religion. There are very few people who are Pagans because they were born into this religion. Although Pagans-by-inheritance may become more numerous in the future, for most contemporary Pagans their religious choice is the outcome of a period of seeking and is seen to express something very fundamental about who they are. This effect is enhanced by the fact that Paganism is neither an obvious (except, perhaps, to the chooser) nor a popular religious choice. At best, to be a Pagan is to have your religion poorly understood or misunderstood completely. At worst, it may mean that you must be secretive about your religion and religious practices. This means being very careful about revealing or being honest about one of the most primordial aspects of one's identity. It also tends to engender a consciousness that others, those in more traditional religions, are socially rewarded for being open and honest about their religious beliefs. Comparisons are inevitable.

Second, identity can be seen from the perspective of the individual's perception of the self as a certain kind of person. Identity "define[s] the self *in relation to* others" (emphasis in the original). Here, "the traits and behaviors expressed by one individual are dependent on and responsive to the behavior and expectancies of the other parties in the relationship." Thus, "relational identities reflect the influence on the self-concept of societal norms and expectations associated with occupying particular roles or social positions, and the nature of the specific interpersonal relationships within which that role is carried out." Because the choice to become Pagan is usually the outcome of an intense period of religious searching and because that choice usually means the relinquishment of a previous religious identity, the average Pagan has given a lot of thought to the roles and relationships involved in being a Pagan as opposed to the roles and relationships involved in having a more traditional religious identity. Also, the choice to embrace a "weird" religion by becoming a Witch or Druid, for example, forever alters one's relationships with those both inside and outside that tradition. One of the major ways in which this is done is for the individual to be intensely religious within Paganism and seem unreligious or more traditionally religious in the secular world. Unitarian Universalism has often provided "cover" and an accepting milieu for those choosing some form of Paganism.

Third, identity can be perceived from the perspective of group-based social identities. These refer to "the perception of the self as an integral or interchangeable part of a larger group or social unit." They are "not forged from interpersonal relationships between and among individual group members, but rather from common ties to a shared category membership." In this perspective the "boundaries between self and other group members are eclipsed by the greater salience of the boundaries between ingroups and outgroups." This means that the fortunes and misfortunes of the group become events that are responded to personally. There are many reasons why a person might wish to base his or her religious identity in some form of Paganism. But, whatever the reason, it means that one's perspective on the world shifts radically.

For example, suppose an individual has said the Pledge of Allegiance many times, not thinking much about the part that says "under God." Then suppose that same person becomes an Isian (follower of the Egyptian Goddess, Isis). All of a sudden "under God" becomes a phrase that marks the self as "other," not wholly America, because the God referred to is clearly the Judeo-Christian God, not Isis. Then, when in 2002 the Ninth Circuit Court of Appeals hands down an opinion that calls the words "under God" into question as an unconstitutional establishment of religion (*Newdow v. U.S. Congress*, 292 F.3d 597), the Isian is impelled to look more seriously at the Pledge and what it is asking him or her to do. News coverage and politicians' statements make the Isian aware of the pervasiveness of the invocation of God in American public life. When people who support the word "under God" state that invoking God is central to American identity and traditions, the Isian may perceive that devotion to Isis, rather than God, is trivialized and that Isians are outsiders in the political system into which they were born. This is reinforced when the U.S. Supreme Court in 2004 unanimously strikes down the circuit court opinion on a technicality, refusing to consider the constitutionality of "under God" (*Elk Grove Unified School District v. Newdow*, 2004 U.S. LEXIS 4178). Thus, members of many minority religions continue to be forced to pledge their allegiance to their country in such a way that their religious choice defines them as member of the out-group, not quite genuine Americans. What is commonly referred to as "ceremonial deism" can easily seem to an Isian (or a Hindu or a Santerian or a Buddhist) an unconstitutional establishment of Christianity as America's official state religion.

Fourth, identity can be perceived as collective. This perspective focuses on the "shared representations of the group based on common interests and experiences," as well as "an active process of shaping and forging an image of what the group stands for and how it wishes to be viewed by others." It is because of such experiences as that outlined previously and others to be discussed later in this book that there is currently a movement among Pagans to present a more united front to the public. This grows out of a desire for the Pagan point of view to be heard and respected. For example, when the circuit court ruling discussed above was released, a group of Pagan leaders from diverse traditions released a statement supporting the removal of the words "under God" from the Pledge of Allegiance, pointing out that this would merely return the Pledge to the way it was said before the 1954 addition of "under God," which was designed to distinguish a Christian United States from a "godless" Soviet Union. It is, in short, a relic of the Cold War of the twentieth century and, in the words of the Pagan leaders: "A return to this non-religious language honors the beliefs of all Americans, and encourages all of us to affirm our solidarity as a nation" (Press Release, July 4, 2002).

In making this statement, they indicated that they wished to be recognized as being fully entitled to their collective identity as Pagans *and* their collective identity as Americans. Both religious communities and nations are collective entities that "stage expressive and ritualistic actions to secure their identities" (Cohen, 1985, 693). To say the Pledge using the words "under God" involves being inauthentic with relation to most Pagans' religion while not saying it deprives Pagans of the opportunity to affirm their patriotism. Characterizing the necessity to make this choice as silly or without importance (as most politicians and commentators did at the time) trivializes both identities and renders the Pledge a mere form without substance.

Because Paganism is, for most, a chosen identity, becoming Pagan usually involves a major shift in one's perspective on one's former religion— usually Judaism or Christianity. A convert to Paganism (or some other non-Christian religion) can come to see the crucifix was a rather gory object to be placed at the center of a religion that professes to be primarily about the love preached and practiced by Jesus. Correspondingly, communion, the most important ritual in most Christian sects, could be perceived as a form of ritual cannibalism, especially with reference to those sects that believe in transubstantiation. Both of these new perceptions can come as a shock to one who was raised as a Christian. On the other hand, the seasonal celebrations of Paganism calls one's attention to the bounty and beauty of the earth and the emphasis on the cycle of life that helps one come to better terms with the inevitability of death. Both can seem more healthy ways to order one's spiritual life.

The "two competing yet complementary aspects of human identity [are] separation from and connection to other human beings" (Note, 1984, 1472). To some extent, the choice to adopt a nontraditional religion is a statement about separation from all those who insisted that the individual (usually during childhood) be socialized into a particular religion, as well as from those who supported or carried out that socialization process. This is not necessarily rebellion against authority figures. Rather, it can be an expression of the conviction that their choice was not the best one for that individual and that the search for religious authenticity has led that individual elsewhere. In the case of a nontraditional religion, the choice expresses a willingness to take the riskier path—the one less traveled by (to borrow from Robert Frost). And it *can* make all the difference. This voluntary refashioning of a very primal part of one's identity is an expression of the contemporary "desire for authenticity and external recognition—finding one's true self and having it acknowledged by others" (Huddy, 2001, 138; Taylor, 1994). Many Pagans with whom I have spoken referred to their choice as "coming home," meaning that for the first time they felt their religious practice was an authentic expression of who they were.

Where does law enter into all of this? Guyora Binder and Robert Weisberg (1997, 1152, 1167) conclude that a system of law can be judged "according to the society it forms, the identities it defines, the preferences it encourages, and the subjective experience it enables" and that "we can 'read' and criticize law as part of the making of a culture." They add: "Traversing a social and moral terrain charged with legal meaning, individuals and groups can define themselves and one another by reference to legal norms." In the United States until slightly before the twenty-first century, a legal system that was strongly Protestant Christian, was comfortable for all but a small minority and assimilation (either forced or voluntary) was the solution. Now, pride in one's authentic self and one's heritage seems to be replacing the desire to assimilate found among previous waves of immigrants. At the same time, many of those born here are questioning their religious heritage.

When the Constitution was written, Christian homogeneity was the rule. The Establishment Clause was intended to keep one Christian sect from gaining the exclusive support (financial and otherwise) of the government. During the twentieth century, the battle was between Christianity and secularism. What seems to be impending as the twenty-first century begins is a far more complex situation. It raises the question of the meaning of the Establishment Clause in a different way. Certainly, until now, Christianity has been the normative religion of the United States and its government. One might even say that it has been the established religion. The main challenges have come from Christian sects with unusual practices and from secularists. For the most part, the law regarding free exercise and establishment has been made within this milieu.

Given current immigration patterns and the religious mutability of contemporary Americans, it seems that the First Amendment legal battles of the future might center more around whether the favoritism shown to Christianity is still acceptable in a country with more and more citizens who are outside that tradition. According to Daniel B. Salmons (1995, 1245) "what is needed is a fuller vision of what religious exercise often means to those engaged in it—one that takes into account the deeply symbolic and expressive nature of religious practice and the fundamental and defining role such worship plays in shaping human identity." The Christian majority is certainly fighting to make this happen for itself and is having substantial success in both the legislative and judicial arenas. The fact that most non-Christian religions are still relatively small with little political clout and legal protection is likely to change as they acquire larger numbers and greater political will.

The religious neutrality test established by *Employment Division v. Smith* will only work when one religious perspective does not dominate the political system. Until that happens, there may be little challenge to the link between American identity and "the need to believe in [the Christian] God . . . in order to be considered a 'true American'" (Huddy, 2001, 129). But "when state action deprives the individual of full membership in the political community because of his choice of a particular religious affiliation, the state interferes with free exercise" (Note, 1984). Given the dominance of Christianity in the U.S. legal system and the growing religious diversity of its population, one of the battle grounds of the twenty-first century may well be, not just equality before the law as it is practiced in the courts, but also equality in the more expressive aspects of the law, such as that of the national motto: "In God We Trust." If they can muster the political and legal savvy of native-born Americans, Pagans may well end up in the forefront of the struggle for true, substantive neutrality, rather than the unrealistic, formal neutrality represented by the *Smith* rule (Greenawalt, 1990). To get a sense of the battlefields upon which this war may be ranged, it is time to turn to the more concrete ways in which Paganism, as a non-Christian religion, has run into problems with our legal system.

CHAPTER 3
THE CHALLENGE OF CHRISTIAN HEGEMONY

Most, if not all, Christians consider Christianity to be the one true religion. In connection with this, Christianity is a proselytizing religion. For centuries, Christians have devoted much time and money to missionary efforts directed at those who do not share their beliefs. There is a range of ways in which this proselytizing imperative is directed. In some cases, the missionary efforts are aimed at persons in other countries who hold religious beliefs other than Christianity. Alternatively, some Christian sects try to convert Americans with non-Christian beliefs. As was discussed in chapter 1, the Native American population was an early target of Christian conversion efforts. Finally, members of some Christian sects aim their missionary efforts at members of other Christian sects. Most notable here are the Mormons and Jehovah's Witnesses who periodically show up on the doorsteps of most Americans patiently and politely asking for a chance to convince and convert. In most cases, conversion efforts are motivated by a genuine concern for persons who are outside the "fold." But, this genuine concern can sometimes turn to anger when the objects of the missionary effort resist the gift they are being offered.

The Doctrine of Christian Discovery firmly established this Christian proselytizing imperative as the norm in the settlement and governance of the lands that now compose the United States. In fact, there are nineteenth-century U.S. Supreme Court cases that call the United States a "Christian Nation" and declare Christianity part of common law (Banner, 1998; Green, 1999; Modak-Turan, 1998). The European invaders used the term "paganism" as an all-encompassing term to indicate religion that was non-Christian. Many of the early Christian settlers of North America believed that anyone who did not accept their faith (and sometimes their denomination) were doomed to spend eternity in hell. Thus, those who were not coreligionists became candidates for conversion—by persuasion at best, by force at worst.

Frequently, the government tacitly or actively aided in this effort, because government policymakers unquestioningly accepted the assumption that the one true religion was Christianity, particularly in its Protestant versions. In the eyes of some of the most zealous, those who stubbornly refused to choose the one true religion became the enemy, the worshippers of false gods. When this religiously ethnocentric impetus was carried to its logical extreme, pagans were perceived as a danger to the welfare of the community. They were not just the misguided worshippers of false gods; they were under the influence of Satan and, thus, posed a threat to all good Christians (Cookson, 2001, 3–5).

Many contemporary fundamentalist Christians retain this hostile and frightened stance toward all—Christian or non-Christian—who do not accept their sometimes extremely literal or idiosyncratic interpretations of the Bible and of Christianity. For example, Jay Rogers (1999a) in an online article, "Witchcraft and Satanism: Are they one and the same?" casts his net far beyond Witchcraft: "Contrary to the deceptive stereotype, no black masses or wild sex rituals are necessary to be a follower of Satan—simply deny the love and authority of God by living your life the way you want to. You can even be religious, attend church regularly, tithe, perform good works. If it's a religion based upon your own terms, you are still comfortably fulfilling the dictates of Satan's most primary law: 'Do what thou wilt.'"

Even to moderate or liberal Christians, the word "pagan" carries vaguely negative overtones. But, whether Christians consider pagans evil or simply misguided, there is no question about the need to convert them to Christianity, if possible. Proselytizing is basic to all forms of Christianity. When people cannot be converted or—even worse—leave Christianity, many fundamentalist Christians see it as their duty to eliminate such evil people from any position of possible influence in their communities and, if possible, drive them away altogether. Among these zealots are some who think that any means are justifiable in the effort to achieve this end. Their ideas and their words are frightening to Pagans, because they evoke visions of the Burning Times and the fear that it could, in some form, happen again. This fear is exacerbated when fundamentalists build alliances with political leaders and parties.

This problem becomes more acute when the Pagans in question are or are perceived as Witches. Since a large number of contemporary Pagans—probably a substantial majority—do self-identify as followers of Witchcraft or Wicca, this identity arouses even deeper fears and feelings of revulsion among some Christians. Even otherwise, tolerant Christians are likely to react more negatively to the term "witch" than they do to "pagan." For this reason, actual instances of discrimination or persecution seem to disproportionately involve those who identify themselves (or are identified by others) as Wiccans or Witches. This has given rise to much debate in the Pagan community about the wisdom of using the term "witch." Some think that it creates unnecessary problems; others want to reclaim it as an honorable, or at least acceptable, identity.

One of the most troublesome factors in this connection is the passage in the Bible that is often cited by evangelical or fundamentalist Christians: "Thou shalt not suffer a witch to live"[1] (Exod. 22:18). People who cite this passage tend to forget that it is a translation into English from a very different language. Anyone who has done any serious translating knows that every translator exercises a certain amount of discretion. Many words in the original language do not have exact duplicates in the language being used for translation, so a one-to-one correspondence is impossible to achieve. Therefore, the translator must choose words that the translator thinks are appropriate. These choices, in turn, can be heavily influenced by the predispositions of the translator and those who pay the translator, as well as the tenor of the times.

The King James translation was written during the Inquisition and the word was changed to "witch" as a justification for the persecution of those alleged to be witches. Thus, in this and many other ways the ideas and definitions of the inquisitors continue to influence contemporary thinking, even among people who condemn the Inquisition.[2] For many Pagans, and particularly Witches, this passage of the Bible when used by hostile Christians can take on the color of a death threat.

Accusations of Satanism

Nothing causes more frustration and, often, fear within contemporary Paganism than the insistence of Paganism's detractors that Pagans worship Satan. In the United States, the norm is to ask the followers of a religion whom and how they worship. In the case of Pagans, however, they are frequently told whom and how they worship by persons having little or no direct knowledge of their faith and practices—often persons (particularly evangelistic or fundamentalist clergy) who will personally benefit if their false assertions are taken as truth (Cuhulain, 1992, 16–18). When Pagans protest that the accuser's ideas are not accurate and try to correct them, the accusers tend defensively to assume that the Pagans are lying. Often this assumption is accepted by others who, given the extreme nature of the assertions, decide to err on the side of caution.

Like the passage of the Bible discussed above, it is a stunning example of the power of words: If you are a Pagan/Witch, you, *therefore*, must worship Satan, kill babies, hold Black Masses, use spells to harm Christians, and so on. Jay Rogers, whose online definition of Satanism was quoted above, makes this sort of sweeping generalization: "Witchcraft is an ancient religion *requiring child sacrifice* which has resurfaced in our day. A revival of neo-paganism has brought with it a revival of human sacrifice in the form of *abortion*" (1999b, 1, emphasis added). This sort of false accusation supports Roger's passionate antiabortion stance and seems to have been based on the fact that some people actively supporting the right to an abortion had some connection to "a registered nonprofit religious corporation known as the Wiccan Religious Cooperative of Florida" (1999b, 1).

This point of view is not limited to Internet "crazies." Charles Colson, noted for his work with Prison Fellowship Ministries, a program that has been praised by many leading politicians, for its work in running prison rehabilitation programs, holds a point of view that is not much different. Cybercast News Service has printed a commentary by Mr. Colson in which he uses the authority of a Princeton professor to accuse modern pagans (in which he includes secularized Christians and Jews) of using abortion as a form of child sacrifice to false gods (CNSNEWS.com, December 11, 2000).

Within the mainstream of contemporary Pagans, there is an insistence that Satan is not even relevant to Paganism. The Witches Anti-Discrimination League (WADL, 1998–1999, 1) responds to this issue thus: "Pagans (no matter what tradition or sect) do not worship the Devil. The Devil (or Satan) are [*sic*] Judeo-Christian concepts and do not have any bearing on the beliefs of Pagans. We do not believe in the Devil, therefore it is impossible for us to worship him." A popular website maintained by The Witches' Voice Inc., answers the assumption similarly: "Satan is a part of the Christian and Muslim religions. Since Pagans are neither Christian nor Muslim, Satan is not part of their deity structure at all. We believe that each and every human being is completely responsible for his or her own actions. To us, evil is a choice, albeit a bad one, that a human might make, not an embodied entity to blame our actions upon" (Walker, 1999, 2).

One of the central symbols of Paganism, the pentagram (or pentacle),[3] tends to be used by critics as "proof" that Pagans are Satanists. Interestingly, neither the Star of Bethlehem nor the stars on the American Flag, both represented by pentagrams, are perceived in the same way. Pagans interpret pentagrams in many ways. Perhaps the most common interpretation is that the five lower points represent the four elements: Air, Fire, Earth, and Water. The topmost point represents Spirit. Satanists usually turn the pentagram upside down, but (as Pagans point out) this is no different from the Satanist tendency to invert the Cross. Then why is the pentagram regarded as an exclusively Satanist symbol while the Cross is not and the Star of Bethlehem is not (e.g. WADL, 1998–1999, 4)? The usual answer is that pentagrams are "the universally recognized symbol of Satan" (Letter appearing in a newspaper in Haverhill, MA, reprinted in Walker, 1997, 2). In her dictionary of symbols, Barbara Walker (1988, 72) points out that the situation is quite complicated: "The most widely revered of all esoteric symbols, the pentacle has received many alternate names: pentalpha, pentagram, Solomon's seal, Star of Bethlehem, Three Kings' star, wizard's star, Star of Logres, devil's sign, witch's cross, goblin's foot, or (in Germany) *Drudenfuss*, the Druid's Foot. From this assortment of names it can be seen that the pentacle is associated with magic, paganism, deviltry and Christian mysticism all together." As the Witches' Voice website points out: "A symbol is simply an image or mark in itself. It is the mind and the beliefs of the beholder which attribute to it a particular meaning." When asked if Witches do blood sacrifices, the same source responds: "Goddess NO! Wiccans believe in the sanctity of all life" (Walker, 1999, 3).

The Pagan Educational Network (PEN, 1998, 2), under the heading "Setting the Record Straight" states that "[w]itchcraft has nothing to do with Satanism. Satan is a Judeo-Christian concept and the Craft has nothing to do with either Judaism or Christianity. Witches abhor manipulative and exploitative acts, such as are often attributed to Satanists. Witches do not accept the concept of a personification of evil. They do not seek power through the suffering of others." By way of clarification, they add: "Witches are essentially healers, whether they heal broken bones or broken spirits. Witches are not anti-Christian (or against any other nurturing faith). Pagans of all paths respect the individual's right to freedom of worship. Pagans do not proselytize or 'recruit.' Instead, they trust individuals to discover the spiritual path most appropriate for them."

This does not mean that there is no such thing as Satanism. As a matter of fact, in 1994, at least one U.S. District Court in *Howard, v. United States* (864 F. Supp. 1019) officially recognized Satanism as a religion entitled to the protection of the Free Exercise Clause of the First Amendment and enjoined the Federal Correctional Institute at Englewood in Littleton, Colorado to permit a prisoner the time, space, and implements to perform his religious rituals.

Mainstream Pagans do not consider Satanism part of Paganism. The current version was founded by Anton Szandor LaVey who became interested in the occult after a varied career that allegedly ranged from professional oboist to police photographer to lion trainer. He began teaching classes that evolved into a magic circle that met to perform rituals. "On WALPURGISNACHT (April 20) in 1966, LaVey shaved his head and announced the founding of the Church of Satan. He shrewdly recognized the shock value of using the term *church* for worshipping the Devil and recognized people's innate need for ritual, ceremony and pagentry. He performed satanic baptisms, weddings and funerals, all of which received widespread media coverage" (Guiley, 1989, 309, emphasis in the original). He wrote five books: *The Satanic Bible*, *The Satanic Rituals*, *The Satanic Witch* (originally published in Europe), *The Devil's Notebook*, and *Satan Speaks*. He also made several musical recordings (Obituary, *The Washington Post*, July 9, 1997). The tenets of the group he founded are more about selfishness and hedonism than blood sacrifices.

One of LaVey's early followers, Michael Aquino, broke with the Church of Satan in 1975 and with a small group of fellow dissidents founded the Temple of Set. Set (or Seth) is an ancient Egyptian deity whom "members do not consider evil but merely a prototype of Satan" (Guiley, 1989, 310). The Temple of Set officially regards itself as a more sophisticated formulation of Satanism and as "the only legally recognized 'Satanic' institution in the world" (Temple of Set, 1997–1999, 2). It sees Set as "a more complex, less stereotypical metaphysical image than that of the Judaeo/Christian Satan" (Temple of Set, 1997–1999, 3–4). Setians distinguish themselves from Pagans by asserting that they are a consciousness-worshipping, not a nature-worshipping religion and that this is a superior, more intellectually demanding path. They offer "a process for creating an individual, powerful essence that exists above and beyond animal life. It is thus the true vehicle for personal immortality" (Temple of Set, 1997–1999, 2). In this sense, they are more in the tradition of religions of transcendence such as Christianity and Islam, than in the tradition of religions of immanence such as Paganism.

According to D. H. Frew, an expert on Satanic and occult crime, "both groups routinely expel persons if they are found to be breaking the law. . . ." (Frew, 1991, 4). Neither advocates the sorts of blood sacrifices normally attributed to Satanists. In fact, the Five Satanic Rules of the Earth posted on the Church of Satan website explicitly state: "Do not harm little children" and "Do not kill non-human animals unless you are attacked or for your food." Their attitude toward human adults is harsher: "When walking in open territory, bother no one. If someone bothers you, ask him to stop. If he does not stop, destroy him" (LeVay, 1967, 2).

Frew (1991, 4) writes that, as of 1991, reliable estimates put the number of Satanists in the United States at fewer than 10,000.[4] He regards the Church of Satan and the Temple of Set members as "religious Satanists." He distinguishes them from "the kind of twisted, criminal practitioners that [talk show hosts] and others tend to focus on" whom he calls "self-styled Satanists." These he sees as the major problem for law enforcement: "It is this latter category of individuals who, getting their 'occult knowledge' from pop occult books, Creature Feature movies, and (most significantly) Christian anti-Satanism and anti-occult books, live up to the stereotypical image of the devil worshipper." He is in basic agreement with most Pagans that "[T]hese individuals are not motivated to commit crimes by Satanism; they are disturbed persons inclined towards criminal behavior who find a justification for their actions in devil-worship." Kerr Cuhulain in his *Law Enforcement Guide to Wicca* agrees: "As law enforcement officers we ought to be investigating crimes, not censoring religions. If a person commits a criminal act, we should bring them to justice regardless of their religious beliefs" (1992, 18).

Often, however, Pagans are faced with accusations of Satanism in situations that do not involve criminal activity.[5] For example, one of the problems that Pagans face stems from their strong preference for worshipping outdoors in natural settings. In our increasingly urbanized society, this often means worshipping in a member's yard or a public park. This makes them vulnerable to obstructionism, harassment, and threats. For example, in one situation where a group of Witches wanted to celebrate an important religious holiday with a service in a city-owned park, they were almost forced to cancel it because they received threats of violence from people who identified themselves as Christians. When this became a public issue, the organizers of the ritual were accused of being Satanists by a local Christian minister and two members of the City Council. This led to a highly charged City Council meeting in which several residents of the city expressed their fear of Satanism. In fact, one member of the Council appeared on television holding garlic and saying that he needed protection against evil spirits. The police, however, took a strong stand in favor of the Pagans' religious rights, assuring the public that there would be a police presence and that anyone causing trouble would be arrested. This made it possible for the ritual to be held (E-mail, October 2, 1996; October 3, 1996).

It should be added that the Witches also got support from many Christians, Jews, and Native Americans. In fact, it is often the case that mainstream Christian leaders publicly support Pagan religious rights, but incidences of such support vary greatly from region to region in the United States and, even within regions, from incident to incident. In this case, the police were the protectors of the Pagans' religious rights. Sometimes, however, the police can be the problem.

A newly formed coven was holding a new moon ritual in a member's yard. A neighbor noticed the ritual and called the police. The first person leaving the yard was stopped, handcuffed, and accused of being a Satanist. Her car was searched and her books and ritual tools examined. Finally, she was released without being charged. Subsequently, an unmarked police car followed another member of the coven. One of the coven members appealed for help to a national Pagan rights organization that informally investigated the situation. A representative of this organization arranged for the local police department to consult with a police expert on Satanism and occult crime. In this way, the problem was solved informally (E-mail, March 11, 1996; March 12, 1996). There have, however, been other such incidents in other places. One of the most notable happened at a Pagan festival. Such festivals are very important in the Pagan community. They are usually held in rural, relatively isolated campgrounds, attract members of many different Pagan traditions and last from three days to a week. At the end of the festival in question, the police stopped festival attendees as they exited the site and searched their cars. The only reason for the search was festival attendance (E-mail, August 6, 1996; June 24, 1997).

Such incidents illustrate the problem. When people think they "know" that Pagans are Satanists and that they "know" what Satanists do, they can become unnecessarily alarmed and take extreme measures to counter a threat that does not exist. If they were correct in their beliefs, they might be justified in taking extreme measures to ensure the safety of the community. Frequently, however, their "information" is simply a set of assumptions dating back to the Inquisition. If they make no effort to check their assumptions against verifiable facts, they can seriously violate the rights of people who are peacefully practicing their religion and are no threat to the community. Often, when information is provided and when the alarmed people are willing to reconsider their assumptions, the problem goes away, as it did in the above incident where the local police were informed and reassured by a fellow policeman whom they regarded as credible. The psychological impact, however, on Pagans can be considerable. They have to decide how much harassment and possible harm they are willing to undergo in order to practice their religion in appropriate ways and settings. And sometimes the harassment can be considerable.

Michael Thompson was the minister of the Spindletop Unitarian Church in Beaumont, Texas. His congregation included a chapter of the Covenant of Unitarian Universalist Pagans (CUUPS), an affiliate organization of the national Unitarian Universalist Association since 1987. Rev. Thompson's problems started one day in May 1996 when a few of the Spindletop CUUPS members were doing yard work at the church and a group of children walked over from a nearby ball park. The two groups mingled and the children learned that several church members were Pagans. There was no allegation that children were harmed in any way, but the fact that there were Pagans in the Spindletop congregation alarmed various members of the community. Shortly afterward, Reverend Rozell (a local Baptist minister), representatives of the ballpark, the police, and an employee of the local newspaper all visited the church. There were also some threats, but then things seemed to quiet down.

In July, however, the public was invited by Rev. Rozell to attend a seminar on the occult that he was holding in his church. Rev. Thompson and six of the eight CUUPS members came to the meeting. The meeting attendees reported: "We were told that we were expected to remain quiet and that any breech of silence would be quelled by the many law enforcement officials present." During his opening comments, Rev. Rozell held up a piece of paper, saying that it had been given to him by Rev. Thompson and that it contained the names of the Pagans in the Spindletop Church. Rev. Thompson protested that he had not given the list to Rev. Rozell and objected to what he saw as an attack on his congregation. When told to be quiet, Rev. Thompson refused and dropped to his knees. The police carried him out. Three Spindletop members followed him and were told to return to the meeting or go home.

The remaining Pagans described their experience: "The rest of us sat mortified and frozen by our fear" (Members, 1996, 88). Subsequently, there were several speakers. The final one was a sheriff's deputy. The Pagans described his remarks as follows: "To the thunderous amens and hallelujahs of the Highland congregation, deputy McCauley claimed himself to be a 'Christian policeman' and stated that he was not going to tolerate pagan religious practices. . . . 'I can see you smiling,' he said, pointing to some of us, 'but you won't be.' We weren't smiling, we were terrified. A cry went up in the congregation, 'Hold Satan at bay! . . . Cast the devil in the pit!' " The Spindletop Pagans then added that

"[I]t wasn't the inquisition and it wasn't the holocaust, but it was the scariest moment most of us have ever experienced" (Members, 1996, 88).

Rev. Thompson was taken to the County Correctional Facility and charged with the misdemeanor of trespassing, which was punishable by a fine of as much as $2,000 and/or 180 days in jail. He was released later that night on a $500 bond. The next day he held a press conference to give his side of the story. He was accompanied by a rabbi and two Christian ministers who said that, while they did not endorse Paganism, they did support freedom of religion. In 1998, after a request for a change of venue was denied, Rev. Thompson was convicted of trespass and sentenced to six months' probation and a $200 fine.[6]

From the perspective of religious freedom, the fact that such incidents happen at all is significant. If Pagans who are within the shelter of a widespread and accepted denomination, such as Unitarian Universalism and who have done nothing more than reveal their identity as Pagans can arouse so much fear and hate, what might happen to a Pagan without a Rev. Thompson to speak for them? And, furthermore, what happened to Rev. Thompson (not a Pagan) when he did try to come to their aid? Incidents such as this have a chilling effect on Pagans. They rightly fear persecution, so many choose to keep their religious beliefs and practices secret.

It is important to note that such incidents are not common. There are many Christian leaders who are aware of and concerned about intolerance toward other faiths. For example, a coalition of evangelical Christian leaders recently called for toleration of religious freedom. The group noted that some churches have not shown "proper respect for the rights and dignity of others" and it repudiated "coercive techniques, dishonest appeals, or any form of deception" (*Chicago Sun-Times*, June 9, 2000). Another example is the statement of James Clement Taylor, a member of the Eastern Orthodox Church, who has written: "Dear brothers and sisters in Christ, these people of Wicca have been terribly slandered by us. They have lost jobs, and homes, and places of business because we have assured others that they worship Satan, which they do not. We have persecuted them, and God will hold us accountable for this you may be sure. . . ." (Taylor, 1999, 2).

It is also important to note that evangelical and fundamentalist Christian ministers tend to be in the forefront when incidents of accusation of Satanism and harassment occur. In fact, early in November 2000, in Smithfield Virginia more than 30 laymen and pastors from the area held a meeting to prepare a "strategic plan" for dealing with Pagan gatherings in that area. Their primary target was a yearly Pagan festival,

Gathering of the Tribes, that was held on privately owned property. According to a local news reporter, the ministers did not see the situation as involving religious freedom, because "the pagan movement [is] evil" and "there is a higher authority [God] at work" (Manner, 2000).

This group basically decided to pray away the Pagans, as did the pastor and members of the Living Word Church in Houma, Louisiana. In the latter case, however, it went farther. They also filed a complaint against the Witches citing a very old Louisiana law that forbids fortune telling. This activated the ACLU of Louisiana that had been trying to get the law abolished as a violation of the protection of free speech in the U.S. Constitution. Although, the local authorities decided not to prosecute because of the freedom of religion issue, the Wiccans were left vulnerable to periodic harassment until the law is taken off the books— a law that is never used in nearby New Orleans where there is a thriving business in many forms of divination (Wehmeyer, 2000). Finally, one of the most emotionally devastating instances of Christian ministerial condemnation of Pagans was when Rev. Jerry Falwell publicly included Pagans among those, such as gays, lesbians, feminists, the ACLU and others, whom he tried to blame for creating an atmosphere that encouraged the terrorist attacks of September 11, 2001.[7]

The most insidious infringement on religious rights is a social, political, and governmental climate that discourages the members of a religious group from openly professing and practicing their beliefs and forces them to hide, or even lie about, their deepest spiritual convictions. This robs them of the freedom to express a basic component of their identities. It would seem that this could not happen in a country that prides itself on religious freedom and even takes it upon itself to pass laws chastising other countries for their lack of religious freedom and persecution of Christians. It would also seem that there should be a legal recourse for persons in this situation. Law in the United States, however, was written by Christians and for Christians. It assumes that any genuine religion will have certain Christian characteristics, such as monotheism. Often the people who administer the law make the same assumptions.

Nontraditional Religious Identity and the Law

The identity of religious people strongly reflects the denomination to which they belong and its beliefs—official and, sometimes, unofficial. This is true for both Pagans and their detractors. Most Pagans feel deeply that it should be their right to be open about their religious identity and beliefs. After all, isn't that what the Constitutional First Amendment guarantee of Freedom of Religion is all about? Many do not realize that the First Amendment only offers protection against adverse governmental action. It is not a shield against discrimination by private parties. Moreover, they do not realize that Supreme Court interpretation further narrowed this protection when in *Employment Division v. Smith* the Supreme Court struck down the *Sherbert* test requiring the demonstration of a compelling governmental interest before the state can burden religious practice. Now the test is whether the government action is religiously neutral on its face. As was discussed in chapter 1, this means that the more similar a religion is to the prevailing Christianity, the more likely it is to receive protection. Conversely, the more different it is, the less protection it can expect. Pagans hope for the same protection as is extended to Christians; as a practical matter, however, they expect less, because even well-meaning government officials can easily make Pagan worship difficult or impossible through sheer ignorance of their religious beliefs and practices. Malice is always a threat, but it is not the only basis for violations of Pagan religious rights.

Thus, for Pagans a major part of their identity is left vulnerable and the First Amendment is a very limited source of protection. Currently, it is more useful as an ideal to be invoked than as a legal remedy that Pagans might hope to pursue successfully in the court system. The other major source of protection within the legal system is the constitutions and statutes of the 50 states—*if* the state has relevant legislation and *if* the protections of the legislation extend to religion and *if* the type of problem they are having is covered by their state's legislation. Most state codes and constitutions contain some sort of protection for religious practice, but it varies widely in nature and scope.

Many, but not all, state constitutions have provisions that confer a more-or-less blanket protection against state interference with religious expression. Some are very straightforward, such as the Massachusetts provision: "No law shall be passed prohibiting the free exercise of religion" (Mass. Const. Ann. Amend. Art. XVIII, Sec. 1 (2000)). Others, however, are more verbose and therein lies the potential for problems that might affect Pagans. For example, the Mississippi Constitution provides that "[t]he rights hereby secured shall not be construed to justify acts of licentiousness injurious to morals or dangerous to the peace and safety of the state. . . ." (Miss. Const. Ann. Art. 3, Sec. 18 (2000)). Similarly, the Washington Constitution provides that "the liberty of conscience hereby secured shall not be so construed as to excuse acts of licentiousness or justify practices inconsistent with the peace and safety of the state" (Wash. Const. Art. 1, Sec. 11 (2000)). Another example is the California Constitution that provides: "Free exercise and enjoyment of religion without discrimination or preference are guaranteed. This liberty of conscience does not excuse acts that are licentious or inconsistent with the peace or safety of the state" (Cal. Const. Art. I, Sec. 4 (2000)). Maryland's constitutional provision removes protection for an individual's practice if "he shall disturb the good order, peace or safety of the state, or shall infringe the laws of morality. . . ." (Md. Dec. of R. Art. 36 (1999)). Earlier in the Maryland provision, it is strongly implied that the morality is assumed to have a monotheistic orientation: "That as it is the duty of every man to worship God in such a manner as he thinks most acceptable to Him, all persons are equally entitled to protection in their religious liberty. . . ."

Such constitutional provisions are not unusual at the state level and implicit in these seemingly reasonable provisions are potential pitfalls for Pagans. For example, many Pagans are not monotheists. Also, there are points at which the Pagan approach to morality diverges from the Christian norm. This is particularly true with reference to attitudes toward the human body and toward sexual activity. Given that Paganism is a religious path that holds the earth and nature sacred, most Pagans regard nudity positively and sex as a gift of the Goddess (or gods) (see e.g. 112 *Green Egg*, 1996). The Charge of the Goddess, one of the more widely recognized sacred texts in Wicca, contains the following passage with reference to nudity: "You shall be free from slavery, and as a sign that you be free you shall be naked in your rites." Subsequently, it addresses sex: "Let My worship be in the heart that rejoices, for behold—all acts of love and pleasure are My rituals" (Starhawk, 1989, 90–91; Farrar and Farrar, 1984, 297–298).

Most, if not all, Christian sects have a very different view of the human body and sexuality. It is easy to imagine a situation in which a court might find that Pagans were involved in licentious or immoral acts in connection with nudity, not sharing with the Pagans before it a view of the body and its procreative functions as sacred. For example, among Pagans social nudity is considered quite acceptable under the right conditions. Pagan events that are in appropriately secluded locations generally have a "clothing optional" policy—no one is forced to be nude, but those who choose nudity or partial nudity participate normally alongside their clothed fellow Pagans. In addition, some traditions practice ritual nudity in private homes or very secluded locations. Even those who do not ordinarily go farther than "clothing optional" may incorporate nudity in initiations.[8] All of this can be traced at least as far back as Gardnerian Wicca (Berger, 1999, 94; Hutton, 1999, 231, 399; Luhrmann, 1989, 48–49).

Even more controversial is the "Great Rite," or ritual sexual intercourse. It is much more often practiced symbolically than physically and when practiced physically it is usually done so in privacy (i.e. not in front of the rest of the coven) (Luhrmann, 1989, 48). In *The Witches Bible Compleat*, Janet and Stewart Farrar (1984, 48–49) explain its meaning:

> To [Witches] sex is holy—a manifestation of that essential polarity which pervades and activates the whole universe, from Macrocosm to Microcosm, and without which the universe would be inert and static—in other words, would not exist. The couple enacting the Great Rite are offering themselves, with reverence and joy, as expressions of the God and Goddess aspects of the Ultimate Source. "As above, so below." They are making themselves, to the best of their ability, channels for that divine polarity on *all* levels, from physical to spiritual. That is why it is called the *Great* Rite.
>
> It is also why the "actual" Great Rite is enacted without witnesses—not through shame but for the dignity of privacy. And it is why the great rite in its "actual" form should, we feel, be enacted only by a married couple or by lovers of a marriage-like unity; because it *is* a magical rite, and a powerful one; and charged with the intensity of intercourse, by a couple whose relationship is less close, it may well activate links on levels for which they are unprepared and which may prove unbalanced and disturbing. (Emphasis in the original)

The more common symbolic Great Rite is usually performed by placing the blade of a ritual knife (the God) into a ritual chalice (the Goddess).

Judges whose own background is in the Judeo-Christian tradition with its strictures against nudity and its restrictive attitudes toward sex, could easily see the beliefs and practices just described as instances of licentiousness or immorality. When these strictures were introduced into state constitutions, it was assumed that there were commonly held definitions of both licentiousness and morality. Much has changed since then and such passages today represent a trap for persons who have non-Christian religious attitudes toward the human body and sexual activity. Although the country is becoming more religiously diverse, the judiciary is still overwhelmingly Christian and has the corresponding attitudes about physical and sexual modesty.

The other major recourse for Pagans who need to protect themselves against prejudice is antidiscrimination legislation. Such statutes exist on the federal, state, and local levels. Federally, Title VIII of the Civil Rights Act of 1968 prohibits discrimination in the provision of housing and specifically mentions religion as a protected category. Although it exempts religious organizations from its reach when the housing is operated for religious, as opposed to commercial, purposes, this is of little concern to Pagans. Of more concern is the exemption that applies to rooms or apartments in dwellings where there are four or less units and the owner actually lives in the dwelling. In places and times where available housing at affordable prices is scarce, this could significantly limit the choices of Pagans.

Of considerably more significance are the laws in which the states use their police powers to forbid religious discrimination. State codes vary greatly and some offer more extensive and comprehensive protection than federal law. Others, however, extend very little—if any—protection. In some states, people may be protected against religious discrimination in housing; in others, they may not. In some states, they may be protected against discrimination in employment; in others, they may not. There exist comprehensive statutes, like that of Connecticut which provides: "It shall be a discriminatory practice in violation of this section for any person to subject, or cause to be subjected, any other person to the deprivation of any rights, privileges or immunities, secured or protected by the constitution or laws of this state or of the United States, on account of religion, national origin, alienage, color, race, sex, blindness or physical disability" (Conn. Gen. Stat. Sec. 46 (a) (1999)). This statute makes the covered conduct a misdemeanor, except where property damage of $1,000 or more is involved in which case the act becomes a Class D felony. In addition, Connecticut has a Penal Code provision against intimidation based on bigotry or bias that includes religion as a protected category (Conn. Gen. Stat. Sec. 53 (a) (1999)). Many other states, however, have no such provisions.

The cases based on religion that have usually been brought under state antidiscrimination legislation have involved persons who invoke their religious rights as a reason to be allowed to discriminate against another person's civil rights (Cordish, 1996). For example, a landlord might not want to rent to an unmarried couple because of a strongly held religious belief that homosexuality and sexual intercourse outside of marriage are sins. Thus, it becomes a case of the state's interest in protecting the availability of housing for all of its citizens against a citizen's claim that enforcement of the fair housing law would burden the right to freely follow relevant tenants of a particular religion: a civil rights claim coming into conflict with a free exercise claim.

Although there have, to my knowledge, been no such cases involving Pagans that have been decided on an appellate level to date, the Pagan situation raises the possibility that both sides in such cases might be invoking a religious basis in their arguments before a court. In other words, the landlord might be claiming to be religiously exempt from an antidiscrimination housing statute while the prospective tenant might claim to be discriminated against on the basis of their religion. Hypothetically, a fundamentalist Christian landlord might not want to rent an apartment to Pagans who, he asserts, worship Satan whether they are willing to admit it or not. Since there have been highly inconsistent court decisions in cases that have involved persons wanting to discriminate because of religion (Cordish, 1996), it is impossible to predict how a court might deal with such a freedom of religion versus religious discrimination case. It is, however, probable that the outcome would be influenced by the court's willingness to regard Paganism as a legitimate religion entitled to the same protections extended to Christian religions. In addition, community knowledge of and attitudes toward Paganism might play a part.

Another way in which the law affects Pagans has to do with the way in which much law impacting religion is written. Until quite recently, Christian legislators commonly used their majority position to write their beliefs into the law (Conkle, 1993–1994, 4–6). Every time Pagans use money, they see "In God We Trust" and are reminded that, while they might be Goddess worshippers, polytheistic, or pantheistic, the United States is officially monotheistic and the deity is "God." Correspondingly, many public buildings carry the same reminder.

Now, there are those in the Christian majority that are marshalling considerable political pressure to have the Ten Commandments posted in schools, courtrooms, and other public places. Most commentators trivialize this Christian dominance as "ceremonial deism" (Epstein, 1996). Another point of view was recently expressed by a Pagan in a religious rights online group: "The popular religions get what they want (10 commandments in public places, crosses allowed in prisons and schools but not pentacles, 'In God we trust' on our money, prayers to Jesus at the inauguration [of George W. Bush], 'Jesus Day' and 'day of prayer' governmental proclamations, etc. etc. etc. etc. ad nauseum. . . .) and the unpopular ones are harassed/legislated against, whether on a local level (zoning laws unevenly enforced, police seizures, animal sacrifice is illegal, Pagan and Native American inmates harassed and sacred items handled, etc.) or federal; 'Charitable Choice' will not include Pagan, Wiccan or atheist groups. That's why this list exists, and presumably why you're on it—the inequities Pagans have to live with on a daily basis and are working to correct."

As was noted previously, in 2002, a federal circuit court found one element of ceremonial deism, the words "under God" that had been added to the Pledge of Allegiance by Congress in 1954, unconstitutional under the Establishment Clause in *Newdow v, U.S. Congress* (292 F.3d 597). The political outcry was deafening. For example, most members of Congress (Democrat and Republican alike) marched to their chambers and ostentatiously recited the Pledge emphasizing the words "under God." Virtually no one, politician or press commentator, accurately described what the court had done. It was repeatedly reported that the decision had struck down the Pledge, not just the two words "under God." For the most part, the leaders of non-Judeo-Christian religions remained silent fearing, perhaps, the response they would get if they spoke out. Those who did protest got little or no press coverage.

In addition, there is much in the law that more subtly favors Christian religious beliefs and practices. For example, much legislation that touches on religion in some way, clearly assumes that all religious people are monotheists. Examples would be the phraseology of the Maryland Constitution and the United States motto that have already been quoted. Even in Connecticut, a state in which religious freedom is relatively well protected, there is an assumption of monotheism: "It being the right of all men to worship the Supreme Being, the Great Creator and Preserver of the Universe . . ." (Conn. Const. Art. VII [1999]). While this sort of verbiage is usually not of direct harm to Pagans and other religious people who are not monotheistic, the quotation above demonstrates that it can convey to them the impression that theirs is a second-class religion (Greenawalt, 1985, 391; Epstein, 1996; Solum, 1990, 1093; Simson, 1994, 520). In situations of harassment or discrimination, it can make them wonder if the legal system will be there to protect them in the way it would be for a Christian who was experiencing similar harassment or discrimination. As is discussed in more detail later, many other legal provisions that are facially neutral assume a Christian way of belief and worship and Pagans have run into problems with many of them—particularly since they are administered by a judiciary so steeped in Christian culture that it cannot help seeing religion in terms of that cultural heritage.

The Judiciary

When faced with legal problems, many Pagans quite reasonably assume that they can find equal justice by resorting to the judicial system. After all, their civic socialization inculcated the notion that the United States is a land where freedom of religion reigns supreme. As it turns out, however, all religions are not treated equally within the court system any more than they are treated equally in the law. The American judiciary often exhibits the same problem as the Supreme Court and the laws just discussed. The farther a faith group departs from Christian norms, the less likely it is that judges will recognize its beliefs and practices as religious and worthy of protection. This failure of understanding demonstrated by the Supreme Court majority in the *Lyng* decision, discussed in chapter 1, is a vivid example; property rights clearly trumped the ability to practice a non-Christian religion. Moreover, the less similar a religion is to the Christian pattern, the more likely it is that a legislative body will unwittingly create a legislation that violates religious rights, but appears "facially neutral" to legislators, law enforcement officials, and courts. Finally, even when the law is truly neutral, judges may administer it in ways that reflect their own Christian socialization (Karst, 1992, 517; Note, 1987b, 1625–1631). Culture is, at least in part, about assigning meaning to behavior. The same might be said of judging. Yet, judges are "acculturated to the meanings prevailing within at least one particular group." For most judges, this is Christianity. "The assumptions thus ingrained are usually left unarticulated, and nothing is more difficult than to stand outside them" (Karst, 1994, 358).

The problem was illustrated by Stephen J. Stein (2000, 60) in an article where he discusses the growth of religious diversity in America and the challenge it presents to the legal system. Conceding that religion clauses of the U.S. Constitution "deserve continuing preeminence and respect," he calls attention to the fact that "the possible matters of contestation regarding religion in the future are likely to become more and more complex and less and less related to the historical concerns that informed those clauses." He asks: "How, for example, should the legal and constitutional concessions granted to organized denominations, including tax benefits, zoning variances, and medical exclusions, apply to a self-declared shaman who operates a website for his virtual congregation out of his home, collects free-will offerings from his followers, prescribes a variety of remedies for everything from a toothache to cancer, uses 'recreational drugs' for spiritual ends, and is far more 'religious' than nine out of ten Americans?" In his opinion, "[o]ur best hope in the future may be wise legislators who will craft new tolerant legislation, and even wiser judges who will apply democratic principles to issues involved with the free exercise of religion." More immediately, what should be done about a Maryland-based Wiccan High Priestess and Founding Elder of the Nomadic Chantry of the Gramarye who holds her rituals for her approximately 50-member congregation in her own home or, weather permitting, in a sanctuary space in her back yard?

In 1998, two members of High Priestess Rosemary Kooiman's congregation who lived in Fairfax County, Virginia wanted her to officiate at their wedding. The only problem was that they planned to hold it in Virginia. She had already married people in Maryland where marriages can be performed by "any official of a religious order or body authorized by the rules and customs of that order or body to perform a marriage ceremony" (Md. Family Law Code Ann. Sec. 2–406 (1) [1999]). In Virginia, however, the determination of who has permission to perform marriages is not left to the religious organization, but is primarily controlled by the circuit courts of the counties and cities (Va. Code Ann. Sec 20–23 [1999]). In May of 1998, High Priestess Kooiman applied for a permit.

The matter was brought to the attention of the Hon. F. Bruce Bach, Chief Judge of the Fairfax County Circuit Court. Unsatisfied with the papers submitted, Judge Bach held a hearing, requiring her to prove that she was the "minister" of a religious organization. In his decision[9] Judge Bach noted: "Kooiman presented documents showing the organization obtained tax exempt status from the United States Government and the State of Maryland in 1995. However, Kooiman was unable to present any 'religious' literature that memorializes her group's beliefs or doctrines. Similarly, no 'handbooks' or 'guidelines' for the high priestess were introduced at the hearing. In fact, Kooiman did not provide any evidence to show the Nomadic Chantry of the Gramarye is connected in any way with the Church of Wicca or any broader organization." What this judge wanted was the kind of documentation that ministers, priests, and rabbis can produce easily, because they are members of relatively large, organized denominations with published theological documents that apply to all member congregations. Paganism does not work that way.

There is no single authoritative "Church of Wicca" that serves as an administrative and theological superstructure for all those who religiously identify as Wiccan. There is no "bible" or catechism that all are bound to study and follow. There is not even a theology that all Wiccans are required to accept. In Paganism, virtually all power, theologically and otherwise, lies with individuals (solitaries) or small groups (i.e. what Christians might call congregations). The small groups may carry any of a number of designations, such as circle, coven, hearth, grove, or nest. Both individuals and groups may be "eclectic" in that they devise their own belief systems and practices, drawing on a variety of traditions.

Alternatively, they may identify with any of a number of relatively widely established traditions, such as Gardnerian Wicca or the Reclaiming Tradition of Witchcraft.

In the Pagan world, a "congregation" of approximately 50 is considered quite large. The authority of the Pagan religious leadership of such a group is based on the followers' willingness to seek and accept spiritual guidance. The followers are not bound to their group or to Paganism the way that a Catholic is bound to the Roman Catholic Church. The members of such groups are free to leave their ritual group or Paganism with no threatened dire consequences—either in this life or the next. If the couple wanting to be married accepts High Priestess Kooiman as their spiritual leader and wishes to have her officiate at their wedding, that is sufficient for most Pagans.

Further, Judge Bach assumed ("without deciding") that the Nomadic Chantry of the Gramarye met the definition of a religion, a definition he took from the *Random House College Dictionary*. He stated that the issue was "whether Kooiman is a minister of a religious denomination as contemplated by the [Virginia] Code." He then went on to find that she was not. His reasoning showed that, in spite of having had the opportunity to educate himself using the hearing and the detailed explanations contained in the application that High Priestess Kooiman submitted, he was judging her application on the basis of standards that were only appropriate when applied to the kinds of religious organizations with which he was familiar and not on the basis of standards appropriate when applied to Pagans. First, he insisted that her group have a formal affiliation with the "Church of Wicca," an organization that does not exist in the sense that it is an overarching church organization, such as the Roman Catholic Church, the African Methodist Episcopal Church or the Presbyterian Church (U.S.A.). In fact, the Church of Wicca is simply one sect within Paganism—but one that was mentioned in a 1986 Fourth Circuit case, *Dettmer v. Landon* (799 F.2d 929), involving a convict who wanted to participate in the correspondence course that group provides.

Second, he insisted that she show significant evidence that she was "elected" or "selected" by her congregation to be their leader. This assumes a much more hierarchy than is characteristic of Pagan groups. In fact, many Pagan groups expressly reject the kind of hierarchical administrative arrangements that are characteristic of most Christian organizations and congregations. He held against her the fact that when testifying in the hearing she said that there was "no difference" between her and the general members of the Nomadic Chantry of the Gramarye.

What she was expressing was a widely held and proudly egalitarian Pagan belief that leadership is shared and fluid. Group organization tends to be minimally hierarchical or non-hierarchical (and, in some cases, even antihierarchical).

Most American Pagans are reluctant to claim spiritual or administrative superiority, even when they are acting as group leaders. Leadership positions often tend to rotate routinely among members of a primary ritual group. Designations, such as "Elder" and "High Priestess" are earned and leadership positions are subject to the willingness of the followers to accept a person as their spiritual leader. Thus, Judge Bach concluded "the simplicity with which Kooiman obtained her minister-ial status and the commonality between the high priestess and the members does not support Kooiman's contention she is a 'minister' for the purposes of Virginia Code Sec. 20–23." The judge obviously did not appreciate how complex consensual organizations are or the fact that leadership does not have to be hierarchical to be effective.

Supported by the American Civil Liberties Union, High Priestess Kooiman applied for a rehearing, but was refused. Then she applied to the Circuit Court for Alexandria. It deferred to the Fairfax County Circuit Court and refused her application. Finally, she submitted the same paperwork to the Norfolk Circuit Court and it treated the matter routinely granting her permission to perform marriages in the entire state of Virginia (*The Washington Post*, September 28, 1998). According to local Pagans, the circuit courts in southern Virginia had been handling such cases for over 20 years and, thus, had become used to processing such applications. As a result of this case, however, a Pagan resource center based in Norfolk began to work on legislation that would amend the Virginia Family Law Code to limit the discretion of circuit court judges in the matter of granting such applications. To date, however, they have not been successful.

The Kooiman case involved a judge who was trying to act in a neutral manner, but who was limited in his ability to do so by his own internalized and unquestioned assumptions about religion based on the prevalent norms for church organization within the Christian tradition. There is no indication of whether Judge Bach had a religious affiliation or whether he was religiously devout (Carter, 1989; Griffen, 1998). The interesting thing is that he did not seem to be aware of the limits to his understanding or (if he was aware) of the fact that his religious bias was driving his legal reasoning. It is significant that at one point in his decision he opined, "to authorize a marriage celebrant in this situation would mean that every self-proclaimed leader of a small cult could perform marriages in Virginia." At this point in U.S. history, the term "cult" is generally used pejoratively, but it is worth remembering that Christianity was once regarded as a cult.

During recent years, there has been a lively debate among interested legal scholars about the "religiously devout judge" (Carter, 1989) and the place of religion in the decision making processes of the judiciary. Most sources (e.g. Smith, 1998) trace this debate to Kent Greenawalt's publication of a book, *Religious Convictions and Political Choice* in 1988. In it, Greenawalt pointed out that the occasional reliance by judges on their personal religious convictions is not improper (239). Gregory Sisk, Michael Heise, and Andrew Morriss (2004, 614) claim to have empirically demonstrated that religion is "the single most prominent, salient and consistent influence on judicial decisionmaking [on religious freedom issues]." They make specific reference to "religion in terms of affiliation of the claimant, the background of the judge, and the demographics of the community," independent of other variables widely used in empirical research on judicial behavior.

Another impetus to the discussion has been the recent increase in religious organizations' overt attempts to influence the confirmation processes of federal judges. Although those who have engaged in this debate disagree about much, they all seem to accept the fact that no judge can completely divorce his religious convictions from his deliberations as a judge. They differ principally on the extent to which and the way in which religious convictions should play a role in the judicial process.

The argument is very wide ranging. At one extreme is William P. Gray Jr. (1998a) who argues that the religious protections of the First Amendment should apply only to the federal government and that the states should be free to determine all matters regarding religion for themselves, including (it would seem) establishing a religion if they so choose.[10] He bases his argument on the fact that some of the states had established religions when the Constitution was ratified and continued to have them for some time thereafter. He feels strongly that the Supreme Court was wrong in making the First Amendment applicable to the states through incorporation into the Fourteenth Amendment. Needless to say, he sees no problem with judges who openly express their religious convictions in their courtrooms and has strongly supported Alabama Judge Moore who displayed the Ten Commandments prominently in his courtroom and invited Christian clergy-led prayer before court sessions. In direct response to Gray, Robert R. Baugh (1998) points out how the United States changed between 1791 and 1868: "Our

Nation's history following the passage of the First Amendment shows a complete abandonment of state established religions. Consequently, by the time the Fourteenth Amendment was adopted, freedom to exercise religion had come to mean that states would not impose religious views on their citizens" (Baugh, 1998, 556). He concludes that posting the Ten Commandments and having a Christian prayer before court sessions is clearly unconstitutional. Gray is unimpressed (Gray, 1998b).

Thus, it would seem that the legal system is, so to speak, "stuck" in the past. Originally, freedom of religion was a guaranty that all Christian sects would be permitted to worship freely. The corresponding Establishment Clause was primarily designed to ensure that none of them would be able to get preferential treatment from federal and, later, state government. This system made sense when the United States was overwhelmingly Protestant Christian. As time passed, however, Catholics, Jews, atheists, and agnostics became more able to assert their rights in the legal system. The legal concept of religion continued to adhere to the basic Christian mode—with room for those who were not religious but ran afoul of the law because of deeply held values that played a religion-like role in their lives. Christianity (in the form of ceremonial deism) flourished and expanded in the face of the twentieth century's threat of "godless communism." Again, there was enough homogeneity in religious beliefs and forms to make this generally unobjectionable.

Now, in the twenty-first century, the homogeneity is waning. More and more Americans and those aspiring to American citizenship are not Christian. The "fabric of our society" called upon so often by the supporters of ceremonial deism is changing and is changing rapidly. It is no longer a matter of Protestant Christian sects jockeying for power among themselves. It is also no longer a matter of all types of Christians facing off against those who are not religious. Now it is a question of whether, in the face of growing religious diversity, Christianity and its concomitant monotheism may be said to have become equivalent to an established religion. In chapter 7, a close look at ceremonial deism supports the notion that it has (Epstein, 1996; Note, 1987a; 1987b, 1620–1623; 1987c, 1651–1659). This has many consequences for Pagans, as well as others outside the Judeo-Christian fold. One consequence is the constant necessity to "prove" that your religion is just as valid a religion as Christianity or Judaism. It is to this problem that we now turn.

CHAPTER 4
PAGANISM AS A RELIGION

Thus far, the discussion has referred to Paganism as a religion without directly addressing that assumption. It is now time to consider whether Paganism is truly a religion for legal purposes, to outline the ways in which it is similar to or departs from generally held notions about what a legally recognized religion should be like and to take a closer look at the sorts of activities usually associated with religious organizations and practices. The definition of religion for legal purposes is one of those tasks that, upon closer examination, turns out to be much more difficult than it seemed at first glance. As is discussed in more detail below, most of the confusion associated with defining religion is due to a series of decisions made by the Supreme Court in the second half of the twentieth century that attempted to extend the concept of religion beyond its usual theist boundaries. Fortunately, the Supreme Court's agonizing over nontheistic belief systems does not affect the status of Paganism as a religion. The overwhelming majority of Pagans (if not all) are theist and clearly fall well within the federal courts' definition of religion.

Legal problems arise, however, because the differences between religions within the Christian tradition and many of those outside of it tend to be poorly understood or completely misunderstood by the general population, chief executives,[1] legislators, government agency decision makers and, as discussed previously, many judges (especially state and local judges) (Idleman, 1998; Note, 1987b). Thus, despite their theism, Pagans tend to run afoul of the law in connection with their status as a religion and methods of worship. More specifically, legal problems tend to arise around the places of worship preferred by Pagans, the training and status of Pagan clergy, the objects that they use in worship and Pagan religious holidays.

The Legal Definition of Religion

It would seem that the definition of religion should be a fairly straightforward one. And, so it seemed to the writers of the First Amendment.

They used the term, "religion," without making any attempt to define or delimit it. Given the history recounted in chapter 1, this is not surprising. Religiously, the people of the 13 original colonies were firmly within the Christian tradition—excepting, of course, Jews, the indigenous population, and the African slaves, all of whom (particularly the latter two) were considered targets for conversion, rather than as a people with a religious tradition to be respected.

In the years since the Constitution was ratified, however, the issue of what constitutes a religion has become much less clear. There are two basic problems. First, as the United States has become more and more religiously diverse and socially egalitarian, the issue of what should be considered a religion for legal purposes has become much more complex than it seemed to the country's early leaders. This problem was compounded further at the time of the Vietnam War when it became necessary for the courts to distinguish religious imperatives from personal moral codes in dealing with conscientious objectors. Second, with time and experience it has become more and more obvious that in many cases the Free Exercise Clause and the Establishment Clause may call for mutually contradictory results (Hammond, 1998).

Until the middle of the twentieth century, the Supreme Court had very little to say about religion and when it did speak it was assumed that religion necessarily involved theism—monotheism to be exact. In 1961, however, it broke from that tradition and in *Torcaso v. Watkins* (367 U.S. 488) it found that a preference for theistic religions over nontheistic ones (such as Buddhism or Ethical Culture) violated the Establishment Clause (Greenawalt, 1984, 759). This lasted until 1965, when the Supreme Court's opinion in *United States v. Seeger* (380 U.S. 163) established the parallel belief test. This was done within the context of the Vietnam War in response to a request for conscientious objector draft status by three men who did not believe in a traditional Supreme Being. The test established by this case asks "whether a given belief that is sincere and meaningful occupies a place in the life of its possessor parallel to that filled by the orthodox belief in God . . ."[2] (166). Sincerity was also required. After this case, the federal courts and administrative agencies have continued to struggle with issues revolving around claims that involve belief systems that are not theistic (e.g. 29 CFR 1605.1). In cases where theism of some sort was clearly involved, however, the federal courts have tended to ignore the whole issue of how religion should be defined for legal purposes (Donovan, 1995).

This clearly places mainstream Paganism in the category of religion. With relatively few exceptions, followers of the three major streams of contemporary Paganism (Wiccans/Witches, Druids, and Norse) are polytheistic, animistic, or pantheistic (including panentheism).[3] Many focus on a Great Goddess (and, sometimes, a Great God), but also revere traditional manifestations of them, such as Isis, Astarte, Cybele, Freya, Odin, or Lugh. Also frequently included are spirits of particular places, faeries, and other "mysterious ones." Thus, in most cases involving contemporary Pagans it is not necessary to deal with the morass the Supreme Court has created around the definition of religion for First Amendment purposes. Because most Pagans are theistic, they clearly fall into the category encompassed by the federal courts' interpretation of religion.

With direct regard to Paganism, the most significant federal court case to date was handed down by the Fourth Circuit Court of Appeals in 1986. *Dettmer v. Landon* (799 F.2d 929) concerned a convict who was taking a correspondence course with the Church of Wicca. As some subsequent judges have failed to understand, the Church of Wicca is not an organization that encompasses all sects of Wicca. Rather, it is a distinct variant of Wicca founded by Gavin and Yvonne Frost. From their home in West Virginia, they offer correspondence courses in Witchcraft from their School of Wicca. It is this feature that has made them attractive to people, like the convict in this case, who are not able to affiliate with Pagan groups in which they might obtain religious education in a more face-to-face way.

In *Dettmer v. Landon*, the convict was taking a course with the Frosts and requested the prison administration that he be allowed certain items to be used in what the Court called "ceremonies for private meditation" (799 F.2d 929, 930). Two issues were before the Court. The first was whether a church based in Witchcraft teachings and ritual was "religion" for First Amendment purposes. The second was whether the prisoner was entitled to the objects he claimed to need for religious use. Regarding the first, the Circuit Court found that "the Church of Wicca occupies a place in the lives of its members parallel to that of more conventional religions. Consequently, its doctrine must be considered a religion" (799 F.2d 929, 932). With regard to the requested objects, the Court considered them on an item-by-item basis, evaluating their potential for threatening the prison's security. For example, the convict requested a hooded robe, but was only allowed a robe with no hood. In the case of his request for candles, salt, and incense, the Circuit Court found the prison administration's security concerns to be reasonable and disallowed those ritual objects.

There is considerable confusion among the numerous cases that prisoners have brought concerning their right to practice their religions while incarcerated. For example, in 1996, the U.S. District Court for the Southern District of New York found that the possession and use of tarot cards by a Wiccan prisoner was a "disruptive, dangerous, and not easily countered force," because they could be used "to gain psychological control or influence over other inmates" (*Reese v. Coughlin*, 1996 U.S. Dist. LEXIS 9206). On the other hand, in 2002, the District of Columbia Court of Appeals overruled a lower court that had upheld a prison rule forbidding the consumption of alcoholic beverages, because the consumption was part of a Catholic communion (*Levitan v. Ashcroft*, 281 F.3d 1313).

What is most interesting about these two cases is the enormous power given to tarot cards by the court which did not seem to understand that tarot cards are most commonly used by Wiccans as aids in personal decision making and spiritual counseling—not spell casting. Assuming that the inmate could be restricted to using the cards in solitary worship, it is difficult to see the disruptive potential. Alcoholic beverages have a much more obvious potential for disruption, but they are more familiar and their religious use well established. Thus, the court was willing to trust that the priest could keep the wine under control. The only clear message this sends is that, if you are a prisoner, your items of religious worship had better be familiar as religious objects to the judge or court hearing your case. It should be noted, however, that the *Reese* court did not question Wicca's status as a religion.

As American Paganism evolved through the second half of the twentieth century, however, the most important definition of religion was not that of any federal court. Rather, it was the one used by the Internal Revenue Service for determining tax-exempt status. In 1961, a pair of undergraduates at Westminster College in Fulton, Missouri, Timothy Zell and Lance Christie, found in Robert A. Heinlein's novel, *Stranger in a Strange Land*, the elements of a new religion. As Timothy Zell remembers it: "Heinlein's novel introduced us to the ideas of Immanent Divinity ('Thou Art God'), Pantheism ('all that groks is God'), Sacraments (water sharing), Priestesses, social nakedness, extended families as a basis for community, loving relationships without jealousy, and joyous expression of sexuality as divine union." He described Heinlein's religious impact on himself and his group: "By defining 'love' as 'that condition wherein another person's happiness is essential to your own,' SISL [*Stranger in a Strange Land*] changed forever the parameters of our relationships with each other, especially in the sexual arena. And all this in the context of a legal religious organization—a 'church' " (Zell-Ravenheart, 2001, 11). This group evolved into the Church of All

Worlds. In 1968, it was incorporated in Missouri and began publishing a newsletter, *Green Egg*, that later became a leading Pagan magazine. In 1970, the Internal Revenue Service (IRS) gave it the tax exempt status of a 501(c)(3) "Religious and Educational Organization."

It proved much more difficult for the Church of All Worlds to obtain tax-exempt status in Missouri. In 1971, it filed the necessary papers to be exempt from the Missouri sales tax. The Department of Revenue declined the application on the basis of a determination that the Church was merely a not-for-profit organization, not a religious organization. The Missouri Revenue Department's attorneys argued that the Church of All Worlds could not qualify as a religion because it did not show primary concern about "the hereafter, belief in God, the destiny of souls, Heaven, Hell, sin and its punishment, and other supernatural matters." In fact, "the general counsel for the Revenue Department said that any legally defined religion must include as its primary purpose the securing of an afterlife" (Adams, 1972).

Thus, the Church of All Worlds was expected to conform to a Christian-like belief system in order to be deemed a religion. Neither Judaism nor Unitarian-Universalism (both of which were regarded as religions in Missouri) could meet all aspects of these criteria. Finally, in 1974, with the help of the American Civil Liberties Union, the Church of All Worlds received exemption from the sales-use tax. The Church currently has "nests" (the rough equivalent of congregations) all over the United States and is an influential segment of contemporary Paganism.

The Church of All Worlds paved the way for a host of other Pagan organizations to obtain tax-exempt status. The pattern experienced by the Church of All Worlds, however, still seems to prevail. Numerous Pagan organizations have been able to obtain federal tax-exempt status from the IRS since this pioneering effort. It is sometimes difficult, however, to deal with IRS forms that are written from the perspective of Christianity. For instance, Pagan applicants must figure out how to explain the religious education of their youth in the context of a question about "Sunday School" or the preparation of their priests and priestesses in response to a question that assumes the existence and use of "schools for the preparation of its ministers" (Feofanov, 1994, 378).

Nevertheless, even though it sometimes takes years, most Pagan organizations have been able to obtain federal tax-exempt status with only a little more than the usual amount of bureaucratic hassle. This seems to be attributable to the fact that the IRS has developed two primary criteria for decision making: (1) whether the religious beliefs professed by the organization are held sincerely and (2) whether the organization's activities include behavior that is illegal or contrary to clear public policy. The applicant Pagan organizations have seldom had any problem with these. The IRS's main interest seems to be in the raising and handling of money and property by tax-exempt organizations. Sorting religions from nonreligions is not a preoccupation unless fraud is involved.

In 1985, Senator Jesse Helms and Representative Robert Walker tried to put an end to this practice by introducing a bill into Congress that would have stripped all "witchcraft" institutions from their tax-exempt status. As Catharine Cookson has observed, this would have been costly to "small Wiccan organizations, as well as their members, since covens would have lost bulk mailing privileges and contributions from religious adherents would no longer have been tax exempt." Moreover, since other government agencies frequently look to the IRS when deciding the credibility of nonmainstream religions, it would have denied legitimacy to Wiccans on a much broader basis (Cookson, 1997, 738). The bill was passed by voice vote in the Senate, but was kept from becoming law by a vigorous lobbying effort. Paradoxically, it became the impetus for Pagan religious rights organizational activity to emerge on a broader basis. This has led to a widespread, interconnected, and coop-erative educational and religious rights organizational cluster that currently makes considerable use of the Internet for development and communication.

As was the case with the Church of All Worlds, it is often at the state and local level that many Pagan organizations run into more significant problems. For example, one Pagan organization had a very difficult time convincing a local property tax assessor that they did not have a build-ing for their church, but considered the land itself their "church." Another Pagan organization spent years fighting for tax exemption for their land in Winnebago County, Wisconsin. Finally, it filed a religious discrimination suit against the town and won a summary judgment that their civil rights had been violated. The case then went to a jury for a determination of damages. The jury refused to award damages (Hayes, 1996, 7).

Ozark Avalon, a Wiccan organization, is located on an 87-acre parcel of land in Missouri. It was incorporated in Missouri in 1997 and recog-nized as a religious organization by the IRS in July of 1999. When it applied for Missouri property tax exemption, however, the Assessor of Cooper County in which the property was located found the land to be agricultural land and refused to classify it as tax-exempt religious property. The denial was appealed to the Copper County Board of

Equalization and it decided Ozark Avalon was not a church. Then Ozark Avalon appealed to the State Tax Commission where in 2001 its right to a tax exemption was upheld and the earlier decisions overturned.

In *Ozark Avalon v. Lachner* (Appeal Number 00–50500) the State Tax Commission hearing officer drew on both constitutional and statutory provisions. He stated that the property was being operated in a not-for-profit manner for charitable purposes in a way that was for the benefit of the citizens of Missouri. Citing the 1977 case *Missouri Church of Scientology v. STC* (560 S.W.2d 837) he stated that there was "a minimum requirement" that there be "a belief in the Supreme Being." With regard to this, however, he focused on the use of the word "the" and found that "the definite article requires devotion to the specific deity. Spiritual devotion to just any deity cannot suffice." This deity, he found, was most likely "the God of Abraham, Isaac and Jacob-Allah." He concluded that "such a standard in effect restricts the definition of religious worship or religion to conventional orthodox religions."

Pointing out that if the deity of one group is supreme, then the deity of other groups cannot be supreme, he observed that using the *Scientology* standard in a literal, strict way puts the courts in the position of "determining what is or is not of a religious nature for a given group." He concluded that in the Ozark Avalon case "the concept of God in an orthodox Jewish, Christian or Islamic sense is not the criterion to be applied in reaching a determination of whether Ozark Avalon's belief concerning God and Goddess is devotion to the Supreme Being." Rather, "the term Supreme Being must be given the widest possible reading and definition." Anything else would violate equal protection. He got around the monotheism issue by finding as a matter of fact that "Ozark Avalon believes in God and Goddess as the manifestations of a single deity," comparing it to the Christian belief in Father, Son, and Holy Ghost.

As for the absence of a church building, he did not find that such a structure was required: "It is clear that the religious activities of Ozark Avalon require a different type of facility, specifically open air, out of doors, than what Catholics, Baptists or Methodists might need." He saw the Ozark Avalon property to be "more in the nature of a church camp site." These, he pointed out, come in varying sizes and are exempt from taxation throughout Missouri because of their use for religious purposes. Thus. His conclusion was that "the size of such facilities is not a factor to deny exemption so long as the actual, regular and primary use is consistent with the overall religious purpose." Finding that the property was being used for a religious purpose, he granted it tax-exempt status. Thus, a Pagan group won another victory, but as is often the case, it was left with a significant debt as a result of its court battle.

In 1982, the Supreme Court of Georgia decided a somewhat different property tax related case. It was *Roberts v. Ravenwood Church of Wicca* (249 Ga. 348). Ravenwood Church was denied an *ad valorem* tax exemption for a dwelling owned by it and used for religious worship. The lower court found that Ravenwood Church did conduct religious worship and that the property was used "extensively and predominantly for religious worship" (249 Ga. 348, 349). It found, however, that Ravenwood Church was not entitled to the exemption because it rented several rooms in the building. Ravenwood Church then got affidavits from other churches stating that those churches had been given tax exemption, even though they allowed nonreligious groups to use church property. The superior court ruled that the exemption denial deprived Ravenwood Church of equal protection.

On appeal, the Georgia Supreme Court held that the activities of Ravenwood constituted religious worship. In doing so, it established a primary use standard for such determinations in Georgia. In a footnote the Supreme Court also made the point that "it could be argued that the subject property is used exclusively as a place of religious worship on the ground that those people who are residing on the property are studying the Wiccan religion" (249 Ga. 348, 351). The dissenters would have imposed a definition of religion that required a relationship to God. Chief Justice Jordan argued, "I do not believe that such cults or beliefs qualify as a religion under the meaning of that term as understood by our founding fathers when they drafted the Constitution of the State of Georgia 'relying upon the protection and guidance of Almighty God.' God has been defined as 'the Being perfect in power, wisdom and goodness whom men worship as creator and ruler of the universe.' Webster's Seventh New Collegiate Dictionary" (249 Ga. 348, 352–353). Again, there arises the argument that if it isn't like Christianity, it isn't religion. This time, at least, it was a dissent.

Tax-exempt status, however, has more than one benefit. First, and most obviously, it can help in fund-raising for Pagan organizations and projects. Second, the blessing of a tax-collecting agency, particularly one with the reputation for toughness enjoyed by the IRS, has been the factor most relied upon by Pagan litigants when called upon to prove that their variant of Paganism is a legitimate, legally recognized religion. On occasion, it is also useful to have a Pagan organization officially recognized in some other way, as in states where churches are officially registered or incorporated.

The issue of whether Paganism is a religion can also arise outside of the courts. A notable example is the case of Cathedral of the Pines. It was established in 1946 by the parents of a young man who had been killed in World War II. It is a scenic parcel of land in New Hampshire near the Massachusetts border west of Nashua. Within it there is an Altar of the Nation that was recognized as a national war memorial by Congress in 1957. Since then, it has advertised itself as "a place of spiritual nourishment for people of all faiths," as well as "a national memorial to patriotic sacrifice" (www.cathedralpines.com/welc.html).

In 1995, AppleMoon Coven requested use of the grounds for a wedding. Many groups, including Bahais, Hindus, Quakers, and Rosicrucians had held, and still hold, services on the Cathedral of the Pines grounds. AppleMoon, however, was summarily refused. When AppleMoon asked for a reason, the answer was that services had to "be conducted by clergy who are graduates of an accredited school of theology with at least a Master's level degree and who are ordained in a recognized legal process" (E-mail, August 13, 1996). The High Priestess who was to conduct the service was recognized as clergy permitted to conduct marriage ceremonies in Massachusetts. Pagans, however, do not maintain theological seminaries[4] nor do they "ordain" their clergy. This was suspect as a requirement, because Quakers do not have formal clergy and Rosicrucians are not, strictly speaking, a religion.

What was really happening became clear during the ensuing negotiations when the Director of the Cathedral referred to AppleMoon as a "Godless lot" trying to make a mockery of the Cathedral and of "Almighty God." When further efforts by AppleMoon to document their religious status failed, they got in touch with the New Hampshire Commission for Human Rights, which subsequently began an investigation of the situation. At that point, the Cathedral's director threatened to reincorporate as a religious organization in order to legally deny the Pagan's access. Under the planned new charter, the Cathedral grounds would only permit services by those "who worship the God of Abraham" (E-mail, August 13, 1996).

In 1996, the New Hampshire Commission for Human Rights preliminarily ruled in favor of AppleMoon (*DesRochers v. Cathedral of the Pines*, PAR 5596-95) finding that the Cathedral had discriminated against AppleMoon Coven by denying it access. It found no evidence that any other religious group had ever been refused use of the facility. In addition, it stated that "numerous civic, fraternal, and patriotic organizations, and individuals" had been permitted to use the facility. The Cathedral, it said, may well have adopted or revised its clergy policy in response to AppleMoon's request. Furthermore it found that: "Requiring Masters' degrees and proof of ordination from a recognized theological school is not a standard which has been applied to all groups, even after the adoption of the policy on clergy. For example, Bahais, who have no recognized clergy, regularly conduct services at the Cathedral, and did so in August 1995. Discretion was most likely used in deciding to schedule services by Buddhist or Native Americans, whose credentials as clergy might be different from those of Christian ministers or Jewish rabbis."

On the topic of monotheism it observed that although the Cathedral had argued that AppleMoon was not monotheistic, in the past the Cathedral had permitted services by clergy of faiths that were neither monotheistic or Judeo-Christian. Its final finding was that there was "direct evidence of hostility by the decision-maker . . . toward Wicca." The bottom line was:

> The evidence and the facts during the Commission's investigation warrant a finding that the reasons given by respondent [the Cathedral] for excluding the complainant [AppleMoon] from the Cathedral of the Pines were a pretext for discrimination. Nothing in the Cathedral's founding documents or history suggests that it is meant only for use by "mainstream religions." Respondent has allowed representatives of many different faiths to conduct services at the Cathedral, both public and private, and has not always required that they have masters degrees or ordination from "recognized" theological schools. Respondent has allowed non-Judeo/Christian religions access to the facilities of the Cathedral.

The Commission then instructed the Cathedral to come to some agreement with the coven.

The Cathedral Board of Trustees remained adamant. By this time, however, the media attention the dispute was getting put additional pressure on the Cathedral to settle. Also, the former Director had left his position for unrelated reasons and the Chair of the Board of Trustees took charge of the situation. Under the auspices of the Commission, the Chair, and the High Priestess of AppleMoon drew up a settlement agreement that "the Cathedral will assure access to the Cathedral, for individual and corporate worship to members of the Wicca Religion . . ." and that "[t]hose Wiccans and neo-Pagans who are to conduct services at the Cathedral, whether public or private, must be recognized as qualified clergy or the equivalent thereof under the standards of their faith and any applicable state law" (PAR 5596-95, Sec. 5b).

Places for Worship

Although there are a few Pagan temples in the United States, for the most part, Pagans prefer to worship out-of-doors whenever possible. In scattered spots, Pagan groups or individuals have managed to acquire relatively large parcels of land that they have dedicated to Pagan worship. Examples of significant pieces of land owned and controlled by Pagan groups or individual Pagans are Circle Sanctuary in Wisconsin, Four Quarters in Pennsylvania, Moonridge in Maryland, and Diana's Grove in Missouri. While these are valuable spiritual resources for Pagans who live within a reasonable traveling distance and while they afford prime locations for worship and study, they do not begin to meet the Pagan need for land on which to practice freely.

Large numbers of Pagans—probably a majority—live in urban or suburban areas and, except for major holiday rituals, they tend to worship in small groups usually consisting of 13 or fewer individuals. Normally, their only options are to worship in someone's home or back yard. Home worship is prevalent in urban areas where large backyards are not common and during periods of inclement weather. Alternatively and when weather conditions permit, Pagans may try to make arrangements to worship in public parkland. The latter is more likely to occur in connection with the celebration of one of the eight major Pagan holidays than it is for regular weekly, monthly, or lunar rituals. Both options can present significant challenges.

Home worship is a significant legal problem in the United States, affecting not only Pagans but also other non-Christian religious groups, most notably Orthodox Jews. Usually the barriers to home worship take the form of zoning restrictions or the selective enforcement of zoning and building codes (Reynolds, 1985; Cookson, 1997, 734–735). Specific cases tend to arise when someone in the neighborhood registers a complaint with local zoning authorities. Most frequently, the basis for the complaint is traffic congestion, parking problems and/or noise. Since zoning cases tend to remain in state court systems and because the Supreme Court has never dealt with a zoning case involving the status of home worship under the Free Exercise Clause of the First Amendment, the law in this area is unclear (Smith, 2000, 1158).

On the federal level, the 1995 case *LeBlanc-Sternberg v. Fletcher* (67 F.2d 412) would seem to be the most applicable to the Pagan situation. It concerns a group of Orthodox Jews who were moving to Ramapo, New York. Orthodox Judaism requires daily prayer and, for certain purposes, the presence of a "minyan" (at least ten males over the age of 13) is required. Furthermore, during their weekly Sabbath and certain religious holidays, Orthodox Jews are required to walk to their places of worship. In Ramapo there was a zoning requirement that places of worship could only be built on a lot of two acres or more. This was not feasible for the relatively small Jewish community in Ramapo, both because it would be prohibitively expensive to construct such a synagogue and because the requirement for all to walk to the synagogue would make the choice of a workable site nearly impossible. The solution for the Orthodox Jews was a provision in the Ramapo zoning law providing for meetings in "home professional offices." It permitted clergy to have offices that could be used to meet with their congregants. This was interpreted by Ramapo officials to permit "home synagogues" in which rabbis could conduct services for groups not exceeding 49 individuals.

Airmont was an unincorporated area within Ramapo. Troubled by the practice of allowing home synagogues, several citizens of Airmont organized the Airmont Civic Association in order to campaign for incorporation which would, in turn, give Airmont control over its own zoning practices. During the campaign preceding the referendum for incorporation, it was clear that the goal of the incorporation proponents was to put Airmont in a position to try to keep out Orthodox Jews through hostile zoning laws and enforcement. In 1989, the citizens of Airmont voted overwhelmingly to incorporate. This precipitated a number of cases challenging Airmont's right to incorporate for the purpose of excluding Orthodox Jews. All three of the resulting Second Circuit Court of Appeals rulings were unanimous and favored the Orthodox Jews. It was held that the Jews' rights were violated under the Free Exercise Clause of the U.S. Constitution (relying on *Lukumi* precedent[5]) and the Fair Housing Act. Like the *Lukumi* case, its scope is probably limited to cases in which it can be clearly shown that the governmental action was motivated by targeted religious animus.

Several aspects of these rulings are potentially useful in the defense of Pagan and other non-Christian home worship. First, in order "to give meaning to the Orthodox Jews' right to worship in Airmont, the [Second Circuit Court issued an injunction that] located that right in a rabbi's home" (Smith, 2000, 1172). Thus, it can be argued that this created a precedent that free exercise has a locational component. It is not clear, though, that this will affect the pattern of facially neutral land use laws that limit or forbid home worship (1173). In the Airmont case, there was clear evidence of targeting the Jewish community that brought the *Lukumi* precedent into play. In the absence of such a clear record of animus toward a specific religious group, the *Smith* rule protecting facially neutral laws would probably prevail. Second, the Second Circuit Court limited the discretion of local zoning authorities. Traditionally, the courts have allowed considerable discretion in connection with local control of land use. Here, again, "if zoning boards, which are naturally sensitive to majoritarian pressures, reject the minority church's request, the church may have no effective recourse" (1174–1175). After all the *Smith v. Oregon* majority made the following observation: "It may fairly be said that leaving accommodation to the political process will place at a relative disadvantage those religious practices that are not widely engaged in; but that [is an] unavoidable consequence of democratic government . . ." (110 S. Ct. 1595, 1606).

Among Pagans, the most widely publicized home worship case was that of the Church of Iron Oak in Florida, a group affiliated with the Aquarian Tabernacle Church and tax-exempt under section 501(c)(3) of the Internal Revenue Code. Although most of the activities of Iron Oak took place in a rented facility in Melbourne, Florida, on some of the eight high holy days of the Pagan calendar, the High Priest Paracelsu (Roger Coleman) and High Priestess Omi (Jacque Zaleski) would invite members of Iron Oak to their home in Palm Bay to celebrate on their one-acre home site. These celebrations usually consisted of a simple outdoor ritual and a potluck afterward.

None of their immediate neighbors objected, but a woman who lived farther down the street objected violently. She asserted, without evidence, that the rituals being held involved nudity, animal sacrifice, and child torture. This led to an incident where the people coming onto and leaving the property were pelted with oranges by local youths. She also claimed that there was excessive noise and that the cars of the attendees blocked the street to emergency vehicles. Police who were called to the scene found the noise level to be reasonable and traffic unimpeded. The one objecting neighbor was referred to the zoning board where she made a formal complaint. Finally, this neighbor would come and stand outside the property trying to see who was coming and going and what was happening on the property. Her complaints to the zoning board also led to some police surveillance.

Palm Bay first issued a zoning violation citation, withdrew it and then issued it again. The City Manager wrote a column for the local paper in which he responded to an editorial that urged the city to leave the Wiccan Church alone. In the course of that response, he twice mentioned the exact address of the property, thus opening the members of Iron Oak to potential harassment. All of this surveillance and publicity led several members to leave the church due to fear of job loss and other negative consequences. The High Priest and High Priestess finally went into federal court to ask for a temporary restraining order against Palm Bay citing their constitutional rights under the Free Exercise Clause of the First Amendment, the Due Process Clause and the Religious Freedom Restoration Act of 1993, as well as several sections of the Florida Constitution.

During the hearing, the representatives of the city said that it would be fine for the couple to hold weekly outdoor barbecues, but that they could not combine them with worship. This was very upsetting to several Christian ministers in the city because many of them held frequent prayer meetings and other church activities at their homes. The city's position also raised questions about the legality of home weddings and baptisms. At the hearing two Christian ministers testified for Iron Oak, not because they supported it on a theological basis, but because an adverse ruling would call into question many Christian activities that also took place on home sites. This development clearly indicated that the zoning requirements were being selectively enforced.

In October 1994, the Federal District Court turned down Iron Oak's request for a temporary restraining order on federalism grounds noting that "though vital freedoms are at stake, this Court is bound by notions of State sovereignty to permit the City of Palm Bay to consider the present facts and interpret its own laws in light of constitutional precedents" (*Church of Iron Oak v. City of Palm Bay*, 868 F. Supp. 1361, 1363). The Court did not dismiss the complaint, but simply decided not to exercise its equitable authority on the incomplete record that it had before it. It wanted to wait for a decision by the Palm Bay Code Enforcement Board. That hearing was held shortly thereafter. The Board heard testimony from several witnesses, including the supervisor of the Code Enforcement Unit for Palm Bay and members of the Christian clergy who routinely held home worship and who had never been cited or otherwise bothered by the City of Palm Bay. Subsequently, the Board voted unanimously not to charge Zaleski and Coleman with a zoning violation. This looks like a win and it was a win. The financial repercussions, however, were significant. The couple was left with $22,000 in legal fees and other costs as a result of the case.

They then made a decision to go into the federal court system. They asked for several things. First, they wanted a declaration that their home worship was constitutional and protected under the U.S. and Florida Constitutions. Second, they wanted the Federal District Court to enjoin Palm Bay from taking further zoning violation actions against the couple because of home worship activities. This was important because the city could, theoretically, issue a citation every time the couple held a home worship service, thus subjecting them to ongoing harassment. Finally, they asked for costs and reasonable attorney's fees. To make a long story short, they lost this case and finally had to give up the fight because of inadequate funds to pursue an appeal.

In the end, two major factors worked against them. First, the Board found no violation so, technically, they had won their case at the local level. Federal courts are very reluctant to get involved in situations where there would seem to be a satisfactory resolution of the case at the local level. Second, they did not have deep pockets. At every step along the way, they were hampered by their lack of funds. Although they appealed to other Pagans many of whom contributed generously with legal help, money, or in other ways, relatively few Pagans are wealthy. Thus, even with a generous outpouring of support by their coreligionists, the Church of Iron Oak ran into the very basic fact that in our legal system money matters. The more money you have, the more likely you are to prevail or, at the very least, to be able to exhaust all of your legal options. The financial repercussions, however, were significant. As noted above, the couple was left with $22,000 in legal fees and other costs as a result of the case. Fortunately, the District Court denied the motion of Palm Bay for attorneys' fees (Case No. 94-1043-CIV-Ord-22 Order). But the case also had a highly disruptive effect on the lives of the High Priest and Priestess and on their congregation. The city had lost, but it managed to inflict lasting wounds.

Usually, home worship for Pagans involves only members of the circle, coven, grove, kindred, hearth or nest, and their invited guests. It is rare for a home worship meeting to be advertised and open to the public. Pagan groups may also rent a private area for worship. This tends to happen when a festival, workshop, or multi-day intensive is being held. Such events usually have too many attendees to be held in an ordinary home or back yard. Rituals that are held in parklands or in other places that are open to the public tend to take place on major Pagan holidays and it is understood that uninvolved members of the public may observe the worship service. Frequently, members of the public who are present are invited to participate.

Rituals that have this "drop-in" feature are often called open circles. To date, one of the most politically controversial open circles is the one at Fort Hood, Texas. It is called the Fort Hood Open Circle and for three years after it was formed, it held its religious education classes and rituals with few problems. Then, in the spring of 1999 the Fort Hood

Wiccans permitted a reporter from the *Austin American-Statesman* to observe and report on a ritual they held to celebrate one of their important spring holidays, the vernal equinox. When this article was published, there ensued a furor with Christians telephoning Fort Hood and threatening to disrupt the rituals.

This also brought the Fort Hood Open Circle to the attention of a member of Congress, Representative Robert L. Barr (R-GA). With virtually no information about Wicca in general or the Fort Hood Open Circle in particular, and relying entirely on what his own imagination generated when the words "Wicca" or "Witchcraft" were used, Representative Barr took it upon himself to write to the commanding officer of Fort Hood demanding an end to the practice of Wicca on the base. He stated that the military was using taxpayer dollars to further the practice of Witchcraft in the military. In this connection, he asserted that the protections of the First Amendment Free Exercise Clause do not extend to people in the military. He even threatened to hold hearings and introduce legislation to stop the practice of Wicca in the military.

The Department of Defense (DOD) had a different point of view. In its Directive 1300.17, *Accommodation of Religious Practices within the Military Services*, issued in 1988 the DOD in the first substantive sentence of the directive stated: "A basic principle of our nation is free exercise of religion. The Department of Defense places a high value on the rights of members of the Armed Forces to observe the tenets of their respective religions."

Previously, the Fort Hood Wiccans had been meeting in a living room, but the group became too large for home worship. A staff sergeant in the group asked about the requirements for official recognition. They needed an off-base sponsor and chose the Sacred Well Congregation[6] of San Antonio that had been founded by a 30-year Army veteran. They needed a leader (High Priestess) and selected a six-year veteran of the military police who had won the soldier-of-the-year award and was currently working in the pediatric unit of the base hospital. She had been raised as a Witch.

The Army chaplains and the Wiccans negotiated some basic ground rules that the Open Circle would observe in their activities. For example, although some Wiccan groups worship "skyclad" (unclothed), the group agreed with the Army chaplains that this would not be appropriate on the base. As for the athames (ritual knives) most Wiccans use to delineate a worship circle by cutting it in the air, they promised that their athames would never be used to cut anything corporeal. The Wiccans were allowed to wear pentagrams, but only small ones worn unobtrusively. When the Fort Hood commandant finally approved the Fort Hood Open Circle as its first Wiccan group, the Wiccans were permitted to use a grassy campsite for their sacred ground and were assigned a Christian chaplain as liaison. Along with their rituals, they began to hold religious education meetings twice a week.

Since Representative Barr is from Georgia, the more directly affected member of the House of Representatives was Chet Edwards (D-TX) in whose district Fort Hood was located. He took a more calm and reasoned approach: "As a Christian, I have serious differences with the philosophy and practices of Wicca. But it would be terrible policy to require each installation commander to define what is a religion and decide which religions can be practiced by American citizens" (*Austin American-Statesman*, May 28, 1999).

The Army adhered unwaveringly to its policy; the base spokesperson said that the Wiccans' presence proved that people with differing religious beliefs could all work together successfully. Although rebuffed by the Fort Hood Command, Representative Barr continued his battle against Pagans in the military. It is worth noting that Congressman Barr was sent informational letters from Pagan individuals and organization, in an attempt to explain why his ideas about Paganism were not based on fact. There is no evidence that any of the information had any impact on Representative Barr who continued to make the same baseless allegations. Instead, he attempted to legislate his position by adding an amendment to the National Defense Authorization Act of 2000 that would have outlawed the practice of Wicca on military bases. The rider was quietly removed while the bill was still in committee. Barr's anti-Wiccan crusade, however, continued to get a great deal of press coverage.

Meanwhile the fervor spread as a group of conservative Christian organizations called for all Christians to boycott the U.S. military by refusing to be recruited or to reenlist. Paul M. Weyrich, a radio talk show host and president of the Free Congress Foundation led this effort. Although initially mentioned as a supporter, the Christian Coalition quickly disassociated itself, as did the American Family Association. The vice president of the American Freedom Institute observed: "This brings back the specter of the Salem witch trials. In addition to being wrongheaded, conservative calls for a boycott of the military are politically suicidal. Support for the military is a bedrock conservative principle" (*Austin American-Statesman*, June 1, 1999). Hal Seimer, president of the Austin-based American Freedom Institute, was also a voice of reason: "What's insane about it is that we fight for the freedom to practice religion in public, and now the conservatives who seek to deny these groups their right to worship are espousing the philosophy of 'freedom of religion for me and not for thee' " (*Austin American-Statesman*, June 11, 1999).

In August, hoping to shift press attention away from Fort Hood, the base commander restricted news coverage by forbidding the photographing of the Pagan rituals. The base chaplains also began refusing to speak to the press on this topic. A local ultraconservative Baptist minister, who had been an early and constant opponent of the freedom to worship of the Fort Hood Open Circle, countered this move by organizing a march against Wicca, calling it a March Against Wickedness. His march was scheduled to start in Killeen, Texas (a town near Fort Hood in which this minister's church was located) and to end at a local metaphysical store in a neighboring town. About 40 persons participated in the march. When they arrived at their destination, they found more than a hundred Pagans, some supportive Christians and a number of protective police officers waiting for them. The Pagans danced and sang of peace, harmony, and love, offering the marchers ice water. As the marchers left, the Pagans began to pick up the trash generated by the event, hoping that at least the children among the marchers would see them as a positive force.

Thus far, this may also look like a win for the Pagans. In October, however, the Fort Hood Open Circle found their stone altar broken. Other objects that they used in worship were vandalized, many smashed and thrown into a nearby dumpster. It clearly looked more like a hate crime than a childish prank, given the size of the altar stone. After a short investigation, the case was closed and the vandals were never identified. The following spring, the circle's worship area was vandalized twice. Again, the offenders were not identified, but the base did erect a fence to try to limit the access of unauthorized persons to the Open Circle's worship space.

The Fort Hood case illustrates two sources of harassment with regard to Pagan religious worship. The first source is the politician seeking electoral support from the fundamentalist Christian voting block. It was clear that Congressman Barr knew little or nothing about what Paganism really was. It was equally clear that he was not interested in finding out anything about Paganism. He simply seized on words such as "pagan" and "witchcraft" and gave them caricatured meanings for demagogic purposes.

The second and, by far, the most common is the fundamentalist Christian, who assumes and insists that the Inquisition or Halloween caricatures of Witches and Pagans represent absolute truth and tries to stamp out the perceived wickedness. On occasion, when these fundamentalists are ministers or politicians, they seem to be playing to their constituencies, much as did Congressman Barr. Another variation is illustrated by the distant neighbor who took it upon herself to interfere with the home worship activities of Iron Oak. An additional example is the person (or persons) who attempted to disrupt a Pagan festival in Virginia in 2001 by making unsubstantiated complaints to the police, posting signs about Jesus at the entrance to the private festival grounds, and shooting a gun near the borders of the festival grounds. Whether a local minister was involved is unclear.

A thankfully rare type of person who steps forward to harass Pagans who are trying to worship is one who has deep psychological problems and who vents their hatred on minority religious groups like Pagans—an easy target in contemporary American culture.[7] One Pagan group that worships at a site in the American west where there are petroglyphs has been harassed for years by a mentally unstable person and the legal system has been unable to protect them, although he was prosecuted for assault and served several months in jail. He and some associates continue to try to restrict access to the site, physically threatening persons wanting to use the site for worship. Thus, the Pagans post on their web site the following warning: "Anti-Pagan disruptors may be at [the site] on festival days. I have successfully fought numerous legal battles against the mentally disturbed, self-appointed 'inquisitor' of this disreputable group, but if you plan to be in the area and wish to visit [the site], directions to find it will be provided. Visit at your own risk!" (http:// members. nbci.com_XMCM/technopagans?HOME>HTM).

For the most part, Christians in America can look forward to their worship services as a peaceful and inspiring break from the turmoil of daily life. They do not have to assemble at their places of worship in the face of potential or actual harassment. They do not fear that their presence at worship will expose them to physical and verbal attacks, job loss or community ostracism. Although most Pagan groups manage to worship undisturbed, the sorts of events recounted above happen just often enough so that every Pagan feels vulnerable. Accusations of zoning violations, disturbing the peace or worse can lead to costly efforts to establish innocence.

Such legal battles or prolonged periods of harassment can also lead to personal loss. The High Priestess and High Priest of the Church of Iron Oak are no longer together, although each remains active in Paganism. Many of the Iron Oak congregation returned to the "broom closet" or became involved in other organizations. The Fort Hood Open Circle must worship under the constant threat of vandalism. It is not easy to worship as a Pagan—one must always be willing to pay a price, be it psychological or physical—or both.

In 2000, the Religious Land Use and Institutionalized Persons Act was passed by Congress and signed into law by President Clinton. The supporters of the bill were particularly concerned with the issue of discriminatory land zoning. In fact, at the time a Brigham Young University study found that "relatively unpopular, minority religions account for 50 percent of court cases involving location of churches, even though they have only 9 percent of the population" (*desertnews. com*, July 28, 2000). The supporters of the bill used this study to demonstrate the need for such a provision. Whether it will be any help to Pagans in their home worship problems remains to be seen. The wording of the bill, however, does not limit its scope to the erection of structures, but includes "use" of land (Sec. 2000cc-5(5)), so it is not (in theory, at least) limited to the erection of religious buildings. It may also afford protection to those Pagan groups who do decide to erect temples or other worship-related structures. The key is how this law will fare in the courts, particularly the U.S. Supreme Court, since it is expressly intended to blunt the impact of *Smith v. Oregon* and to restore some of the protections of the Religious Freedom Restoration Act struck down by the Supreme Court.

Ordination and Clergy Status

The Christian practice of ordination of clergy has its origins in the Jewish custom of consecrating rabbis by the laying on of hands. In Christianity it has become a ritual intended to invest people with ministerial or priestly authority. According to the *Encyclopedia Brittanica Online*, "The essential ceremony consists of the laying of hands of the ordaining minister upon the head of the one being ordained with prayer for the gifts of the Holy Spirit and of grace required for the carrying out of the ministry." Usually, there are educational prerequisites, such as a Master's Degree in Divinity, and a preordination period of supervised practice. During the ceremony, there may be a public examination of the candidate and a charge regarding the responsibilities of the ministry.

In the contemporary United States, ordination is usually done within a hierarchical framework when some higher official or ecclesiastical body makes the decision that a person merits ordination. Self-ordination is not, however, unheard of in contemporary Christianity. Self-ordained ministers claim a calling from God to the ministry and attract followers through some combination of personal charisma and the power of their message. Because there are no institutionalized ties between the minister and his or her congregation, people are usually free to come and go according to their perception of the efficacy of the self-ordained person's ministry. Absent any financial or other irregularities, these self-ordained Christian ministers are usually accorded the same privileges and perquisites as their institutionally ordained brethren—or, at the very least, their power to solemnize such sacraments as marriage is rarely, if ever, questioned in the courts. Also, the Society of Friends (unprogrammed), now considered mainstream, does not have ordained clergy and functions with few or no legal problems. Many nontraditional religions, such as Buddhism, do not have ordinations in the Christian sense. This lack of ordination can be a problem when the issue of ordination arises in a legal or governmental context and the official involved is looking for an excuse to discriminate against a nontraditional religion.

The issue of ordination is troublesome in contemporary Paganism for several reasons. First, many contemporary Pagan traditions began in a casual way, inventing and reinventing themselves as they evolved. They have tended to adopt structures and rules that worked for them and that, in some cases, were based on a fragmentary historical record. Even the more scripted traditions, such as Gardnerian Wicca, have been influenced by such events as its movement into the United States from England. Few, if any, of these institutionalized ordination, choosing instead to select their liturgical leaders in other ways. Second, because contemporary Pagans were, in many cases, rebelling against their Jewish or Christian roots and a pervasive Christian cultural milieu, the founders and developers of these traditions tended to reject either explicitly or implicitly the traditional Jewish or Christian ways of institutionalizing a religious tradition. This made them resistant to adopting a form like ordination that is so closely tied to Judaism and Christianity. Third, many Pagans practice in an eclectic way, believing themselves to be their own spiritual authorities and rejecting any efforts to organize or pin them down to any structured and delimited set of beliefs and practices. In fact, some Pagans can fairly be characterized as dogmatically eclectic. Finally, a large number practice as solitaries. They either belong to no tradition or identify with a particular tradition, but are not directly involved with any organized group within that tradition.

For most Pagans, whether their Priestess or Priest is properly ordained is not an issue. They become affiliated with a particular tradition, coven, circle, nest, kindred, hearth, or grove because it suits their spiritual needs at the moment. If it ceases to fill those needs or if the leadership of their group no longer affords them adequate spiritual sustenance, they simply move on. They ordinarily do not experience the kind of pressure to remain loyal "to the faith" that is present in Jewish and Christian traditions where family spiritual heritages as well as claims of exclusivity may be operative.

For Pagan clergy, ordination is most likely to become an issue when they interact with the rest of the world, particularly the legal system. Then, in order to gain certain privileges, like being able to marry couples in their faith, they are forced to formulate what they are about in terms that adherents of Jewish and Christian religions can understand. In many states, the government is seen as having a significant interest in the institution of marriage. In such states, to a greater or lesser degree, the person officiating over the ceremony of marriage may be regarded as an official of the state needing some sort of authorization or approval by the government (International Clergy Association, 1999). The same applies to other functions over which the government has control. Thus, Pagan clergy also have to fit into the Christian mold sufficiently to be allowed to do such basic spiritual tasks as minister to their hospitalized sick and prisoners, as well as act as chaplains for their military.

While some, such as the High Priestess whose story appears in chapter 3, rebel against the idea of being forced to conform to what they see as alien or inappropriate methods of gaining their credentials, others accommodate to varying degrees and in varying ways. One of the easiest ways to satisfy official demands for ordination is to get an ordination from the Universal Life Church (ULC). A member of the Pagan clergy can simply go to the web site and obtain official-looking papers attesting to his or her ordination. There are also other web sites that offer ordination, as well as "mail-order" ordination companies. Many Pagan clergy have seized upon such opportunities as the easiest way to appease government bureaucrats. Others, however, have reservations about such practices. They point out that it is easy to get ULC ordination for household pets (it seems that many cats, in particular, have been ordained by the ULC). If Paganism is to be taken seriously as a religion, they think, the use of an ordination that does not distinguish between humans and household pets invites disrespect, no matter how esteemed and qualified the Pagan clergy so ordained. On the other hand, when the Utah legislature passed a law making Internet ordinations invalid, the

Universal Life Church brought suit and in 2002, the Federal District Court found the law an unconstitutional violation of equal protection (*Universal Life Church v. Utah*, 189 F. Supp. 2d 1302).

Some unconventionally ordained clergy (whether Pagan or of other faiths) may do harm by taking on tasks, such as pastoral counseling, for which they do not have adequate training, in situations where those relying on them may be particularly vulnerable. Then, there is the larger problem of legal liability. In a country, such as the United States, where most congregations belong to large and well-organized denominations, these organizations can (at least potentially) be held legally responsible and civilly liable for the actions of their ordained clergy. Where training in a denomination-controlled program or an accredited theological seminary is involved, there is some way of ascertaining the background and training of clergy. Where affiliation to a larger religious organization is involved, there is some way of enforcing clergy accountability.

In response to these imperatives, some of the larger, more organized Pagan traditions or organizations have developed programs for ordination or the Pagan equivalent. One of the most demanding programs is that of the Church of All Worlds (CAW). The CAW has a very complex organization of rings and circles the achievement of which is associated with increasing levels of status and the right to perform certain functions. For ordination, the CAW requires that a person have completed the qualifications of their sixth circle and have been recommended for the seventh, as well as having achieved unanimous approval from the Priesthood Council. This process is quite long, arduous, and seemingly seldom achieved. Other Pagan organizations with well-developed ordination programs include the Aquarian Tabernacle Church and Cherry Hill Seminary. The Covenant of the Goddess requires proof of appropriate training and experience, as well as recommendations. This process usually takes a year or less. Other Pagan organizations offering ordination programs that are not seminary modeled vary greatly in what they require and how long the process usually takes. Some Pagan clergy seek further credibility by becoming Unitarian–Universalist ministers or being accredited by organizations such as the American Humanist Association.

Questions about ordination and clergy status have tended to arise most often in connection with the task of performing marriages. The legal qualifications for performing marriages are determined by state law and the 50 states differ greatly in the extent to which they become involved in the determination of who has clergy status for this purpose. One of the states creating the most problems for Pagan clergy is Virginia in which local judges and clerks of the court have the discretion to grant or refuse permission to perform marriages. As we saw in chapter 3, a judge placed in this situation usually falls back on his or her Jewish or Christian-based concept of what constitutes proper clergy status for purposes of marriage. This may often, but not always, result in a refusal to license Pagan clergy.

The Virginia approach has led to a great deal of inconsistency from county to county and even from judge to judge. For example, in Newport News, Virginia, a Pagan Priest seeking authority to marry a couple told the person in the Clerk of the Court's office that his sect did not grant ordination papers. He was asked to bring in whatever documentation he thought might satisfy the legal requirement. He returned with a certificate from his coven designating him as Priest, an excerpt from the *Encyclopedia of American Religions* listing his coven and the national organization with which it was affiliated, an excerpt from the local library's *Directory of Community Services* listing the coven as a community service organization and a copy of the U.S. Army Chaplain's Handbook describing Wicca. His paperwork was quickly and efficiently processed, he was administered oath, got his license and shared a friendly handshake with the officials who processed his request (E-mail, May 8, 1999).

A Priestess had a very different experience in Williamsburg, Virginia. Her application included the same documentation that was used in Newport News, but the county clerk referred the application to a judge because the Priestess did not have a traditional certificate of ordination. Without giving a reason, the judge refused to grant her a license to perform weddings. Instead of just taking her credentials to Newport News or Norfolk where (based on past experience) they would have been accepted, she decided to stand up for her religious rights. Subsequently, the American Civil Liberties Union (ACLU) became involved because they thought that Virginia's inconsistent practice from county to county and from judge to judge indicated a need for a change in the law that would take the discretion to determine appropriate clergy status away from court officials. Seeing this as a potential test case, the ACLU argued on her behalf that her documentation met the requirement for granting a license. Perhaps not wanting to become involved in such a test case, the judge then changed his mind and gave her a license (*The Washington Post*, July 3, 1999).

The fact that the person performing the ceremony is legally regarded as an agent of the state does not mean that the state necessarily makes a decision about whether the person is worthy to be recognized as clergy.

Many states allow a Notary Public to perform weddings. This official status is usually easy to obtain and allows the Priest or Priestess to perform the Pagan wedding ceremony desired by the couple and then sign the certificate as a Notary Public making the marriage legal. Another way to get around the system is for the Pagan group to incorporate as a church or religious society. An ordination committee may then be formed to issue certificates of ordination. Most Pagans reject such subterfuges on the ground that they should not be required of nontraditional religious groups, if they are not required of Jewish or Christian groups.

Some states try to stay out of the clergy recognition business altogether. In these states, if the couple is legally eligible to be married, if the proper paperwork is filed, if the fees are paid and if the witnesses are present, the marriage my be performed by any clergy recognized by the couple or their faith community as qualified to do so. This approach essentially sees the role of the clergy as blessing and acknowledging the marriage and the role of the state as recording and acknowledging it. The actual sacrament is seen as being performed by the bride and the groom.

Texas is often cited as a state that wisely stays out of the business of deciding who is clergy and who is not. There the couple must obtain the marriage license and blood tests. A Pagan Priest or Priestess (or any other clergy that the couple may choose) can perform the wedding ceremony. The only requirement is that the bride and groom must profess before witnesses their intent to be lawfully married. The marriage is finalized when the witnesses sign the license and it is returned to the state to be filed. No one has to be made an agent of the state. Thus, Texas need not officially concern itself with the credentials of the person performing the wedding ceremony.

Another area where the issue of clergy status arises is in the provision of chaplains to hospitals, prisons, law enforcement, and the military. As was evident from the story of the Fort Hood Open Circle, the military, while not perfect, is a place where Pagans have been able to gain a significant amount of recognition. Currently, most military chaplains are Protestant clergy and all chaplains are trained to minister to persons of diverse faiths. Although the U.S. military does not have fully accredited Pagan chaplains, several Priests and Priestesses have been able to establish cordial working relationships with individual Chaplain's Offices and, thus, have been able to minister to members of the armed forces, both on bases and in military hospitals. Most notable in this area has been the Temple of Isis that supports the Isis Invicta Mission for Pagans serving in the United States Armed Forces.

It is much more difficult for Pagan clergy to obtain chaplain privileges in law enforcement, hospitals, and prisons. Since these institutions are under state or local control, there is a great deal of variation in their willingness to accept chaplains who are not Jewish or Christian. The lack of some official Pagan presence can, in turn, create problems for Pagan patients. One Pagan who is a registered nurse has reported that in his medical center some staff members have refused to care for Pagans, in one instance calling the patient "a devil-worshipper wearing a penta-gram." In another case, a pregnant Pagan woman was "scoffed at" by her physician when she asked for some religion-based modifications in her birth process. They were not exceptionally unusual. For example, one was not to have an episiotomy or C-section unless absolutely necessary because she wanted her birthing process to be as natural as possible. When she went into labor, the preadmissions employee refused to designate Wicca as her religion, saying "I can't put that in the computer. I can't in good conscience do that. I don't believe in it." After refusing to continue with the admissions process and yelling, "You can't do this to me, this is my religion and you have to follow my wishes," a supervi-sor intervened and typed in Wicca. The new mother filed a complaint and got no response. With the help of an open-minded new chaplain, however, the Pagan nurse was able to gain some recognition as a lay resource person for Pagan patients (Ream, 2002). This, however, solves the problem in only one of thousands of medical institutions.

Most hospitals do not recognize Pagan clergy as official visitors. Many require proof of ordination creating the same problems as in the licensing of marriages. On the other hand, the license that permits Pagan clergy to perform marriages can often be used to obtain chaplain status at hospitals. When patients are admitted, they often face a check-list of religions that does not include theirs and makes no provision for "write-ins." At present, Unitarian–Universalist ministers seem to be the chief hospital recourse for most Pagans, although some Pagan clergy have managed to develop a relationship with individual hospitals that permits them to be summoned to minister to their sick, as well as to make regular rounds as do Jewish and Christian clergy.

In at least one law enforcement case the bias is blatant. According to *The Sacramento Bee* (November 17, 2001), Law Enforcement Chaplaincy-Sacramento has a requirement that all chaplains be follow-ers of Jesus Christ. This organization gets financial support from Sacramento City and County, as well as payroll donations from law enforcement personnel. If requested, they will summon clergy from another faith, but maintain that if persons of other faiths are not satisfied with that, they should form their own chaplaincy. According to the same source, the International Conference of Police Chaplains, representing 2,700 police chaplains, has a logo that features the Star of David and a cross.

State prison systems are another frontier where the situation with regard to Pagan chaplains varies greatly from state to state. Although there are many stories of Pagan prisoners being denied the right to practice their religion[8] and of Pagan clergy being barred from prisons, there is also some good news. Patrick McCollum was the first official Wiccan prison chaplain in the United States. A High Priest of the Cauldron of Cerridwen, he is the Statewide Wiccan Chaplain for the California Department of Corrections. In this capacity, he has been able to serve in 13 prisons and to do such things as testify at parole hearings and have his input treated with the same respect as other clergy. He is also involved with the Lady Liberty League Prison Program. This program has made significant progress in arranging for Pagan inmates in several states to be permitted to practice their religion. For example, High Priest McCollum has worked with the Texas Department of Criminal Justice to set up a Pagan religious program that would permit the celebration of Pagan holidays and group study, as well as access to ritual equipment, tarot cards, books, and periodicals. In addition, he is the national liaison between the American Academy of Religion and all U.S. correctional systems.

With Laurel Owen, a Pagan clergy member in Tennessee, he has worked to start a Pagan religious program in Tennessee prisons. Under the auspices of the Lady Liberty League Prison Program, he has helped to resolve many religious discrimination complaints in a number of states. Collaborating with him in this work is High Priestess Selena Fox of Circle Sanctuary who has been performing ministerial duties in prisons since 1980 and is a consultant to the U.S. Department of Justice on religious accommodation for Wiccans and adherents of other nature religions. Another resource for Pagan prisoners is the Covenant of Unitarian Universalist Pagans' prison ministry. Run by the Magnolia Grove Chapter of CUUPS from 2000 to 2002, it enabled interaction between inmates and Pagan volunteers, personally contacted Pagan prisoners who were having problems practicing their faith, as well as worked to inform and educate prison administrators. Currently this is in the process of being converted into a nationwide effort.

Informing and educating prison administrators is only half the job. The story of one Wiccan chaplain illustrates the oft-repeated story of the interference with administrative decision making by political and religious demagogues. In December 2001, Jamyi Witch, an ordained Wiccan priestess, became the first full-time salaried state prison chaplain. The prison is in Wisconsin and the other chaplain was a former Catholic priest who was currently an Episcopalian. Jamyi Witch was no stranger to the Wisconsin prison officials, having previously made a presentation to prison authorities on alternative religions and having served in the Waupun maximum-security prison for two years on a volunteer basis. In fact, her experience and extensive knowledge about alternative religions helped get her the job, as well as the fact that the Warden found her to be "an outstandingly approachable person" (*LaCrosse Tribune*, Friday, December 7, 2001).

The job is largely administrative. The person holding it acts as coordinator of religious practices for all inmates. The only time she functions as a Wiccan priestess is when she is ministering to the approximately 30 Wiccan prisoners. Nevertheless, several state legislators objected to the appointment, one threatening to introduce legislation that would eliminate funding for her position and promote the hiring of chaplains of the same faith as the majority of inmates. In spite of considerable political pressure and threats to have the legislature eliminate Witch's position, the Department of Corrections continued to support her. She is, however, paying a price. She has had to endure many verbal and written attacks, both anonymous and from a group of churches in her hometown (*L.A. Times*, January 7, 2002; *Milwaukee Journal Sentinel*, December 7, 2001). The Waupun Clergy Association, composed of prison chaplains and other clergy who has voted to expel her and a Muslim chaplain from another Michigan prison (*Fond Du Lac Reporter*, October 25, 2002). As of this writing, she is still on the job, but suffering a great deal from stress and fear for her family, because of a constant stream of threats and other overt expressions of bigotry.

Religious Holidays

As the United States has become more religiously diverse, the issue of religious holidays has become more troublesome. For example, in *Fleming v. City of Boston/Boston Public Library* (Massachusetts Lawyers Weekly, 2000, No. 22-004-00) a Catholic employee complained because Jews were being granted paid leave for religious holidays and the Catholic was not. The policy was based on the perception that Jews were not allowed to work on their holy days while the Catholics had no such strictures. This was found to be illegal discrimination. In other situations, Orthodox Jews have been fired for refusing to work on Saturday, their Sabbath while Christians have been fired for refusing to work on Christmas.

In 1980, such cases were addressed by a regulation of the Equal Employment Opportunity Commission (EEOC) (29 CFR 1605.3). Basically, the regulation requires employers to make a reasonable accommodation to the religious needs of employees. Thus, there is no absolute bar to an employer requiring a religious person to work on one of their holidays, just a requirement that every reasonable effort be made to find a way to accommodate the employee's ability to observe the holy day appropriately. All of the cases mentioned in the previous paragraph occurred after the passage of the EEOC regulation and were covered by it. The problem is that reasonableness, like beauty, is in the eye of the beholder.

Whatever the outcome, however, in the cases just discussed there was no question as to whether the holy days were authentic. As in many other cases, followers of minority religions may have additional problems getting their holy days recognized as religious holidays. For example, in 1999 in the school system of a large city, the union contract contained a provision that an employee was allowed to be absent for eight days before penalties would result. "Recognized" religious holidays were exempted from this rule. Wicca, however, was not "recognized" by the public school system so Wiccans who chose to take a day off to celebrate a holy day were disadvantaged (E-mail, September 27, 1999). Likewise, many of the holidays of other nontraditional religions are not familiar to the majority of Americans and can, thus, have their importance dismissed.

More seriously, as the religious diversity of the United States grows, the whole system of making national and state holidays coincide with religious holidays may become increasingly questionable. Currently, only Christmas, Thanksgiving, and (in some states) Good Friday are government-sanctioned holidays. Because Easter always falls on a Sunday, it does not raise the same issue—although the very fact that Sunday is the United States' official "day of rest" is traceable to the fact that Sunday is the day of the week on which most Christians regard as their official day of worship. If this courtesy that has been historically extended to Christian holidays is extended to the major holidays of other faiths, it would present a serious problem for both government and private sector employers.

Just accommodating Jewish or Muslim holy days (as is now done in many school systems) complicates the picture. This very accommodation raises an equal protection issue with regard to a host of other holy days of a host of other religions. As the United States continues to become more and more religiously diverse, this policy issue may come increasingly to the fore. The question to be addressed is twofold. First, which religions should have some sort of recognition or accommodation? Second, for any given religion which holy days should be considered the most deserving of official recognition or accommodation? When one contemplates these issues, a third question arises: Should the government be in the business of recognizing or accommodating religious holy days? It may just get too complicated.

The other major issue that has arisen is the politically sensitive one of which religions to recognize when holy days coincide or are in close time proximity. To date, this has arisen primarily with regard to Christmas displays on public property. Since Pagans and some atheists celebrate the Winter Solstice at approximately the same time as Christians celebrate Christmas,[9] the question of displaying some sort of symbol of the Solstice along with the usual Christmas displays has arisen in many places. In Texas, the American Atheists were successful in getting their Solstice Greeting (a four foot by eight foot sign) displayed near a 12 piece nativity scene (*The Fort Worth Star-Telegram*, December 13, 1999).

Pagans have been less successful. For example, in Watertown, NY a Pagan tried to get permission to add a Pagan display (showing the waxing, full, and waning aspects of the moon) included in the Public Square Christmas display. The city council refused to permit the placement of the Pagan symbol alongside the Christian and Jewish symbols. The mayor's response was that, as a Christian, he could not support this. The city attorney's opinion was that the exclusion of other religions would not be in violation of the constitution and raised the specter of a "slippery slope" that could lead to every religion being represented. The Pagan who raised the issue made a decision not to pursue it in the courts because she felt that it would have too much of an adverse impact on her business (E-mail, September 11, 2002).

The issue of recognizing or accommodating religious holy days promises to be one that, sooner or later, will become more politically volatile than it is at present. As the number of Christians in the United States drops below 80 percent, the situations in which a politician can take a firmly Christian stance against other religions and assume that it will build electoral support will also decrease. Since September 11, 2001, American Muslims have stepped up their mobilization for political action. It is safe to suppose that their political activities will include demands for more demonstrations of respect for Islam, as well as measures to counter what they see as unreasonable discrimination against Muslims. The Jewish community in America already has a substantial influence on American policy because it has been very successful in mobilizing its voters and financial resources to that end. American Muslims are moving steadily in the same direction. The way in which non-mainstream religious groups are treated in the American political system promises to be far more politically contentious in the twenty-first century than it was in the twentieth.

This issue has arisen because Christians are privileged. In spite of "a constitutional guarantee that the government of the United States will be faceless when concerning religion, a system has developed that has absorbed Christian practice at every turn." In fact, Christianity has become so much a part of mainstream culture that "Christians . . . have been blind to the privilege that [they] have experienced" (Duncan, 2003, 617). Without realizing the full import of what they are doing, many Christians take it for granted that the Christian trappings of American culture are natural, normal, and untouchable. This takes the form of a sense of privilege that is not limited to evangelicals or fundamentalists, but for most Americans pervades their lives. In turn, it leads to a sense of entitlement that impels some Christians to try to convert or otherwise impose their religion on those who do not share it. This becomes a particular problem when the Christians are acting within or as the agents of a public organization, such as a child protective services department or a school system.

CHAPTER 5
THE OTHER: RELIGIOUS DIVERSITY
AND THE SOCIAL ORDER

Human beings seem to have a natural inclination to separate people into "us" and "them." Among some Christians, particularly fundamentalist or evangelical Christians, this dichotomy often tends to be equated with good and evil. Catharine Cookson (2001) points to the wilderness myth as a metaphor. Drawing on biblical imagery, as well as European folklore, she reminds us that the Old Testament wilderness was a place where unholy pagans carried out evil rituals in homage to false gods. Harking back to the efforts of the early and medieval Christian missionaries to the tribes of northern Europe, "Christians judged their work to be successful when they . . . cut down the sacred groves where the pagans held their rites" (Nash, 1967, 17–18). The pagans were then persuaded, by one means or another, to become Christians.

The "wilderness represented the Christian conception of the situation man faced on earth. It was a compound of his natural inclination to sin, the temptation of the material world, and the temptation of the forces of evil themselves" (17–18). To many Christians, the way to overcome these evil inclinations within one's self is to call upon the help of God and his son, Jesus. The way to combat them in the world is to convert pagans to Christianity. And, in the more fundamentalist denominations of Christianity, at least, those who do not share their religious beliefs and pagans tend to be equated so this can include some other Christian sects, as well as all non-Christians.

Thus for many Christians, religious groups that are different from Christianity do not just differ from the righteous, they raise the threat of social chaos and immorality. They are perceived as culturally different and, thus, as a source of danger. "Cultural majorities have [historically] sought to force outsiders to conform to the prevailing cultural norms" (Karst, 1986, 305). Thus, "a cultural outsider can become a member of the American community only by relinquishing his or her native culture and embracing the prevailing American cultural norms" (312). "Forced conformity, like other forms of cultural domination is not just a means of securing power or material advantage for members of the dominant culture." In addition, "the coercion of a cultural minority to conform also reassures the majority that its own group identities are secure" (314).

"A believer who sees those who hold competing religious beliefs as belonging to the 'powers of chaos' is likely to use any means available, including the authority and machinery of the state, to combat her perceived adversaries" (Marshall, 1996, 390–391). Since the American law and legal system were instituted and developed primarily by Christians and, to a great extent, reflect Christian ideas about what the proper social order should be, conversion is seen as a way to insure that all are law-abiding and socially conformist. Those who persist in false beliefs and nonconformist religious practices are perceived as a threat to the social order. As Cookson (2001, 5) points out, "nondominant religious groups whose religious beliefs compel them to undertake behavior which violates mainstream society's moral norms, especially tend to be regarded as living in immoral chaos."

When Christian-derived norms are reinforced by legal precepts, it is easy for Christians to feel justified in acting on their "need to convert the wilderness barbarians into a law-abiding, moral citizenry, or even to move forcefully to contain the breach in the boundaries of civilization in order to protect society" (5). Similarly, Stephen M. Feldman (1996, 868) observes, "Christianity can be imposed on members of outgroup religions through the instrumentality of the government so long as legal discourse labels or codes the government action as secular." Thus, "governmental actions that are conducted in the guise of secularity can endorse, propagate, and otherwise support Christianity because, from the perspective of constitutional doctrine, the government has not impermissibly conjoined with religion."[1]

Beginning from the premise that a basic problem for any society is the ability to maintain social order, Stanley Feldman (2003) looks below the familiar problem of overt lawlessness to a more fundamental level of the social order: the stability of the interactions among those who live in a particular society. In his survey of social theory, he finds an emphasis on the importance of the extent to which the members of the society hold common norms and values. In the United States, with its history of a rhetorical emphasis on the importance of the individual, this creates a tension between the values of personal autonomy and social conformity. In looking at people who have a strong desire for social conformity, he observes a number of central characteristics.

First, he finds a basically pessimistic view of human nature. It is not that people are inherently antisocial, but rather that they need to be guided by a set of socially validated norms and rules that lead them to behave appropriately in society. Appropriateness, however, can be seen differently by people with different social and cultural backgrounds. For Christians, the most basic rules are the Ten Commandments. From these, they assert, all American law derives. While this might be an extreme view, given the development of the Anglo-American Common Law System over many hundreds of years, there is some validity to the claim. Those who wrote the U.S. Constitution, the laws of the federal government, and the constitutions and laws of the various states were either Christian or heavily influenced by Christian thought. As has been discussed previously, the paradigm for religion in American law is Christianity—more specifically in its Protestant manifestations.

Second, Feldman notes that those who place great value on social conformity tend to emphasize the importance of limiting diversity in society. They see diversity as "both an indicator that people are not conforming to common social norms and a potential threat to the maintenance of those norms." Moreover, they think that, when necessary, "the threat of sanctions and the use of punishments may be necessary to keep people from misbehaving" (48). To this end, they look toward government power to suppress nonconformity through its laws or, at least, to look the other way when the righteous act to impose social conformity. The former is demonstrated through the legislation and policies that have historically limited immigration, welcoming those who were "desirable" (i.e. Christian Western Europeans who resemble the early colonizers) and placing stringent quotas on those who were considered less desirable (i.e. people from Asia or other non-European places who do not resemble the early colonizers). This, in turn, limited religious nonconformity to the prevailing Christian (mostly Protestant) norm.

A desire to preserve traditional social norms is also obvious in the defiant continuation of officially sanctioned Protestant Christian prayer in public school settings following the Supreme Court's 1962 decision in *Engle v. Vitale* (370 U.S. 421) that teacher-led prayer in public schools was unconstitutional. As an increasing number of officially sanctioned school prayer or prayer-like arrangements have failed legislatively or have been struck down by the courts, many of these same people have begun urging the public schools to hang the Ten Commandments in school rooms, emphasizing their historical importance and downplaying their obviously religious content.

Finally, "the desire for conformity requires commitment to a *particular* set of norms" (Feldman, 2003, 49). In the United States, these norms strongly parallel the norms found in pan-Protestantism as it is expressed in both law and social expectation. This is not a static situation. During the latter quarter of the twentieth century and the beginning of the twenty-first, there has been a strong political drive by the more fundamentalist sects of Christianity to force their extreme and less tolerant norms onto the entire population via governmental policies and laws. This, they are convinced, will impose the correct set of prescriptions for behavior on those who are not inclined to convert. For those who might be so inclined, Christian participation in or influence over various government activities[2] will enhance their ability to proselytize. In any case, it is necessary because they are acting on behalf of a higher authority, *their* God and Jesus—the only higher authority that they believe exists.

Perhaps the most important venue for inculcating social conformity is the home environment during the early years of a person's life and, thereafter, the schools. Those who desire to impose a Christian-derived social conformity are, thus, very concerned with parental religious influences on children during their early years. For the most part, direct pressure on non-Christian parents is discouraged by the individualistic political culture of the United States. Pagan and other non-Christian families are most likely to experience direct attempts to interfere with their child rearing practices when a divorce or some other family problem opens the door to outside, usually governmental, interference. When children enter the public school system, the opportunities for Christian influence multiply greatly, because more pervasive social and political influence becomes possible.

Child Raising and Conformity

Although it is currently not possible to get a definitive count of the number of child custody disputes that involve issues related to the religious convictions of one or both parents, it is clear this does happen with some frequency. In fact, the loss of custody or visitation rights is one of the primary fears of Pagans who are parents of minor children. The sources of this threat are not limited to the use of Paganism as a tactic by spouses during divorce proceedings. Even intact Pagan families may face custody challenges that are initiated by relatives, police, social workers, and adoption agencies. These challenges are usually based on a genuine belief that the children are potentially being harmed by their family's nonconformist (i.e. non-Christian) religious practices. For example, one Pagan foster mother had her three foster children removed as a result of a complaint by another foster mother that she was a "devil worshipper." When faced by a suit for defamation of character, the complaining foster mother explained: "My Bible tells me that I'm supposed to expose the darkness, which is the witches. I did what I was supposed to do" (*St. Louis Post-Dispatch*, August 21, 1994). This is primarily a threat faced by Witches or Wiccans. But there are cases in which Pagans who do not self-identify as Witches or Wiccans are nonetheless accused of witchcraft and, thus, of being unfit or even abusive parents.

In the context of divorce proceedings, Paganism is sometimes used by one of the parties in a manipulative way in order to gain advantage in the dispute by playing on the ignorance and fear of Paganism that often characterizes judges and others involved in the adjudication of parental rights. In such cases, the overriding job of the lawyer representing the Pagan parent may be to educate the court about the actual content of the challenged parental religious beliefs and practices, hoping that the judge has an open mind. In order to better understand this problem it is necessary to consider the legal framework within which custody decisions are normally made.

Both legislation and court precedent regarding the determination of child custody are almost exclusively on the state level. This means that there are theoretically 50 different bodies of law governing this process (e.g. see Eilers, 2003, 105–108). Federal law can only come into play when questions involving a federal question are raised. Here, the U.S. Constitution's First Amendment Free Exercise and Establishment Clauses are the major available potentially relevant sources of law. Despite the possibility of widely differing legal approaches, there is considerable uniformity in the principles used by the various state courts to handle questions of child custody. This has come about primarily because state appeals courts, faced with few or no precedents in their own jurisdictions, have frequently turned for guidance to the precedents created by the courts of other states.

Early English common law gave the father virtually exclusive right to custody of his children except in extreme cases. Around the beginning of the twentieth century, however, the preference for the father changed to a preference for the mother. This was embodied in what was referred to as the "tender years doctrine" and was based on the belief that mothers were more able than fathers to meet the needs of young children. During the 1970s this doctrine was gradually replaced by the principle that in custody disputes between two biological parents, courts should award custody using as a guide the best interests of the child. All state courts in the United States now use the "best interests" approach. There is variation, however, among the various states' approaches to making such determinations. This variation, in turn, has given judges considerable latitude (Freeman, 1998, 75–78; Miller, 1995, 1278–1280; Tyner, 1994).

In custody disputes that involve religious beliefs and practices, courts are sometimes asked to evaluate the relative merits of the parents' religious commitments—or lack of same. When this happens, judges are put into the position of having to balance the best interests of the child against the religious freedom of the adult whose religious beliefs are at issue.[3] In turn, they must keep in mind the possibility that the way they handle this problem can expose them to the charge of violating the Establishment Clause. In response to this dilemma, many courts have embraced the "harm standard." Under the harm standard, the state can claim an interest in protecting its children from harm and this state interest can then be balanced against the constitutional rights of the parents. What this means is that the actual or potential harm to the child must be sufficient to create a compelling state interest in protecting the child by intruding into the constitutionally sensitive area of religious freedom. The intrusion, in turn, must be the least restrictive one that will result in protecting the child from the damage associated with potentially harmful religious practices.

The way a court determines whether the religious commitments of the parent or parents harm or threaten harm to the child can make the court vulnerable to Establishment Clause challenges. In his study of the way in which the various jurisdictions have handled this problem, Gary M. Miller (1995, 1285–1295) has been able to identify three lines of cases. Using the test developed in 1971 in *Lemon v. Kurtzman* (403 U.S. 602, 612–613) he evaluates these three general approaches in light of the limitations imposed by the establishment clause. Under the *Lemon* test the action of the court must (1) have a secular purpose, (2) neither advance nor inhibit religion, and (3) avoid government entanglement with religion.[4]

The first approach Miller discusses finds religion a proper factor to be taken into consideration in determining the best interests of the child if the religious practices at issue affect the general welfare of the child. No actual or threatened harm need be shown. The second approach requires a showing that the religious practices at issue have actually harmed or threaten to harm the physical or mental health of the child. In a modification of this, if the child can be shown to have actual religious needs and is mature enough to be able to make a choice between religion and nonreligion, religion can be considered in determining the child's best interests. But, the religious needs are not decisive. They are merely one factor the court may take into account. Finally, the most restrictive approach requires a showing that the religious practices have caused actual physical or mental harm to the child, before the court can take them into account in determining the best interests of the child.

Miller (1995, 1292–1296) finds that all three approaches pass the first prong of the *Lemon* test: that the court's actions have a secular purpose—the state's interest in the welfare of the children residing within its boundaries. Thus, it is the job of an overwhelmingly Christian bench to evaluate the religion and religious practices of all sects, including non-Christian ones. The first approach, however, fails the second prong: that the effect of governmental action should neither advance nor inhibit religion. A positive consideration of religion would advance religion in three ways. First, it would lead to a preference for parents who are religious and punish parents who are not. Second, it would encourage nonreligious parents to embrace religion. Third, it would increase the number of children brought up in religious environments. On the other hand, if a court considers the negative effects of a religion it would inhibit religion by discouraging its practice. Clearly, taking such matters under consideration threatens to impermissibly entangle the government (via the courts) with religion, potentially violating the third prong of the *Lemon* test.

Miller finds the second and third approaches acceptable under both the second and third prongs of the *Lemon* test. He concludes, however, that within a "best interests" context the second approach is the better one, because it does not require that some actual damage occur before permitting an inquiry into religious practices. It should be noted, however, that Jennifer Drobac argues that religion should only be taken into consideration in custody cases "upon a predicate finding that religious beliefs and practices were actually harming a child (a risk of harm would not suffice)" (Drobac, 1998, 1613).

One of the first hurdles that a Pagan parent (as well as parents belonging to religious groups that are not Jewish or Christian) faces in a custody dispute involving religion is finding a sympathetic lawyer with the proper legal skills practicing in their jurisdiction.[5] Pagan religious rights organizations are frequently asked to help litigants find Pagan or Pagan-friendly lawyers. When the Pagan parent is poor, the problem is exacerbated, since there have been cases where Pagan parents have had trouble getting help from a public defenders' office or have been assigned court-appointed lawyers unsympathetic to Paganism who urge their clients to take actions that are harmful to their legal positions, such as agreeing to court imposed arrangements that raise serious constitutional issues.

Catherine Cookson writes of one Wiccan mother who had difficulty finding a lawyer willing to represent her. "Several of the lawyers she contacted to handle her divorce refused her case out of a fear of paganism, or from a fear that the fact that she was a 'Witch' would prove 'too controversial' " (1997, 733). The first lawyer she was able to retain advised her coven to stop holding religious services until the divorce case was settled. Her husband, in spite of his history of wife and child abuse, got custody. The judge stated that it was child abuse to take the child to Wiccan ceremonies, rituals, or holiday celebrations, ordering that there be no mention of Wicca in the child's presence and that the child have no contact with members of the mother's religious group or with their children who had been the child's playmates.

When religious nonconformity is made an issue in a custody or visitation proceeding, the lawyer usually must attempt to convince the presiding judge that Paganism in general and his or her client's brand of Paganism in particular are, in fact, religion. An unsympathetic or even hostile lawyer is, obviously, poorly equipped to carry out this function. Although, as was discussed in chapter 4, the case is an easy one to make under Supreme Court precedents, most locally oriented judges and lawyers are not well versed in either the applicable Constitutional law or the characteristics of Pagan religious beliefs and practices. Finding a Pagan-friendly and knowledgeable lawyer and an unprejudiced judge can be difficult or impossible (Eilers, 2003, 17–31).

One of the most heavily publicized cases that illustrates this problem was the Conan Brewer case. Mr. Brewer faced an uninformed judge and was represented by a lawyer unable or unwilling to advise him of his rights properly. In this case, the visitation rights of Mr. Brewer were at issue. In the July, 2000 Court Order granting the divorce in the Chancery Court of Lawrence County, Tennessee (Case No. 10041–00), the presiding judge specified: "This Court further directs that during the time Mr. Brewer has physical custody of Sara, there will be no exposure to . . . the teachings of Wicca." This specification was based on the belief of the judge that Wicca is a nonconformist lifestyle, not a religion. It is not clear from the available record what attempt was made by Mr. Brewer's lawyer to demonstrate that Wicca was a religion, although the presiding judge did seem to have some knowledge of its basic tenets.

Had this part of the court order been challenged and appealed, there is a good chance that it would have been overturned on appeal, since there is an ample legal basis for a finding that Wicca is a religion and that Mr. Brewer had a constitutional right to practice his religion in the presence of his child. Had the court treated Wicca as a religion, there is precedent in Tennessee for permitting both parents to expose their children to their religions.[6] Mr. Brewer, however, was permitted to agree to the order by his counsel. This agreement plus the failure of the lawyer to object made it virtually impossible for Mr. Brewer to appeal the ruling when, at a later date, he became aware that he had a good basis for appeal.

Subsequently, Mr. Brewer's ex-wife petitioned the Chancery Court to declare Mr. Brewer in contempt and put him in jail (Petition for Contempt, Case No. 10041–00, Chancery Court for Lawrence County, Tennessee, 2001). This petition was based on the child's first visit with Mr. Brewer. During the visit, she was passively exposed to his religion. Because he was clergy, a high priest, the child was on the premises where two worship services were held (although she did not actively participate) and was taken to a party at a store that sold Pagan goods. In addition, she was exposed to Wiccan ritual attire, jewelry, and "various other things in his home." No attempt was made to give her any formal religious education in Wicca. Mr. Brewer, who by that time had managed to find more adequate legal representation, was found in contempt, but not jailed. It is difficult to imagine a Protestant minister being required to cleanse his or her home of all religious objects and clothing, as well as find childcare in order to protect a visiting daughter or son from any indication of his religion or clerical status.

On some occasions, the accusing parent was a Pagan during the time of the marriage, but subsequently converted to a more conformist religion or denies their former Pagan religious affiliation. In one case, the husband sued for custody accusing the wife of being a Witch arguing that this religious affiliation was harmful to the children. The wife was able to respond by producing photographs of the husband participating in Pagan rituals (*The Daily Telegraph*, February 20, 1997; Drobac, 1997). This time, the mother got custody. Whether she would have without the incriminating photographs remains an open question.

Judges make most custody and visitation decisions.[7] Here, the key factors are the ability of the Pagan's lawyer to educate the judge about Paganism and the willingness of the judge to be educated. A study of the available cases, as well as the experiences of Pagans involved in religious rights organizations, seems to indicate that, when the Pagan's lawyer does a good job of presenting Paganism as a religion and the judge is impartial, the custody and visitation cases are decided on grounds that have little or nothing to do with either parent's religious convictions and practices. When the lawyer is inadequate and/or the judge biased, however, the result is different.

The problem with lawyers has several aspects. First of all, as is the case with most minority religions, there are relatively few Pagan lawyers or law firms and those that do exist are not always located in the jurisdiction where they are needed. Second, many Pagan lawyers are hesitant to be open about their religious convictions. Some are willing to give information to lawyers representing Pagans, but only from deep cover. Third, as mentioned previously, an appropriate lawyer may not want to represent a Pagan. Fourth, when the Pagan parent is forced by a lack of alternatives to retain a non-knowledgeable or unsympathetic lawyer, the Pagan parent often finds the lawyer inept or unhelpful when religious issues are raised. Fifth, non-Pagan lawyers may be given the proper information and documentation regarding Paganism, but not use it or use it ineffectually. This is unfortunate, because the experience of Pagan religious rights activists has led most of them to the opinion that when Pagan parents have competent and sympathetic local attorneys who use the materials the Pagan religious rights organizations have made available, they seldom lose custody on the basis of religion.

Potential Christian judicial bias is another problem that Pagan parents face. The United States is a country where it is possible for a judge, such as Judge Roy S. Moore of Alabama (*The Washington Post*, October 3, 1997) to hang the Ten Commandments in his courtroom, become (as a result) a regular on the Christian tent revival circuit and parlay his label of "The Ten Commandments Judge" into a successful campaign for Chief Justice of a state supreme court (*The Washington Post*, November 19, 2002). Subsequently, in the dead of the night Chief Justice Moore dragged a 5,300-pound granite Ten Commandments monument into the state's judicial building where it was prominently displayed. The U.S. District and Circuit Court of Appeals found this unconstitutional and the case was refused certiorari by the U.S. Supreme Court (*The Washington Post*, November 4, 2003). Although removed from office on ethics grounds, Judge Moore was subsequently urged by his fundamentalist Christian supporters to run for elective office. He is an extreme case, but he is not alone in his conviction about "the sovereignty of [the Christian] God over the affairs of men" (*The Washington Post*, November 19, 2002). As was discussed in chapter 3, many judges share this point of view. Most of them are just not that flamboyant.

A recurring theme in Pagan custody and visitation cases is the way in which many presiding judges deal with the issue of minority and unfamiliar religions in deciding custody cases. There are reports of hearings during which questions about religion predominate or completely eclipse questions about the parenting skills and commitment to parenthood of the people contending for custody. In many of these lower court hearings no complete transcript is created. Thus, the presiding judge is free to make his or her decision based on the perceived harmfulness of Witchcraft or Paganism without creating a record that would make that bias obvious as a basis for appeal (e.g. Bartley, 1995). Appellate courts normally defer to the trial judge. An example can be found in *Warrick v. Lane* (1979 Tex. App. LEXIS 3466, 2):

> Respondent further complains that the trial court violated her constitutional rights under the Texas and U.S. constitutions by allowing testimony as to respondent's religious beliefs and as to the Church of Wicca. . . . Although the trial court made extensive findings of fact, there are no findings whatsoever pertaining to the religious beliefs of any party to the action and there is no mention whatsoever in such findings as to the Church of Wicca or any other form of religion.
>
> The general rule of practice assumes that the trial judge hearing all the evidence has distinguished between the competent and the incompetent evidence and where the former is clearly sufficient, that he based his decision on it rather than on the latter.

Thus, it is impossible to ascertain the role (if any) that the mother's affiliation with the Church of Wicca played in the final decision. Unless a judge wants to make an issue of his or her perceptions concerning the harmfulness to the child of a parent's practice of a nonconformist religion, there is little that can be done.

In general, when a Pagan parent loses custody of a child there are usually serious allegations of parental inadequacy other than the religion of the parent. Most judges, if religiously unbiased and properly informed by counsel, do not regard Paganism as a sufficient source of harm, to deny custody exclusively on that basis. But it does happen and, as illustrated by the *Brewer* case, a biased judge can erect a legal wall between a child and the Pagan parent's nonconformist religion.

Another of the serious problems that religiously nonconformist parents and foster parents face is the religiously zealous social worker. In a Midwest state,[8] a divorced mother who had custody of her child remarried. Subsequently the stepfather abused the child and, as a result, social services put the child in foster care. The father, requesting visitation and eventual custody, was told that he could not see the child unless he agreed never to discuss Wicca with the child. The reason given was that Wicca was not a religion recognized by that state. His court-appointed lawyer sided with the authorities and advised the father sign an agreement that provided: "I understand that I will not, nor will anyone in the household, bring up the subject of witchcraft in the presence of my child at any time, nor will I have obvious paraphernalia out in the home during a visit. Should this occur I understand that my visitations will become supervised immediately."

A hearing was scheduled and several Pagan religious rights activists mobilized on his behalf. When the court was told that Wiccan clergy intended to testify on the father's behalf, the court went into a closed session. The result was that the court permitted the father to discuss Wicca with the child, but not take him to any services. The mother was permitted to take the child to Christian services. Finally, the hearing was held, but the social services representatives (who had apparently educated themselves) called the father's religion "Wicca" instead of "witchcraft." Much of the testimony was directed at the father's religious beliefs and the judge, a devout Christian, showed considerable interest in Pagan theology. The child's attorney took the position that the attack on the father's religion was unfair.

The final outcome was that the father might practice and share his religion with his child and the mother might do the same—a result that is routine when two Christian sects are involved. Both sides were also ordered to respect each other's beliefs and not speak negatively to the child about the other parent's religion. A less fortunate parent was deprived of parental rights after an evaluation that characterized her Pagan beliefs to be "satanic" (which they were not). During the hearing, the judge asked her if she believed in reincarnation. When she answered that she did, he ordered the children to be placed in foster care (E-mail, October 4, 1997). This is of particular significance, since many of the growing nonconformist religious groups, such as Hindus, embrace belief in reincarnation.

Clearly, what was at issue in these cases and is operative in many other similar cases is the fear of persons in the court and child protective systems that the child might be harmed in some way by the parent's nonconformist religion. The nature of the harm is usually not clearly specified or substantiated. In Pagan cases, the religion is usually referred to as "witchcraft" even when that is not an accurate designation, as in the case of a Druid. In one case, a Wiccan went into a hospital to have her first baby and designated Wiccan as her religious faith. As a result, the newborn child was placed in protective custody for the first 30 days of its life (E-mail, March 13, 1996). In another case, a group of anti-Pagan Christians infiltrated the *guardian ad litem* structure and systematically created problems for Pagan parents. Since they had been political supporters of the judge and several went to the same church as the judge, they were able to operate with the tacit support of the court (E-mail, December 15, 1996). In an even more extreme case, a Wiccan grandparent was denied custody of his grandchildren because of his religion and the children were placed in the home of a Christian minister who insisted that they attend his church every Sunday (E-mail, March 26, 2001).

This raises another problem faced by non-Christian parents who lose custody of their children. The institution or foster homes in which the children are placed may be places where their religion is undermined and the children are evangelized. For example, in one case the children were removed on allegations of neglect due to the long working hours of the parents. The children were placed in an institution run by Christian fundamentalists who proceeded to try to convert the children and to impress upon them that their Pagan beliefs were immoral and wrong. Although the institution formally reprimanded one of the involved workers for violating an institutional policy against evangelizing, the worker remained in the employ of the institution. The children's Pagan clergyman was not permitted to meet them privately so that the children could talk in confidence to him. Also, when requests were made to take the children to Wiccan services, the administrators of the facility always found ways to prevent the children from attending the services or spending religious holidays with their family (E-mails, March 7, 2001–April 23, 2001). In another case, a Wiccan grandfather requesting custody was turned down by the social services agency for the express reason that he refused to promise to bring up the children as Christians (E-mail, February 24, 1996). Pagan parents visiting their children in foster care have found their children wearing Christian crosses.

Like judges, many social service agencies are operating on the basis of ignorance and superstitious fears for the safety of the children. They are sometimes amenable to efforts to better inform them. In one case, local child protective services workers visited a mother and questioned her extensively about whether her Pagan beliefs meant that she was a Satanist. The visit was precipitated by an anonymous informant who reported that the mother was involved in the occult. The social workers left, saying that they would return. In this case, a local Pagan leader had a sister who worked in a children's services institution in a neighboring county. At the request of her brother, she contacted the social workers involved and talked to them about Paganism, assuring them that Satanism was not part of the Pagan belief system. After this, the social workers dropped all mention of religion and helped the mother to get additional services for her child's psychological and motor problems (E-mail, October 5, 1995).

Parents practicing Pagan religions are frequently the subjects of reports to social services agencies. In one case, publicized on the Internet (www.helptalen.org), a Colorado mother met with her two-year-old daughter's daycare provider. She requested that the provider avoid religious slurs in decorations and readings for Halloween, explaining that her family was Wiccan. The daycare teacher, who always wore a crucifix and used "Trinity Christian College" stationary to send home official notices, reported suspected abuse and a social worker contacted the mother. The father was charged with abuse on the ground that the "parents are witches" and the child had a small bruise on her buttocks. The child was placed in foster care. Subsequently, teachers in the public school system, working with another ostentatiously devout Christian social worker, managed to keep the child out of his home for a period of years, during which the child was not allowed access to Pagan clergy or services.

In another case, the informant was a workman who was installing tiles in a home. He saw evidence of mother's religious beliefs and notified local children's services authorities. They found potential harm to the child, because "Witches sacrifice children and animals to Satan." The family's religious books and other Wiccan items were called "instruments of satanical torture." A picture of the one- and two-year-old girls playing outside in their diapers was called child pornography because the children's breasts were not covered. The lawyer the mother contacted told her that it was her fault for being involved with Pagans. At last report, the mother was searching for a Pagan-friendly lawyer (E-mail, October 1, 2001).

Finally, Pagan or Pagan-friendly social workers are not immune from problems themselves. In one case (*Morning Star News* [Wilmington, NC], January 16, 1997), a Wiccan social worker employed by the Social Services Department for 13 years was fired. She had been working with a Wiccan mother whose son had some behavioral problems and the situation came to the attention of authorities when the boy's mother appeared on a television show about Witches. Pagan foster parents are also vulnerable. In Ohio, a Wiccan foster mother who lost custody of her foster children filed suit against a couple who were also foster parents. They had alleged that she was a "devil-worshipper," because she was Wiccan. The suit was for defamation of character (*St Louis Post-Dispatch*, August 21, 1994).

When non-Christian children enter school, they also con
scrutiny of persons who may hold deeply prejudiced view;
formist religions. In such cases, the children may be press
form or punished for their nonconformity. As will be evide
section, the parent can also become the object of action
enforce a Christian-oriented conformity.

School System Enforced Conformity

When the public schools become involved in the imposition of school-
based religious conformity, "the government delivers an audience of
potential recruits to a religious majority, which then uses the opportunity to proselytize. In these situations, the government also provides a
forum for the religious majority to announce and celebrate its position
of influence in the community, thus reinforcing the views of those
already committed to the majority faith" (Gey, 2000, 433). The public
schools can be a hostile environment for students who do not subscribe
to Christianity. Here the three major sources of problems are the overtly
religious atmosphere in some public schools, concern about school violence (including gang activity) and the belief systems of individual
teachers and school administrators.

In a 1993 Fifth Circuit case, the majority opinion listed the "acts and
customs" of the schools (*Doe v. Duncanville Independent School District*,
994 F.2d 160, 162, N2):

1. Girls basketball teams from the seventh through twelfth
   grades . . . recited the Lord's Prayer before . . . and after . . . each
   game. . . . They also routinely formed a circle and recited the
   Prayer before practices. . . .
2. The Lord's Prayer was recited during regularly scheduled physical
   education classes for members of the teams.
3. Prayers were said at pep rallies.
4. While traveling from away games, the teams recited the Lord's
   Prayer prior to leaving the school bus.
5. At awards ceremonies honoring the teams, prayers were recited,
   and pamphlets containing religious songs were prepared and distributed by the coaches and/or other school personnel.
6. A prayer was spoken prior to all football games conducted and
   operated by DISD.
7. Prayers began all regular school board meetings. . . . Prayers
   were said prior to each football game, graduation ceremony,

baccalaureate, employee banquet, new teacher orientation, the end of the year banquet, and PTA meetings.

8. Prayers began all regular school board meetings, with the exception of special school board meetings. Prayers were said prior to each football game, graduation ceremony, baccalaureate, employee banquet, new teacher orientation, the end of the year banquet, and PTA meetings.

9. Each school in the district usually staged a Christmas program during its December PTA meeting. During these meetings, traditional Christmas hymns were sung, and the meetings began with a prayer.

10. Gideon Bibles were made available to the intermediate school students, and announcements were made that the Bibles could be picked up in the front foyer of the schools.

11. Doe's history teacher taught the Biblical version of Creation; Christian songs routinely were sung, and the theme song for the choir—required to be sung at all performances—was a religious song.

What it must be like to be an adherent of a minority religion under these conditions can only be imagined. The pressure toward conformity, always a problem with minor school children in virtually all areas of their lives, is overwhelming.

The practices listed above only pressure the children to conform. The use of school dress codes enforces conformity. It is justified as a way of coping with gang activity and school violence. Whatever the merits of this assertion, it has also had an impact on Pagans and other minority religious people, as well as a few more conventional religiously devout students who want to demonstrate their faith through their appearance. Pagan students often experience intolerant reactions by school administrators and teachers, particularly if they are wearing a pentacle. It can be politicized, since Christian clergy and parents often get involved, calling for the banning of what many of them regard as a satanic symbol. It is rare that Christian or Jewish students are forbidden to wear their religious symbols, although such cases occur (e.g. *WorldNetDaily*, April 23, 2003). School systems regularly lose these cases when they are taken to court. In fact, in many situations where a clearly religious pentagram is involved, a consultation with school system lawyers has been sufficient to cause school authorities to back down. In the meantime, however, the problems caused to the Pagan student and his family can be considerable.

Commonly dress codes involve lists of forbidden types of clothing, jewelry, and other forms of attire, including tattoos. Such dress codes raise serious legal questions, most notably issues involving constitutionally protected expression. Among the religious symbols that have been banned have been "the Star of David, rosary beads worn as necklaces, T-shirts bearing the image of Our Lady of Guadalupe, cross tattoos, long hair worn by [male] Native American youths, and various 'Satanic' or Wiccan symbols, such as the pentagram or pentacle" (Kordas, 2000, 1456). Problems continually arise because gangs utilize a wide range of symbols and colors that do include many with religious significance. School administrators are often reluctant to try to ascertain a particular student's motivations for wearing a particular symbol, unless (as in the case of Christian symbols) it seems obvious. Many school districts have, thus, banned various symbols and types of dress without reference to the students' reasons for wearing them.

Attempts to give school administrators flexibility by listing categories, such as "gang symbols" have raised questions about vagueness, allowing school authorities unfettered discretion in deciding the definition of the word "gang" and what qualifies as a "gang symbol." Both of these raise the issue of arbitrary enforcement. In 1997, the Eighth Circuit Court of Appeals held that such a school district rule was unconstitutionally vague in the case of Brianna Stephenson who had a Christian cross tattoo on her hand as an act of religious devotion. The school system compelled her to remove the tattoo in a painful surgical procedure, although there was no evidence that she was involved with a gang or any violent activity (*Stephenson v. Davenport Community School District*, 110 F.3d 1303). This case is unusual, though, since school administrators seldom find the wearing of common Christian symbols objectionable. It might have been the use of a tattoo rather than a more common necklace or pin that triggered the problem.

There have been many cases of Pagan students being forbidden to wear a pentacle when the wearing of crosses or Stars of David were readily allowed, although both of the latter have on occasion been used as gang symbols. One of the most widely publicized was the case of Crystal Siefferly, a student in Lincoln Park High School in a suburb of Detroit, Michigan. Crystal, an honor student with no disciplinary record or gang affiliation, embraced Wicca when she was 13 years old. Although her parents were Christian, they supported her choice. When she was 17, the principal of her high school issued a Gang/Cult Policy. It prohibited students from belonging to a list of groups that included Pagans and Witches. It also forbade the wearing of certain symbols, including the pentagram. So, while the Christian students could openly wear their crosses, Crystal was forced to wear her pentagram (a gift from her parents) under her clothing or not at all.

Crystal and her mother talked to the principal in an effort to explain the meaning of the pentagram and the fact that it posed no threat. He responded that she could not wear it to school. After consultation with several Pagan religious rights organizations and the American Civil Liberties Union (ACLU), Crystal decided to sue the Lincoln Park Public Schools and was represented by the ACLU of Michigan and two other lawyers. The school system stipulated that Wicca was a bona fide religion, but that it was also "employed by numerous other students to assert their gang membership, to deface school property, and to establish their presence in the school. It is *likely* also employed to announce and/ or suggest the presence of students in illegal and disruptive activities including sex with minors, *possibly* forced sex, drug use, and mutilation" (as quoted in Eilers, 1999, 22, emphasis added). The case was settled after an evidentiary hearing in the U.S. District Court. The school system agreed to pay $14,000 to cover Crystal's legal fees, removed the words "Pagans" and "Witches" from the policy, and made an exception for students wearing jewelry or other symbols as signs of religious devotion.

Aside from the personal problems they have caused for many Pagan students, school dress codes raise virtually insurmountable legal problems. If they are too vague they raise problems of arbitrary enforcement, overbreadth, and the suppression of constitutionally protected rights. If they are too specific, they become ridiculous and raise the problem of inappropriate sanctions. As has been pointed out by Rob Killen (2000, 462), almost anything can be considered disruptive or gang-related. In a partial list of items forbidden by dress codes or found to be gang-related he includes: "the numbers 311, 2, 4, 5, 20; . . . Doc Martin shoes; baggy pants; a backward 'R'; the Letters 'BGD' and 'BK'; the colors red, black, white, green and blue; 'Old English'-style writing; peace symbols, crowns; popcorn braids; dollar signs; . . . the color combinations black/gold and blue/black; Converse shoes; winged hearts; collegiate logos; . . . the word 'vegan'; . . . the Star of David; pentagrams; rosaries; and crosses." He quotes one police gang specialist's observation that "the list is endless."

In fact, during the Seifferly hearing, U.S. District Judge Rosen produced a hat for the analysis of a gang expert who said that the hat would be a problem because it was blue, signifying one gang, and had a five-pointed star on it, signifying that gang's rival. The hat was the baseball cap of a U.S. Marshall (*South Bend Tribune*, March 3, 1999). In a subsequent Indiana case, it was pointed out that police badges in that jurisdiction featured pentagrams (*South Bend Tribune*, March 15, 2000). Ironically, even the stars on the American flag are pentagrams. Faced by the possibility of a lawsuit and the precedent of the Seifferly case, that school district changed its policy.

The core problem here is that forbidding symbols that are thought to be gang symbols enforces conformity, but does little to stop or hinder gang activity. Paradoxically, it gives gangs a significant measure of control over both school policy and the rights of their fellow students. As Killen (2000, 463) points out: "Since the justification for dress codes is to prevent violence and disruption in the classroom, the list of prohibited symbols and apparel will continue to grow as gangs adopt new symbols." In addition, while Christian or Jewish symbols such as the cross and the Star of David have occasionally been at the center of such disputes, the pentagram has precipitated many more cases, as have religious objects worn by other students, such as the scarves worn by Muslim female students. School authorities are much less likely to understand their religious meaning or to be sympathetic to the religious motivations of their wearers.

Most school personnel are likely to be Christian, some of them passionately so. This can predispose them to think the worst of their Pagan students. More strangely, there seem to be a number of teachers and administrators who ascribe occult powers to Pagan students and seem almost afraid of them. In some of the most publicized cases, the students accused of practicing Witchcraft have not even been Pagans.

Brandi Blackbear, like many high school students, had a dream. She dreamed about becoming a successful writer of fiction, like Stephen King (a horror fiction writer). When she was in eighth grade a rumor circulated that she had a gun. School authorities searched her locker and backpack and found no gun. They did, however, find the draft of a fictitious story about a student carrying a gun onto a bus. For this act of creative writing, Brandi was given a 19-day suspension. A year later she was suspended for 15 days when school officials accused her of hexing a teacher who fell ill and had to be hospitalized. Their only evidence was a pentagram inside a circle that was drawn on her hand. The assistant principal and a counselor brought her into an office and accused her of being a Witch. She protested that she was not a Witch and did not practice Wicca. Later, her father confirmed that she was being raised as a Catholic (*Associated Press*, October 26, 2000).

According to the complaint filed in U.S. District Court by the ACLU of Oklahoma and Brandi's lawyers, the assistant principal and counselor "repeatedly accused [Brandi] of being a member of Wicca, practicing Wicca and casting spells on other people. Plaintiff, Brandi Blackbear, repeatedly denied these accusations until such point as she was not emotionally strong enough to deny." Finally, she "admitted that she had been reading books about Wicca and that she could be a member of a Wicca coven, although she had been heretofore been studying Wicca independently. Plaintiff Brandi Blackbear admitted this only because of the continued hostility and oppression by the [assistant principal and counselor]." The ACLU complaint continued: "The interview culminated with [the assistant principal] accusing Plaintiff, Brandi Blackbear, of casting spells causing [the teacher] to be sick and to be hospitalized. Based upon the unknown cause of [the teacher's] illness,[9] [the assistant principal] advised [Brandi] that she was an immediate threat to the school and summarily suspended her . . . for a period of fifteen (15) days. . . ." The same two school officials "put much inflammatory and prejudicial language in [Brandi's] personal school file which will continue to hurt and harm her throughout the remainder of her life" (www.aclu.org/court/blackbear_complaint.html).

In a similar case, a straight A student was suspended from school for "practicing witchcraft." She had been reading a book on Witchcraft when several other students asked her if she was a Witch. At first she denied it, but after being harassed about it she said, "Yeah, I'm a Witch." She did nothing more than pointedly stare at the students who were harassing her, but this was regarded as sufficient proof for school officials to suspend her. Later she again denied she was a Witch and said that she had stared at her harassers to get them to stop bothering her (E-mail, January 12, 1998).

The interesting thing about such cases is the readiness of school authorities to take seriously the ability of a student to cast effective spells or hex others. The fact that neither of the young women just discussed was actually a Witch or claimed to have cast a spell did not seem to matter to the school authorities who seemed startlingly ready to act on their personal superstitions with no real proof that an offense had been committed. Even more disconcerting is the fact that in at least one school district the school authorities felt free to exert enough pressure on the student to elicit a false confession.

Suspensions, of course, have not been limited to non-Pagans. Jamie Schoonover, a freshman at Baltimore's Southwestern High School was open about her adherence to Wicca, making it evident in her dress and music preferences. One morning when Jamie and her friends were sitting outside the school waiting for classes to start, another student told Jennifer Rassen that Schoonover had cast a spell on her. Distraught, Rassen went to school administrators who issued a one-day suspension to Schoonover citing her for "casting a spell on a student." Later when the story hit the news media, the reason for the suspension was changed to "allegedly making a verbal threat" (*The Washington Post*, October 22,

1998). Other Pagan students have been suspended for "practicing witchcraft" when they were just behaving like typical teenagers. For example, a Texas Pagan was suspended for three days when she wrote a hostile poem about another girl of whom she was jealous. The poem included a description of how she wanted the other girl's hair to drop out (E-mail, December 17, 1996).

This combination of dislike for persons identified as Pagan or Witch and a seeming fear of their powers may be explained by relatively recent findings regarding the nature of prejudice. There seem to be two dimensions in prejudiced people's reaction toward outgroups. One has to do with liking versus disliking or the extent to which the prejudiced person sees outgroup members as nice, likeable, generous, and moral versus bad, malevolent, mean, insincere, and immoral. The other has to do with the extent to which outgroup members are seen as competent versus incompetent. On an emotional level, dislike would involve stereotyping a person as bad, evil, immoral, or malevolent, while disrespecting them would involve stereotyping them as incompetent, weak, backward, and unsuccessful (Duckitt, 2003, 562–564). Thus, in the cases mentioned above (and more that will follow), the school authorities seemed to dislike the Pagans (or alleged Pagans), but they seemed to have respect for the Pagans' power to affect others in a negative way. Thus, both dislike and fear appear to be part of the dynamic.

Aside from such direct pressures put on school children following nonconformist beliefs, there is a clear Christian bias in the curricula, organized activities and books in many, if not most, public schools. One area that has, to date, not been addressed by the Supreme Court is the singing of Christian music in classes and school events. The consensus, both among legal commentators and the courts that have addressed the issue seems to be that Christian music is "appropriate in a study of choral music [and] essential to presenting an honest portrayal of music in society" (Whitaker, 2003, 360; Kasparian, 1997). But, as Brian Whitaker points out, "there is a dividing line somewhere between the enjoyable performance of a good piece of music in a proper setting and the imposition of one's religious beliefs on others" (Whitaker, 2003, 361). When non-Christian children are forced to sing only Christian songs and the songs of their traditions are not sung or even expressly rejected, a line seems to have been crossed. When the effort to achieve more balance in a public school choral program results in public abuse and harassment, a line is definitely crossed. That was the case with 13-year-old Shana McNelly.

Shana joined the school chorus at her middle school and even won a place on the all-county chorus. When the middle school chorus was preparing for the Spring Concert, however, Shana's mother and a representative of the Appalachian Pagan Alliance met with school authorities and objected to the fact that six of the nine songs were Christian. They suggested that a Pagan song be added, but the school refused. School officials did, however, agree as a compromise to remove the two most overtly Christian songs, "Pie Jesu" and "Did My Lord Deliver Daniel." When the other students found out what had happened they began harassing Shana to the point where she was forced to leave a class and take refuge in the counselor's office. She was threatened with physical violence and, according to the Director of the North Carolina Witches Against Religious Discrimination, received at least one death threat. An entire class sang "Jesus Loves Me" at Shana.[10]

At the Spring Concert, after the program was over, the piano player began playing "Pie Jesu" and the students sang it. When Shana ran off the stage in tears, some students said "Bye, bye Pagan get out of here," and the chorus teacher made no attempt to intervene. The audience stayed and applauded at the end. Chris Cox, a columnist in the local newspaper, commented, "I want to believe that the students themselves orchestrated this little 'in your face' gesture, but even if they did, they did so with the complicity of the adults involved. No one tried to stop it, no one intervened. Instead they piled on. Shana was showered with yet more hateful commentary as she left the building and outside, cars approached playing Christian music loudly and the abuse continued" ([Ashville, NC] CITIZEN-TIMES.com, May 26, 2001). The principal said that he made a decision to let the song continue in order to maintain safety and order. He did, however, talk to "a few students" subsequently and told them that such behavior would not be tolerated in the future. The school refused to publicly apologize or punish the students involved. The principal's position was that "No one was forced to listen. No one was forced to participate. Our school resource officer was here and I did ask her to make sure [the NcNellys] got to their car safely" ([Ashville, NC] CITIZEN-TIMES.com, May17, 2001). At the time this was being discussed on a religious rights Internet list, another mother reported that the music for her daughter's Spring Concert was all Christian and that participation was required for a grade in the class. For obvious reasons, they hesitated to object.

Sometimes, however, objecting can produce a successful result. In another case in South Dakota, a child objected to participating in the chorus at Christmas because most of the songs being sung did not accommodate her beliefs. She and her mother met with the chorus teacher and were told that she would get an "F" for the semester if she did not participate fully. They then went to the principal who "started waffling" until the mother mentioned going to the Superintendent of Schools, the ACLU, the Lady Liberty League, and the media. Then the principal sent the child back to class and summoned the chorus teacher who was informed that she would have to excuse the child from that part of the concert on religious grounds. She was also explicitly told not to let the incident affect the child's grade (E-mail, January 11, 2004).

The problem of hostility to non-Christian religions also extends to the texts used in the classroom and available in school libraries. In many areas, fundamentalist Christians have taken it upon themselves to assure that the books used in the public schools do not promote anything but Christianity. In 1994, this impulse to control the curriculum of public schools gave rise to two court cases, *Fleischfresser v. Directors of School District 200* (15 F.3d 680) and *Brown v. Woodland Joint Unified School District* (27 F.3d 1373). At issue in both cases was the Impressions Reading Series. According to the unanimous *Brown* opinion: "Impressions is a series of 59 books containing approximately 10,000 literary selections and suggested classroom activities. . . . The selections reflect a broad range of North American cultures and traditions" (27 F.3d 1373, 1377). In *Brown* the complaining parents objected to 32 selections, contending that they promoted the religion of Wicca. These challenged sections asked the children to discuss witches or make up chants and some suggested role-playing exercises in which some students would pretend to be witches or sorcerers. The parents conceded that the creators of Impressions and their publishers did not intend to promote or endorse any religious practices. The *Fleischfresser* opinion did not name a specific number of selections, but said that the offensive ones were a relatively small minority.

In both of these cases, the parents were concerned, not just with the presence of material dealing with wizards, sorcerers, witches, giants and other characters with supposed supernatural powers, in *Fleischfresser* they objected to the material because it "Indoctrinates children in values directly opposed to their Christian beliefs . . . and by denigrating Christian symbols and holidays" (15 F.3d 680, 683). The *Brown* plaintiffs argued the using the challenged sections would denigrate Christians and make Christians feel like outsiders. This, in their opinion would amount to discrimination against Christianity "and other popular religions" (27 F.3d 1373, 1382). When viewed along with the choir cases, it is clear that at least some members of the Christian majority wish to suppress any inclusion of religion in the schools' curriculum and activities—unless that religion is one of which they approve.

A similar problem has often arisen with regard to the books in school libraries.[11] The popularity of the Harry Potter series, which has nothing to do with any major Pagan religion, has exacerbated the situation. For example, in 2002, in Connecticut a middle school was subjected to demands from some Christian parents that the Harry Potter series be "removed from the [middle school] library on the grounds that they promote the Wiccan religion." The pastor the River Bend Christian Fellowship, a local church, observed "the Harry Potter books portray Christianity in a 'bad light' and 'has satanic overtones' " (CNSNEWS. COM, July 19, 2002). As was observed by a commentator[12] in the *Milwaukee Journal Sentinel* (JSOnline) on November 5, 2001: "Protestant fundamentalist criticism of Harry Potter is an outgrowth of a larger struggle over how to deal with a popular culture that—unlike the popular culture of the 19th century and early 20th century—is being produced with very little church influence."

During recent years, there has been an upsurge of interest in Paganism, especially Wicca, among high school students and young adults.[13] There are many theories as to why this might be the case. One has to do with the increasing number of television shows, movies and works of popular fiction depicting witches in a favorable light. Seldom do these entertainment sources give an even remotely accurate portrayal of what Wicca or Witchcraft is like in the real world. They do, however, arouse curiosity and, in many cases, lead the teenager or young adult to pursue the topic farther. Currently, the first thing curious young people consult is the Internet and there are hundreds of sites that contain information about Paganism of all traditions. For those still inclined to read books, there are sources such as Silver Ravenwolf's *Teen Witch: Wicca for a New Generation*, a bestseller for its publisher. This can also cause trouble in schools when students turn to their teachers for help. In several cases, teachers have gotten suspended for loaning books on Wicca to students who were doing research. In one case the research was on herbal healing ([Michigan] *Herald Palladium*, March 1, 2000). Most Pagan groups and adherents will not give information to teenagers unless the parents specifically give their permission.

Once a young adult has been introduced to the realities of Paganism, as well as the beliefs and practices of its various traditions, there are those who find it attractive enough to pursue it in a more serious manner. Many are young women who are drawn to a female deity and the leadership roles women currently play within most Pagan traditions.

The editor of a magazine that targets young adults recently observed "stories [about Paganism] just score through the roof. There's a sense of magic that girls get from this that is very empowering" (*The New York Times*, February 13, 2000). Anthony Paige, a former Catholic who wrote *Campus Wicca for the Student Practitioner*, thinks that one source of appeal is the absence of a "sense of sin." He makes the point that while "there is a karmic law, . . . there's no scorn or condemnation" (*Fox News*, December 12, 2002). Because it can be a very eclectic practice and lacks a strong dogma, Paganism also tends to appeal to persons who think of themselves as more spiritual than conventionally religious. Finally, Witchcraft has an appeal for "the defiantly unconventional and the would-be hip" (*The New York Times*, February 13, 2000). John K. Simmons, a professor of religious studies is of the opinion that: "It appeals most of all to the intelligent, poetic young woman who is not necessarily going to go out for cheerleader or date the captain of the football team" (*The New York Times*, February 13, 2000).

One clear manifestation of this trend is the current growth of student Pagan organizations on college campuses. Although there are campuses on which such organizations have been accepted, there have been problems. In one case, the Pagan students found that it was extremely difficult to find a faculty member willing to be their official advisor—a necessity for gaining a line on the campus activities budget and access to other resources normally used by campus religious organizations. Turning to the religion department, the students found that those professors did not consider Paganism a religion. Then they found a junior sociology professor who was willing to be their advisor, only to have the head of his department categorically forbid him to do so. Eventually, they found a tenured, full professor who was sympathetic and willing to act as advisor, but the search was very stressful and almost kept the organization from being formed. And on another campus the Pagan Association was denied membership in the Inter-faith Council, because "according to the Protestant minister, the Catholic Priest, and the Baptist Deacon, [they] did not actually have a faith." In other words, they had "no religion" (E-mail, January 24, 2004).

Other types of problems that Pagan groups have encountered include the refusal of the university to recognize their organization and opposition by student Christian leaders to student government funding of Pagan organizations. On occasion, access to facilities, such as interfaith chapels, has been an issue. Also, there are campuses on which Pagan students have been given "special interest organization" status, but refused "religious organization" status. Related is the fact that Pagan students have seldom been accorded any accommodation for the celebration of their major holidays on campuses where Christian, Jewish, and Islamic students are routinely accommodated. Lehigh University and the University of Arizona have been pioneers in extending accommodation for religious holidays to Pagans, as well as to other minority religions. For the most part, it seems that—slowly, but surely—student Pagan organizations are becoming a part of campus life with relatively little in the way of serious opposition. The key seems to be perseverance and patience, combined with a willingness to educate faculty, administration and non-Pagan students about the sincerely religious nature of Paganism.

Schools, however, are not the only venue where the imperative to impose a certain degree of conformity with Christian religious beliefs and behaviors creates problems for minority religions. Often, as in the case of Muslim women's religious choice to cover their hair with scarves, a nonconformist attitude regarding appearance and dress can become a source of contention and attempts to change the behavior of the adherents of minority religions.

Public Appearance and Dress

There is currently an increasing variation among religious groups in the United States regarding the level of dress or undress considered acceptable. Most Christians regard it as mandatory that certain areas of the body, such as the breasts of females and the genitals of both sexes be covered in public situations. Some Muslim and Orthodox Jews go farther than this and require the covering of the hair and/or part of the face by females.[14] Sikhs and Orthodox Jews require the covering of part or all of the hair by adult males. Pagans tend to conform to the modesty requirements of the dominant Christians when in public. In private situations, some Pagan traditions practice ritual nudity. Ritual nudity goes back at least as far as Gerald Gardner. Even those Pagan traditions that do not routinely practice ritual nudity tend to have clothing-optional policies for some rituals, as well as large Pagan festivals and gatherings that take place in secluded locations.

As a nature-centered religion, Paganism sees the human body (regardless of shape and size) as another manifestation of the sacredness and beauty of nature. They see sexuality in much the same way, but do not necessarily equate the nude human body with eroticism. In fact, like naturists, many Pagans think that a partially clothed human body may be much more erotic than a nude one. Christians tend to view nudity, especially in "public places,"[15] as being lewd or erotic and, thus, likely to give offense. As a result of this attitude toward the human body and Christian influence on the legal system, there are a host of state and local laws that forbid and punish "public" nudity.

In 1991, Chief Justice Rehnquist writing the plurality opinion in *Barnes v. Glen Theatre, Inc.* (501 U.S. 560, 568–569) made clear the Christian basis for public indecency laws outlawing nudity, as well as their relationship to the goal of protecting the social order:

> [The] statute's purpose of protecting societal order and morality is clear from its text and history. Public indecency statutes of this sort are of ancient origin and presently exist in at least 47 States. . . . This public indecency statute follows a long line of earlier Indiana statutes banning all public nudity. The history of Indiana's public indecency statutes shows that it predates barroom nude dancing and was enacted as a general prohibition. . . . A gap during which no statute was in effect was filled by the Indiana Supreme Court in *Ardery v. State*, 56 Ind. 328 (1877), which held that the court could sustain a conviction for exhibition of "privates" in the presence of others. The court traced the offense to the Bible story of Adam and Eve. . . . This and other public indecency statutes were designed to protect morals and public order. The traditional police power of the States is defined as the authority to provide for the pubic health, safety, and morals, and we have upheld such a basis for legislation. . . . Thus, the public indecency statute furthers a substantial government interest in protecting order and morality.

Justice Scalia, concurring, was in substantial agreement with Chief Justice Rehnquist on all of the points quoted above. He did, however, go farther, stating: "The purpose of Indiana's nudity law would be violated, I think, if 60,000 fully consenting adults crowded into the Hoosier Dome to display their genitals to one another, even if there were not an offended innocent in the crowd. Our society prohibits, and all human societies have prohibited, certain activities not because they harm others but because they are considered . . . immoral" (501 U.S. 560, 575).[16] He specifically likened the free speech clause issue in this case to the free exercise clause issue in the *Smith* decision, tying the acceptability of laws prohibiting nudity to laws interfering with the ability to practice minority religions as long as they could arguably be regarded as "neutral." His conclusion was that "moral opposition to nudity supplies a rational basis for its prohibition, and since the First Amendment [Free Speech Clause] has no application to this case no more than that is needed" (501 U.S. 560, 580).

Subsequently, many fundamentalist sects and local congregations have joined in an effort to increase the number of anti-nudity laws and to have existing ones made more stringent. Much of this legislation targets sexually oriented businesses, but because of the way in which these laws and bills are drafted, many of them could potentially outlaw religious nudity. Frequently these efforts have focused on legally defining nudity as inherently indecent, lascivious, or obscene, particularly in the presence of a child. Thus, a host of previously acceptable behaviors might raise legal issues. For example, it might be a problem to have a nude or partially dressed statue of a classical god or goddess where a child could view it. Qualifications in existing laws, like "willfully," "indecently," and "maliciously," that have specific legal meanings could be removed, leaving mere nudity illegal. Laws have been proposed that would punish businesses that allow nudity within their premises, making it impossible for resorts and camps to host Pagan gatherings that wish to include clothing-optional events. In one extreme case, a proposed law criminalized not only bare female breasts but also required that male nipples be covered. Such laws have not usually gained passage at the state level, but some have at local levels. According to the Naturist Action Committee (www.nac.Oshkost.net), bills restricting nudity were under consideration in 28 state legislatures during 2001–2002.

The issue for Pagans is how to deal with state and local laws on nudity that might be interpreted to outlaw nonsexual, non-pornographic, non-injurious nudity that is practiced discreetly in rituals or at Pagan gatherings. Problems have arisen at both the state and local levels. Their first line of defense has been to be extremely careful about where they practice ritual nudity and hold clothing-optional events. The second line of defense has been to exercise considerable care in shielding nudity from the view of anyone who might take offense, sometimes at the cost of the nature-based orientation of their religious beliefs and the related preference for holding religious services and events in outdoor settings. For example, at festivals held in rural campgrounds there is often a group of guards who patrol the periphery of the festival to repel any curious people who might try to sneak within viewing range of nude or partially nude participants. Rituals that properly should be held outdoors are often held indoors. When they are held outdoors, considerable trouble is taken to prevent outsiders from viewing any nudity by having the participants wear clothes in situations where nudity is considered more religiously appropriate or by taking considerable pains to block any potential view of nudity by non-Pagan viewers. Sometimes, however, this is not enough.

In Toledo, Ohio, Spirit Weavers, a branch of the Church of All Worlds, was holding a Beltane ritual[17] on private property situated in a residential area. According to *The Toledo Blade* (May 19, 2001), they "had constructed a fence, put up a tent, and strategically placed plants to try and preserve privacy." There was, however, an open walkway and the ritual could be seen from one angle. A neighbor just happened to glimpse a "naked 'May King' [who] was bound to a pole while [fully clothed] revelers danced around him with multicolored ribbons." The neighbor said, "It was a fleeting glance, but I saw what I saw." Another neighbor who did not view any nudity, but who was concerned said, "We are Christian people, and that type of behavior doesn't fit." A Vice President for the Church of All Worlds who had attended the ceremony clarified its intent: "It's like a wedding ceremony. [The May King] is being bound to the tribe and the Earth."

The police were called and prosecutors indicated their intent to charge the person portraying the "May King" with public indecency, a misdemeanor carrying a maximum penalty of 30 days in jail and a $250 fine. Even the attempt of the Spirit Weavers to ensure the privacy of the ritual became a problem, because it prompted zoning officials to observe that two fences on the property were not in compliance, since one was too high and one was erected without permission. Also, the zoning officials requested that the owner of the property obtain a conditional use permit to operate a church at his residence. The permit requires approval from the township board of zoning appeals.

After many legal hassles and efforts to placate the involved public officials, the Spirit Weavers managed to have the charges of public indecency and zoning violations dropped. They still, however, incurred about $1,000 in costs and $7,080 in attorney's fees. The attorney donated her fee back to the Spirit Weavers, because of what she regarded as "the idiocy and unfairness of the cases" (E-mail, June 23, 2001). The Spirit Weavers, for their part, invested in a large privacy fence around the property in order to prevent such incidents in the future. So, in a sense, they had their religious rights vindicated, but (as usual) it turned out to be a very expensive vindication for a religious group of about 40 members.

Although the organizers of Pagan festivals go to great pains to ensure the privacy of their clothing-optional events, they are not always successful.[18] According to the *Lexington* [Kentucky] *Herald-Leader* (April 26, 2000), a Pagan festival that was returning to the area for the second year[19] was forced to cancel plans for a late-night, clothing-optional, ceremonial fireside dance. They thought that a Kentucky statute that allows nudity for religious purposes would protect them. Thus, they applied to county officials for a "nudist society permit." Subsequently, they were warned that they could be prosecuted for child abuse if children had any access to the dancing. The organizers had planned to hold the ceremonial dancing at a location distant from the children's camping area and considerably after their curfew, but the County Attorney still maintained that the event was a potential risk for minors. Thus the organizers were forced to cancel the ceremonial dancing and, according to the *Lexington Herald-Leader*, indicated that in the future they would probably make the festival an adults-only affair, thus excluding Pagan families from a major religious event. Such cases clearly force Pagans to choose between holding family-oriented gatherings and being able to have Pagan-appropriate ceremonies at those gatherings.

Sometimes the religious nudity practices of Pagans can create problems for the facility where they are held. Camp Gaia is a 168-acre campground in Leavenworth County, Kansas. It had opened as a camp for nudists during the 1940s. In the 1950s Baptists used the facility. Since 1992, it has been owned and operated by a nonprofit organization called Earth Rising, Inc. Until 2001 Camp Gaia regularly hosted Pagan events, such as The Heartlands Pagan Festival and The Gaea Goddess Gathering, as well as several naturist gatherings. It is in a remote location among forests and farmland with no public road frontage. Initially, Camp Gaia had no problem acquiring a required special use permit from the Leavenworth County Planning Commission. In 2001, however, despite a positive recommendation from the Director of Planning for the County, the commission voted not to renew the special use permit (*The Kansas City Star*, October 25, 2001).

Although noise and traffic congestion were mentioned, it was clear that nudity was the main problem. Without any evidence, some of the commissioners expressed the fear that "the nudity the camp allows could foster pedophilia and other illegal sexual activities." This is clear in the following exchange that took place between the camp's attorney, Robin Martinez and an opponent Dennis Bixby. Bixby asked, "Have you even known of 175 naked people getting together and not having sex?" Martinez replied, "I didn't know sex was illegal in Leavenworth County." Bixby's response was, "Sodomy and pedophilia are" (*The Kansas City Star*, October 25, 2001).

The camp owner threatened to take the case to the federal courts on First Amendment grounds, filing for an injunction to allow the camp to continue operating pending a legal resolution of the dispute. The ACLU sent a letter to the country commissioners (*The Leavenworth Times*, October 26, 2001). Ultimately, the legal pressure worked and the dispute was resolved. Earth Rising was issued a perpetual land use permit if it agreed to the following: (1) Payment of a one-time $2,000 land-use fee; (2) Payment of a yearly $1,000 fee for dust control measures; (3) A "quiet time" (below 80 decibels at the property line from 11 p.m. to 8 a.m. on "school nights" and from midnight to 8 a.m. on weekend and holiday nights); (4) Refusal to host groups larger than 750, except for Memorial Day weekend during which it may admit up to 1,500 for the Heartlands Pagan Festival; and (5) Emergency plans to deal with unexpected events such as fire or violent weather. Again, there was vindication, but again it was expensive. The camp lost one event for that year, costing its owners about $5,000. The impact fee and dust treatment fee would cost them an additional $3,000. And then, as always, there were the legal fees (Camp Gaia Announcement, April 9, 2002).

Another issue that can arise at a Pagan festival stems from the fact that many Pagans are professionals and that all Pagan festivals include persons who have clergy status. In most states it is mandatory for such persons to report any suspicions of child abuse to the proper authorities. The problem stems from the vagueness of the mandatory child abuse reporting laws in some states. While the reporting of suspected child abuse is something that Pagans unequivocally support, they are thinking about signs of abuse, such as oddly shaped or placed burns, things a child might say about their home life, frequent injuries, age-inappropriate sexual behavior, or other similar, relatively clear indicators that the child might be the victim of abusive adult behaviors. There are states, however, where in a clothing-optional situation a photograph might incidentally show a child's genitals or show a child in the mere presence of nude adults who might be flirting with each other or show children being touched—clearly non-sexually—by nude adults, as in a diaper-changing situation. Some festivals have tried to address this problem by establishing no-camera policies. This does not, however, alleviate the dilemma of professionals subject the mandatory reporting laws who do not see the latter types of behaviors as abusive, but who may face accusations of violating the reporting laws by others who do.

A Wiccan does not even have to practice ritual or optional nudity to have it impact his or her life. For Shari Eicher it was sufficient to be Wiccan and to be associated with persons practicing ritual nudity. Mrs. Eicher was an ordained Wiccan minister who did not personally engage in nudity. She was also an eleventh-grade English teacher at a local high school in North Carolina. She was pictured fully clothed on a website that contained pictures of other people practicing ritual nudity. The site carried a warning that "visitors not proceed of they [would be] offended by pictures of people practicing a religion while naked." She had taught at the high school for three years and had made her beliefs known to the administration of the school 14 months previous to this incident. She did not usually discuss Wicca with any adult at the school and never with her students. Nevertheless, when the website was discovered, "school officials escorted her off campus after telling her that she was suspended without pay indefinitely." That conformity was an issue is clear from her statement at the time: "All I ever wanted to do is teach, and I thought I was doing a pretty good job. To have someone tell me because I'm not the same I can't do my job, that hurts on a level I can't even explain" (*Fayetteville Online Local News*, January 11, 2000). A meeting held by a group of area ministers made it clear that their main objection to Shari Eicher was the nudity on the website for which they seemed to hold Shari Eicher responsible, passing a resolution and circulating a petition to be sent to the school board and/or the Superintendent of Schools.[20]

Subsequently, the Board of Education released a statement that she would not return to her job. According to a statement released by her husband, Richard Eicher, one major factor was the concern that her effectiveness in the classroom had been undermined by the publicity given the case. The Board also acknowledged that she had not proselytized to students, peers, or anyone in the community. Both parties pledged not to say anything further about this case. Sheri Eicher retained her teaching credentials and her performance ratings and, thus, was positioned to find another job. This did not, however, end her problems. When the Eichers moved to another location, she received a death threat and flyers were distributed alerting the community that the "Scotland Witch" was now living in their community. She swore out a warrant against the responsible person under NCGS Sec. 14—277.1 Communicating Threats. At trial he was found guilty and sentenced to 30 days (suspended), one year of probation, a fine and court costs. The court also forbade him to have any further contact with the Eichers (E-mail, July 27, 2001).

For the moment, statutes and other policies regarding nudity are something that Pagans will just have to accommodate. Because ritual nudity is not practiced in any of the dominant Christian religions, the importance Christians place on physical modesty and the shame-oriented Christian attitude toward the human body, very little legal attention is paid to nudity as part of a religious practice. The legal provisions regarding nudity are usually intended to forbid it. Thus, under the *Smith* rule, laws forbidding nudity in a variety of places and situations are regarded by both the courts and legal commentators as clearly involving religion-neutral behavior (e.g. Conkle, 2001, 2–3). This fact, plus the current crusade by fundamentalist religious groups to make existing anti-nudity laws more harsh and to pass new ones presages a future when Pagans will either have to significantly modify their religious behavior or be subject to litigation as a result of activities that are based on one of their core beliefs, the sacredness, beauty, and sanctity of all human bodies.

Thus far, the discussion attempts to enforce conformity with Christian beliefs and values has focused on issues relating to socialization and the use of the law to enforce what are seen as morality-related community norms. Christians who object to nonconforming behavior, even for religious reasons, are able to claim the high ground. They can cite traditional practices and widely held notions of appropriate behavior and dress. When dealing with fully clothed adults, however, some Christians resort to fear inducing threats and intimidation—often intended to drive the nonconformist religious people out of their communities. Some even see breaking the law as acceptable, the "moral" ends justifying the means.

CHAPTER 6

THREATS, INTIMIDATION, AND THE STRATEGIC USE OF FEAR

As far back as the 1950s, scholars found a correlation between religious fervor and intolerance of nonconformity (e.g. Stouffer, 1955). Building on such findings, Gordon Allport and J. Michael Ross (1967, 434) made a distinction between extrinsic and intrinsic orientations toward religion. Those who have an extrinsic religious orientation approach religion in an instrumental and utilitarian way and tend to use religion for such ends as security, status, and self-justification while people who approach religion with an intrinsic orientation attempt "to internalize it and follow it fully" in the sense that they *live* their religion. Allport and Ross concluded that "the indiscriminately pro-religious are more preju-diced than the consistently extrinsic, and very much more prejudiced than the consistently intrinsic types." Prejudice, in turn, "provides secu-rity, comfort, status, and social support." Also, they asserted, "prejudice itself is a matter of stereotyped overgeneralization, a failure to distinguish members of a minority group as individuals" (Allport and Ross, 1967, 441–442; Feagin, 1964).

Previously, Allport had called attention to the fact that some, but not all, religions use pathogenic appeals: "In some of its forms, religion instills an abnormal degree of terror . . .; it may arouse pathological feel-ings of guilt; it may inculcate superstition" (1963, 189). He asserted that "these pathogenic strains are not found in the great creeds of the world religions, rather they are extrinsic accretions that lead some worshippers away from the intrinsic possibilities of their faith." He adds that "most of the damage that religion does and most of the criticisms directed against it are related to these accretions." That is, "to make religion easy and palatable . . . they fall far short of the total outlook of the creed in question" (1963, 195).

Although all religions support—to some degree—a stance of brother-hood and compassion, Allport argues that, at the same time, nearly all theological systems "contain three invitations to bigotry . . . [that] have led to prejudice, injustice, outrage and inquisition." The first is the claim that a particular religion exclusively possesses the ultimate truth and is the only authority for charting the destiny of humans. "Held rigidly, this position regards the teaching of other religions . . . as a threat to human salvation." The second is the doctrine of election, the concept that the self and one's coreligionists are the deity's chosen people and that this fact justifies persecution and cruelty. "Since God is for the ins, the outs must be excluded from privileges, and in extreme cases eliminated by sword and fire" (1966, 449–450). The third, a theocratic orientation, supports rule by divine right. That is, a government should be moral and to the extent that a certain religion can control the civil government, the ideas and morals stemming from that religion's ultimate truth and the elect status of its adherents can be translated into a legitimate guide for the behaviors, policies, and legal codes of that polity.

In an attempt to refine Allport's work, Bruce Hunsberger has proposed that "religious fundamentalism, and the related concept of religious quest, offer stronger, richer, and more extensive explanations by focusing on the ways in which beliefs are held and the openness of individuals to changes in those beliefs . . ." (1995, 118). Religious quest is marked by an open, flexible, and questioning approach to religion. Fundamentalism, on the other hand, is based on the idea that there is only one truth about the relationship between humanity and the sacred; whatever opposes it is an evil force that must be vigorously fought. Religious life is seen as a battle between good and evil. Hunsberger links this latter orientation to a right-wing authoritarianism that is characterized by three attitudinal clusters: authoritarian submission, authoritarian aggression, and conventionalism.

Right-wing authoritarianism and religious fundamentalism "feed" one another in that both "encourage obedience to authority, conventionalism, self-righteousness, and feelings of superiority" (Hunsberger, 1995, 121). Thus, religious persons who think that their beliefs are the absolute truth, are constantly alert to evil influence, divide the world into right and wrong, do not question their religious beliefs and are right-wing authoritarians. They tend to be highly prejudiced and prone to an aggressive stance toward what they perceive as evil and a threat to the existing social order (Feldman and Stenner, 1997, 767; Feldman, 2003, 67). Such people "are atypical in the overall scheme of things, but they do exist" and they are not limited to traditionally fundamentalist sects, but can be found in many mainstream Christian denominations, as well as other religions. Hunsgerger concludes that "it would seem that it is not religious fundamentalism per se that causes prejudice, but rather it is the tendency for fundamentalists to be right-wing authoritarians that accounts for the link with prejudice" (1995, 126). And, it is the tendency of right-wing authoritarians to be aggressive in their battle between good and evil that leads to the threats, intimidation, and strategic use of fear that characterizes the approach such people take toward those who do not share their religious beliefs.

When these people are confronted with a world in which there is a rapid diversification in religious beliefs, they react strongly by struggling to maintain their traditional way of life. This may include increased political activity in an attempt to gain the support of governmental and legal policies in order to save their dying, yet cherished, way of life by translating it into official laws and policies[1] (Moen, 1995). They may also take an aggressive personal stance toward people in their communities who represent the incursion of religious pluralism that they so fear. Differentiating "them" from "us" and devaluing "them" is central to harassment, threats, and violence against "them" (Staub, 2003, 3). When these fearful and potentially aggressive people comprise a significant majority, they may be able to accomplish their aims through selective law enforcement, as well as by avoiding the complications of the legislative process and the possibility of judicial involvement.

If it is impossible to get minority religious groups to conform to the morals and norms of a dominant *and* aggressive Christianity, there are many ways to harass them and either drive them away or force them at least to appear to conform. Among these are threatening their livelihood by trying to get them fired, driving them out of business or forcing them to move their business elsewhere. Pressure from neighbors or landlords can make living in a certain place intolerable or impossible, especially when the police are sympathetic with the harassers instead of the harassed. Finally, there can be threats of violence or actual violence. Also, the violence can be turned against the self, as has happened twice with young Witches (one in America and one in England) who were bullied to the point where suicide seemed the only way out. In all of these cases there is a definite pattern of police and other governmental officials looking the other way or even participating in the persecution of religious nonconformists. There are also many instances when such officials make a good faith attempt to do their job in an even handed manner—sometimes at the cost of having their personal lives or careers threatened. Increasingly, Pagans, especially those who are police officers, are becoming more proactive in intervening and helping to educate public officials.

Workplace Harassment and Deprival of Livelihood

According to *The Salt Lake Tribune* (January 20, 2003), "Worker complaints of religious discrimination made to the Equal Employment Opportunity Commission (EEOC) jumped more than 20 percent [in 2002], driven primarily by claims of retaliation against Muslims."[2] The article continued that there was a more gradual trend of complaints that had gone up about 85 percent over the past decade. Although these are a small percentage of the total of discrimination complaints, "they are rising at a much faster rate" and are made, not only by Muslims, but by "people who practice less conventional religions." A spokesman for the EEOC was quoted as saying, "You have employees of hundreds of different religions in the workplace . . . and some employers are not aware of their obligations to make accommodations." In addition, "some conflicts have flared over religious practices that are outside the mainstream."

One of these instances, decided in 2001 by the EEOC, was *Hurston v. Henderson* (2001 WL 56204). Hurston, an employee of the U.S. Postal Service and a Wiccan, filed a complaint that "the agency restricted him from wearing his religious shirts, jewelry and in the display of a small cauldron. [He argued] that members of other religions [were] not restricted in the display of their [Christian and Jewish] messages and symbols and that they are not warned about offending others [as Hurston was]." The Administrative Judge who heard the case held that Hurston had, indeed, experienced religious discrimination, but this holding was overturned during the administrative appeals process within the EEOC. The Commission itself subsequently heard Hurston's appeal and reinstated the decision of the Administrative Judge, concluding "the agency permitted [Hurston's] co-workers to subject him to a barrage of humiliating comments and that management unreasonably restricted [his] personal religious expression." They also found "that the treatment created an humiliating, intimidating, hostile, and offensive work environment." As a result of these findings, the EEOC declared Hurston entitled to damages and sent the case back to the Administrative Judge to determine the proper amount.

Mr. Hurston was not alone in being harassed on the job because of his Pagan religion. Threats of firing, harassment, and actual job loss are one of the most common complaints voiced to Pagan religious rights organizations. It is a classic expression of the religious perception that life is a battle between good (us) and evil (them) and that evil needs to be eliminated—at least from one's immediate environment (Hunsberger,

1995). Those with power over employment in the United States today are most commonly Christian and those so inclined can use this power to carry out their core religious conviction that evil must be eliminated.

While Hurston's religious behavior was on-the-job religious expression, some Pagans have experienced threats of firing or harassment for off-the-job religious activities. In one Midwestern state a clinic's X-ray technician was threatened with being fired because she was hosting outdoor rituals on the large parcel of land where her home was located (E-mail, July 25, 1996). Sometimes, the harassment leads the Pagan to leave the job, even though she or he was not technically fired. One such case happened on the west coast and involved a salesperson in a chain retail establishment. He did not flaunt his Paganism, but did wear a small pentacle ring. Over a period of years, two successive managers subjected him to numerous derogatory comments (frequently involving charges of Satanism), discriminatory treatment and forceful attempts to convert him to Christianity. Finally, unable to put up with what he characterized as "daily assaults," he quit his job (E-mail, October 9, 1996).

In these cases, the employee was able to take a proactive role. Hurston could access an appeals process governed by due process, the clinical worker stopped hosting rituals on her land and the retail worker was able to quit. Much more common is a situation in which the Pagan is simply fired—with no explanation or one that is secular, but patently an excuse for an action based on religious grounds. In some cases, however, the firing is explicitly tied to superstitious ideas about the powers of stereotyped Witches. Such cases illustrate the fear evoked in authoritarian, fundamentalist Christians concerning the threat of the "other."

For example, in one case, the company simply refused to acknowledge that Witchcraft was a religion. Shirley Tingley worked for an animal-restraints manufacturing company in Florida. When she was fired, "the lawyer representing the company [said that her] firing had nothing to do with her religious beliefs, and everything to do with her threatening a co-worker—by casting a spell against the woman." Tingley said she was told that a management informant had said that "I was going to put a spell on a little old lady, because she had a job I wanted within the plant . . . I was not given a chance to defend myself or even know who said what about me. . . . I would never do such a thing, never say such a thing." This firing, the company's lawyer protested, had nothing to do with religion, since being a Witch was not a religion (starbanner. com/articles/breaking_news/959.shtml).

In many other cases, the firing is simply an expression of the management's or owner's attitude toward Paganism that may be based on their own fundamentalism or on fears they may have regarding the threat they see the Pagan posing toward their customer or client base. Frequently, only the sequence of events indicates the cause: a person is discovered to be a Pagan and subsequently fired with no other intervening cause for the firing. For example, a woman who had been a successful and valued employee of a blood bank was suddenly let go after she drove to work with new license tags on her van. Her husband had acquired tags that said PAGAN 22. She was asked if that was her van and shortly afterward was terminated (E-mail, June 13, 2001). Another person, employed by a local Domestic Violence/Sexual Assault shelter for nearly nine years was fired when it became known that she was participating in Pagan rituals outside of the organization and on her own time (E-mail, April 20, 2001).

Another Pagan working at a credit union is probably the best example of obvious sequencing. On Monday at 3 pm, he told a manager that he was a Pagan; on Tuesday morning he was fired. The reason given was not production related, but that the manager did not feel he would work out in the long run (E-mail, January 13, 2000). Perhaps most perplexing (and unjust) is the case of Lauren Berrios, an elementary school teacher, who was fired following rumors that she was a witch that seemed to have originated when she taught her fifth grade class about the Salem witch trials. Ms. Berrios is Jewish. The school maintained that the reason was job performance in spite of the fact that she had previously gotten "glowing" evaluations for each of the previous two years she had taught at the school (*Newsday*, June 20, 2001).

Usually, when the firing is accompanied by an express mention of religious reasons, there is some recourse to the courts. If the employer, however, is a religious organization it may be allowed to hire and fire according to the religious affiliation of the prospective or current employee (Brant, 1994; Hodson, 1994). This may have been what made the Salvation Army willing to be candid about why it decided to fire a Pagan who worked in its Domestic Violence Shelter as a Victims' Assistance Coordinator. The basis given for her firing was twofold: (1) that she made personal use of a copy machine and (2) that she was Wiccan and was reproducing related manuals and rituals, contrary to the Salvation Army's religious mission. In his 1989 decision (*Dodge v. The Salvation Army*, 1989 U.S. Dist. LEXIS 4797, 5) the judge found it "extremely improbable to assume . . . that [Dodge] would have been terminated solely because of the use of the machine for personal matters." His conclusion was that "it is obvious that [Dodge] was fired because of what she was copying and what she believed, not for the mere act of copying."

Although he noted that the Salvation Army was allowed to terminate some of its employees on religious grounds, Ms. Dodge held a position that was substantially supported by government funds and thus the religious exemption did not apply. Because of the government funding, the firing on religious grounds represented "excessive government entanglements exist with the religious purpose of the Salvation Army" in the supervision of a government grant, thus rendering the discrimination on the basis of religion a violation of the U.S. Constitution's Establishment Clause (1989 U.S. Dist. LEXIS 4797, 13). Although this decision seems to be a victory for Pagans, it is a mixed one, because the judge repeatedly equated Wicca with Satanism in his decision.

In another court case, however, the employee was fired because she raised an Establishment Clause issue. In Republic, Missouri in 1991, the Board of Alderpersons voted to use a logo on the city flag and seal that contained the Ichthus, a traditional Christian fish symbol. At the time, Jean Webb was employed by the local newspaper and wrote an editorial criticizing the inclusion of the fish symbol. Not only did she lose her job, but in the words of the 1999 court decision (*Webb v. Republic*, 55 F. Supp. 2d 994, 996): "After authoring the editorial in the city newspaper opposing the city seal, Webb received hate mail and harassing phone calls from citizens of Republic. . . . Webb's children were ostracized as a result of her criticism of the city seal. . . . Eventually, Webb even moved from the community rather than endure the harassment." Together with the ACLU, she sued the city and was granted a motion for summary judgment: "The Court finds that no genuine issue of material fact remains in dispute on whether the fish symbol . . . is a religious symbol. No reasonable person could conclude otherwise and it would be disingenuous of the Court to create a controversy where none exists" (5 F. Supp. 2d 994, 999). The town was enjoined from displaying the symbol because it violated the First Amendment of the U.S. Constitution.

Harassment is not always a precursor to firing and employees are not always positioned to take their case to legal authorities. For example, one employee of a Catholic Nursing home did not see any alternative but to take the abuse, because she needed the job and was afraid of endangering it—realistically so, because of the religious exemption that such an organization could claim (E-mail, September 17, 1998). Another Wiccan working as a corrections officer for a state penal system was subjected to such persistent persecution that the stress led to sickness. As a member of a government employees' union, she thought she could turn to them for help. When she contacted one of their lawyers, however, the attorney dismissed her as a "kook," making fun of her and demanding documentation that Wicca was a legitimate, recognized religion and that she was, in fact, a Wiccan. Finally, the lawyer rejected her case saying that the complaint of years of harassment and persecution were too general to be pursued (November 11, 1998).

Finally, it should be mentioned that many cases of religiously motivated harassment and firing stem from the employee wearing a pentacle. As was discussed earlier, in such a context the wearing of the pentacle has the same meaning for the Pagan as the wearing of a cross does for a Christian. It is not required for their faith, but is simply an affirmation of that faith and the seriousness with which the wearer is following their religious path. Being asked to remove it or to put it underneath clothing so that it will not be seen does impinge, not only on free exercise rights, but also on freedom of expression. For others, however, it can be much more serious. Muslim women are sometimes asked to remove their headscarves as a requirement for employment. Like many Pagan cases, if the woman is able to pursue the case into the legal system, she is likely to win (e.g. *The Washington Post*, April 19, 1996). There is no way, however, if knowing how often the woman just walks away defeated in her quest for gainful employment.

Vulnerable Businesses

Like any other religious community, Pagans have certain religious books and other items that are connected with their worship and that need to be purchased somewhere. In order to meet this need, small Pagan businesses have sprung up in various locations throughout the United States. In order to have a viable customer base, many of these stores also carry merchandise that is used by persons of other minority religions, as well as persons who might loosely be referred to as "New Age." Like the people just discussed and like small business owners anywhere, these entrepreneurs depend upon their businesses for a livelihood. Thus, when they are harassed or evicted, they and their families are deprived of a means of obtaining the necessities of life, such as food and shelter. The same happens when potential shoppers are discouraged from patronizing a business by threats and demonstrations.

In order to start a small business, most entrepreneurs have to find a space to house their business. For Pagans, this means finding a landlord who is willing to rent space to a business that might be or become controversial. Often, Pagan small businesspersons are initially able to find space for their stores. When the final arrangements are being made or after the store has opened, however, the landlord may realize the potential for problems and terminate the rental agreement. Often this takes place after the Pagan has made a significant investment in inventory and advertising. One Pagan businessman, after being rejected by several potential landlords, found a suitable location and an amiable landlord. The ministers of several nearby churches, however, became aware of the nature of the new store and began to harass the landlord. They also organized a boycott of the landlord's funeral business, one that is very dependent on referrals. The landlord then told the Pagan that he would have to close the store. Although the landlord was willing to give him time to find a new place, not collect any more rent and return the Pagan's deposit, he was also breaking a lease. In addition, during this "grace period," he asked that everything be taken out of the display window, thus creating the appearance that the store was unoccupied (E-mail, August 26, 1997).

In a similar case with a better outcome, four or five persons targeted a Wiccan business yelling "Satanism, Satanism." Subsequently, there were threatening phone calls and literature, leading to an investigation by federal authorities. Then, the landlord refused to renew the lease and the store was forced to move to another town. In the new town, however, there was a completely different climate. The Chamber of Commerce welcomed the store and helped the owners advertise. One of the owners stated, "They realized we would harm no one. That we are trying to bring different cultural aspects to the community" (KXAN 36 News [Austin, TX], February 23, 2004).

Of course, the landlords themselves can behave in a prejudiced way when they discover that their new tenant is of a minority religion and that the business is oriented toward the followers of that religion. In one case, the landlord claimed that the businessperson had lied by not stating that she was Wiccan and then made derogatory comments about witches (as well as Indians, teenagers, and homosexuals). He stated that he did not want such people, rituals, or sacrifices on his property (E-mail, April 10, 1997). Of course, the types of people he mentioned patronize most businesses without incident and the owner of the business was there to sell merchandise, not hold rituals or make sacrifices. Even computer-based businesses are not immune, if persons in the area become aware that such a business is operating out of their locality. An experienced computer-based businessperson moved into a new area. When her neighbors discovered the local origin of the Pagan-oriented computer-based business, she was threatened and harassed to the point where, after living there for only two months, she was afraid to leave her house (E-mail, July 22, 1997).

When a business finds a space and becomes established, it does not mean that problems will not arise. In the case of one popular café owned by a Pagan and used as a gathering place for Pagans, the landlord came in and asked if it was a gathering place for "devil worshippers" (E-mail, May 1, 1998). Subsequently, the businessperson received an official eviction threat, listing as violations several types of behavior that were commonly practiced by other businesses in the plaza in which the café was located. Farther along in the document there was a blanket accusation that the café "may be engaging in certain occult or paganistic practices at the premises." The attached "proof" was a flyer advertising a celebration for a major Pagan holiday that was open to the public and a membership application for a Council of the Magical Arts. The latter was not based in the café and was a regional nonprofit organization that serves as an umbrella group for Pagans from various traditions (Letter from landlord's lawyer, April 30, 1998).

Another Pagan businessperson who also had a shop within a larger cluster of small businesses was told that he would have to change his line of merchandise if he intended to remain. The charge was that his merchandise, unlike that of the other tenants, was not "family oriented." He dealt mostly in Wiccan religious material, along with religious material from other world religions, including Hinduism, Native American Spirituality, Buddhism, and Christianity. There were also books about Jungian psychology and history. Among the more "family oriented" businesses that presumably were considered acceptable were dealers selling semiautomatic assault rifles, weapon-type knives and swords, as well as dealers in exclusively Christian religious materials (E-mail, November 2, 1992).

The minority religion businessperson's problems do not always stem from a landlord. The direct harassment of customers and the business owner are also issues. For example, the owner of a store in a mall was subjected to systematic harassment by a group of fundamentalist Christians who would come into the store in groups accosting customers and telling them they were going to burn in hell or that God was going to destroy them because they were Satan worshippers. Not surprisingly, this caused a significant loss of business, an obvious goal of the harassers. They also told the owner that they intended not only to run her out of business, but also to run her out of town. Appeals to mall security and the local police brought no assistance (E-mail, August 28, 1997).

In a California town, the members of a fundamentalist Christian church made death threats against a store proprietor and her customers.

Members of the church were running for local office on a platform of eliminating any non-Christian influences from the town, including books stores carrying romance novels (E-mail, December 12, 1997). Elsewhere, the proprietor of a small metaphysical shop who was similarly being threatened and harassed by a church group managed to get a restraining order. Not able to continue the harassment, the group turned its attention to the owner of the complex in which the store was located and persuaded him to evict her (E-mail, March 6, 2001). An extreme case occurred in the northwest. A church that was located near an established (five and a half years) Pagan business bought the building in which the business was located and then proceeded to get rid of the business (E-mail, December 24, 2001).

Such harassment does not invariably come from church-based movements. One storeowner was targeted by a city administration that wanted to get rid of "hippie businesses" and "pagan type stores." In this case, the store was mainly a health food store with some New Age items in addition to a deli that attracted a Pagan clientele and hosted small Pagan meetings. The city responded by issuing citation after citation over a period of years, particularly targeting some outdoor organic garden beds on the store's property (*Detroit Free Press*, May 21, 2001). At a court hearing, the city representatives could not cite any specific ordinances that had been violated by the health food store. The judge urged both parties to work out their problems (*Detroit Free Press*, May 22, 2001). Another metaphysical store was targeted by a city council that wrote a zoning ordinance restricting such businesses to industrial areas well away from the shopping public (E-mail, January 10, 2003).

Threats of violence are not unheard of. During 1999, large numbers of Pagan bookstores in Massachusetts were sent anonymous, veiled threats using Biblical references: "Beware for our God . . . is just and will throw your gods into the Pit. . . . Every knee will bend, every tongue confess His name, Jesus Christ, the one true God. . . . This may be your last chance for redemption. You not only practice evil, but encourage others to do so. . . ." The sender was obviously a disturbed person and that alone encouraged the businesspersons involved to take the threat seriously (E-mail, January 14, 1999). In Louisiana, a small shop owner selling books, cauldrons, herbs, and candles was told that her store would be burned down unless she removed her inventory within a few days. She also received death threats. Out of concern for the welfare of her minor son, she made plans to move her shop (*The Advocate ONLINE*, March 8, 2001).

In Brookland, Arkansas, a small (about 35 persons) but vocal group of hostile residents not only targeted a store selling books on Witchcraft, herbs, candles, jewelry, and other Wiccan items, it also targeted the mayor of the town. The group circulated two petitions. One called on the mayor and city council to force the occult store out of town. The other called on the mayor to resign or be impeached because of his failure to prevent the opening of the store. More than 50 people gathered to protest its grand opening, singing Christian hymns and praying. The mayor indicated that he did not know if the protest was personal or political. In any case, the owner of the premises gave the store proprietor a 90-day eviction notice the day after he opened saying that his family was being threatened (*Arkansas Democrat-Gazette*, May 11, 1999).

A widely publicized incident involving a Pagan business took place in Lancaster, California in 2002. Prior to this incident, the storeowner had been subjected to a series of city licensing and zoning demands that had ultimately been resolved but that had also indicated a less than friendly city administration. About a year later, she decided to change the name of the store. In this connection, she held a rededication ceremony in a parking lot behind the store that was the property of the building owner and, therefore, private property. When the service started, several carloads of people parked their vehicles around the worshippers watching quietly. At that point, they were welcome.

Subsequently, however, a family group in a large SUV turned on a Christian Rock station as loudly as possible making it difficult for the Wiccans to continue their religious service. The people leading the service politely asked the family to turn the music down, but the response was that this was a public parking lot and they could do what they wanted. Several men from the group began to walk counterclockwise around the Wiccan circle, praying loudly and reading from their Bibles. Another adult man harassed the 14-year-old son of the proprietor. One of the participants was a politically active clergyman, a volunteer chaplain with the Los Angeles County Sheriff's department and founder and executive director of United Community Action Network. He said, "We weren't there to do anything other than offer alternatives (to Wicca)" (*Antelope Valley Press*, April 5, 2002).

Finally, the Wiccans called the Lancaster Sheriff's Station that was three blocks from the location of the event. According to one report, the sheriff's deputies failed to respond (*Antelope Valley Press*, March 22, 2002). According to another, they did not respond for four and a half hours (CNN.com, April 30, 2002). Although there is a California state law on hate crimes that forbids the disturbance of "any assemblage of people met for religious worship . . . by any unnecessary noise, either within the place where the meeting is held, or so near it as to disturb the order and solemnity of the meeting," it specifies that the service must be "at a tax-exempt place of worship" (*California Penal Code*, Sec. 302). The Los Angeles District Attorney said that since the group was not tax-exempt and in a building, the legal requirements were not met and they would not prosecute. The disruptive Christians were just exercising their First Amendment freedom of speech (CNN.com. April 30, 2002).

The Los Angeles County Sheriffs Department has an official policy posted on the Internet that assures citizens "the department is dedicated to . . . the immediate investigation of reported hate crimes and hate-related incidents," including "harassment, intimidation or other crimes designed to infringe on" religious rights (http://www.lasd.org/public-info/hate-crime.htm). Again, you apparently have to have a church building of some sort to be taken seriously as a religion. One Pagan religious rights activist wondered how the incident would have been handled if the same thing happened at an outdoor Easter sunrise service. Interestingly enough, the one group that did try to support the Pagans was the Antelope Valley Interfaith Council that, in turn, was influential in creating widespread support for the Wiccans in the region.

A somewhat similar incident happened later that year in Florida when a group of Pagan drummers gathered inside a public park gazebo to practice drumming in anticipation of participating in the annual Christmas parade. The drumming circle had been advertised in a local paper's religion section. The ads alerted the members of two local fundamentalist churches. Led by their clergy they decided to imitate the "Walls of Jericho" story in the Bible. A reporter describes it as follows: "One hundred people walking in circles chanting, counting and tooting on horns. An average onlooker probably wouldn't even have noticed a smaller band of people with drums huddled inside the park gazebo, surrounded by the larger group" (*The Independent Florida Sun*, January 3, 2003).

One of those present called it "spiritual warfare." A participating drummer had the following reaction: "they were trying to circle around us like a pack of wolves." An uninvolved onlooker said, "It was wrong, just wrong, for the larger group to do what it was doing. . . . You could see by their actions they were there to disrupt and disband the smaller group. It didn't feel right to me." One of the participating ministers, however, passed it off as a harmless game. The police who were present agreed with the minister and made no effort to help the drummers. Afterward, however, at the request of the drumming group, a police officer was assigned to follow the Pagan float in the Christmas parade in order to protect the safety of the participants—a tacit admission that there was a problem (*The Independent Florida Sun*, January 3, 2003).

A Place to Live

Aside from a means of earning a living, one of the most basic human needs is for shelter. In places where housing for all income levels is abundant, Pagans can move away from a bad situation. Usually this type of mobility is found in urban areas where there is already a certain amount of anonymity protecting people from those who might take offense at their religious choice. But, if their religious affiliation becomes known for some reason, they are subject to problems from two sources, their landlord and their neighbors.

Usually one's right to have privacy in one's domicile is one dearly held by Americans. For renters, however, the privacy is not so complete, because there are a number of reasons why outsiders might legitimately gain entry to a rented living space. For example, one Pagan had a neighbor whose water pipes burst causing damage in his apartment. The person sent to clean his carpets noticed his altar and other Wiccan-related objects in his apartment. Subsequently, he was notified that he had to pay his rent in five days. When he made the payment, the manager refused to give him a receipt, after which he got a summons to appear in court for nonpayment of rent. The court order was dated one and a half hours after the rent had been paid. When he tried to contact the management, they refused to talk to him (E-mail, February 14, 1997). This meant that he would have to try to get documentation that he had paid the money and might even have to ask the court to order an examination of the landlord's books. It is another of those instances in which there is no problem until a Pagan's religion becomes known and then there ensues some form of harassment with no obvious connection to religious discrimination except for the sequencing of the events.

The landlord does not have to find out what is in your home to identify your religion. A member of the U.S. military and his family was stationed in Louisiana and living in a mobile home park that they particularly enjoyed because of the abundance of trees and wildlife, as well as the safety and quiet. This soldier was completely "out" at his job on the base and his wife had been wearing a pentacle when they signed the agreement for the lot rental. They did, however, invite a small number of Pagans over to celebrate a full moon. Subsequently, the landlord phoned them and asked about the candles, the robes, and what they were doing. They responded that it was a church function and where told that they were not allowed to hold "Church" at their house any longer. Then they got a five-day eviction notice that said they "didn't fit in with the community" (Pagan Unity Campaign, May 3, 2002). Such eviction notices are legal in Louisiana "for good cause." They appealed to the Equal Housing Authority. Their contact talked to the landlord. He accepted the landlord's reasoning that they must have held other circles before (they did not) and, thus, had no case. The Military Equal Opportunity staff was willing to try to mediate the disagreement, but the landlord refused to cooperate. The family was finally forced to move (Press Release and E-mail, May 19, 2002).

Even owning a home can be no guarantee. A Pagan couple had a mortgage that was 85 percent paid off when some of their neighbors decided that they did not want practicing Wiccans in their neighborhood. They poisoned one of the family dogs and harassed the 11-year-old son on his way to the school bus. Finally, the Wiccans took the responsible neighbors to court in an attempt to enjoin them. The judge questioned them closely on their Wiccan faith and whether it meant that they where Witches. They were given a week to stop practicing their faith in their home or to move (E-mail, September 12, 1998).

In a somewhat different case, the owner of a 46-acre farm was holding religious services under the name of Greendome Temple. They were hauled into the local municipal court on disorderly conduct charges related to drumming during the ceremonies. A First Amendment defense was disallowed and the judge seemed more interested in the neighbors' complaints that Satanic rites were being held than in the testimony of two police officers who said that the noise was not excessive. Sound level measurements taken by the landowners were also ignored, because the judge thought that drumming was excessive noise regardless of the level. The judge finally found them not guilty, but warned them that further charges would be brought if there were more complaints (E-mail, November 22, 1996). Evidently, the owner was able to overcome his problems, since currently Greendome Temple is a thriving spiritual center.

Even a long history in the same spot is no guaranty against harassment. In 1976, a pagan-oriented church was founded in a large midwestern city and chartered by the Secretary of State for the state in which it is located. It has been in the same location since 1982. During the late 1990s, the church began to be harassed about property violations by city officials. It soon became evident that the sources of the complaints were some of the neighbors of the church property. The city's actions ranged from specifying the exact height of mowed grass to repeatedly condemning the church building in spite of improvements designed to take care of any possible code violations. The neighbors killed pets, tore down surveillance equipment, and threatened the clergy and their families with weapons. As of 2002, they were unable even to find a lawyer to take their case (WARDlist, November 18, 2002).

Violence

While the previous materials have contained treats of violence or actual instances of violent behavior, the importance of violence is so great that it deserves a focused consideration. At a time when violence in and associated with the public schools has gotten widespread media attention (and, consequently, school administration attention) little attention has been paid to violence toward minority religious children. In fact, not only have the adults in the school system tolerated such violence, but often their policies have encouraged it. Thus, despite other characteristics that may or may not make Pagans targets for violent behavior by their fellow students, their religious identity may make them targets from a very young age. In many instances, intolerance toward Paganism has led directly to violence or threats of violence against Pagan students and, in one instance, the suicide of a 12-year-old Pagan student who was being harassed.

In at least one case, the Bible was the weapon used in the physical attack. This case also involved a teacher who was preaching in class that anything non-Christian is wrong, as well as a school administration unwilling to act when the mother of the Pagan child reported the teacher's behavior (E-mail, March 9, 1997). Incidents in other schools have involved slamming into the Pagan student, as well as yelling and screaming and threatening "to jump the student" outside the school (E-mail, November 19, 1996). In the latter case, the Senior Druid of the local grove and a respected professional intervened with the school administration to try to alleviate the problem.

One right that many Christians demand and are given is the right to hold prayer meetings in public schools. This right is often not respected when Pagans are involved. In one case, a male student who led morning Wiccan devotions was accused by the school administration of Satanism and ordered to stop his religious activities. His group had Bibles thrown at them, a dead possum hung outside their meeting room, members pulled out of class and searched for weapons and, most seriously, death threats. The mother of the student leading the group met with school authorities and tried to educate them, as well as give them reading material on Paganism. They refused, however, to protect the children, stating, "the people of———County are not going to accept this religion." In addition, some of the Pagan student's teachers call him "that satanic person" or "the devil worshipper" (E-mail, March 13, 2001).

In another case, a Pagan student was isolated in a school district that was dominated by fundamentalist Christians. On several occasions, the entire school attended tent revivals or other fundamentalist Christian services during school hours. Her parents who were also Pagans repeatedly refused to sign the permission slips that would allow her to attend. She was called derogatory names, such as "Satan worshipper." She was also accused of eating babies and being a lesbian, because she was not a Christian. She was forced to attend regular Bible study classes during the school day; derogatory names were written on her locker in permanent ink and the school would not paint over them or move her locker. She was repeatedly attacked when she was accessing her bottom row locker by having her head bashed at least ten times, cutting her lip, her forehead, and bloodying her nose. When she wrote a paper about religious freedom, a teacher told her to "keep quiet because you'll get in trouble." A school bus driver regularly questioned her about her religious practices in front of the other students. Through all of this, she remained in the school and participated in extracurricular activities. She was finally pulled out of school when one of her friends told her parents that she was considering suicide (*KnoxNews*, February 14, 2003). As of this writing, she is being home-schooled and her parents have filed a federal lawsuit charging the school system with failing to protect her against violence (*KnoxNews*, April 14, 2003). She is not the only Pagan student who has considered suicide.

Constant harassment and bullying have recently gotten considerable attention in the media as a source of student violence. On the other hand, relatively little attention has been paid to the relationship between bullying and suicides (a form of self-directed violence). One Pagan student who was teased and bullied until she committed suicide is considered a religious martyr among many Pagans. Tempest Smith, was a 12-year-old student in Lincoln Park Middle School.[3] According to *The Detroit News* (March 7. 2001), Tempest was bullied constantly since elementary school because she wore dark clothing and was seen reading books about Wicca. Much of the bullying took the form of chanting Christian hymns at her. According to her mother, Tempest said "she told her teachers about it all the time." The mother also talked to school officials about the problem, asking for their help. The teachers and counselors, however, seemingly made no attempt to intervene (*The Detroit News*, July 4, 2001). At her funeral, many of her classmates acknowledged that they had teased her ruthlessly and expressed regret. The school district, however, did not adopt measures to discourage teasing and bullying. Finally, the mother filed a lawsuit, charging the school district with religious discrimination saying: "There should be rules in place so that children in the future won't have to experience what my daughter went through" (*The Detroit News*, July 4, 2001).[4] In the meantime, Tempest's mother has organized The Tempest Smith Foundation (TEMPEST = Train, Educate and Motivate Parents, Educators and Students in Tolerance).

Children are not the only Pagans to experience bullying. One tenant was subjected to constant bullying by a fellow tenant over a long period of time. This involved such things as a physical attack on the streets and damage to her apartment and her attached business. The landlord told her to handle it all on her own, including the damage to his rental property. A no-contact order filed at the local police station brought no relief. Also, two friends of the woman were physically attacked. Although the attack was violent enough to draw blood, the local police did not take it seriously. The attacked parties had to push very hard to be permitted to file charges and have it prosecuted (E-mail, October 16, 1997).

College students also seem fair game. One male student ran the Student Pagan Association's booth at a college event. Later that night he was recognized as having done so and was beaten severely by four men. They tied him to a tree and hit him with the intent of getting him to say he was a Satanist. He never did and finally something made them nervous and they left (E-mail, April 8, 2003). Another "out" Pagan was ambushed near his home in broad daylight. He was choked and punched by three men who yelled things such as, "Die Witch Die." The local police were unresponsive. In that case, the person was lucky enough to have a witness who, after some pressure, admitted to seeing the incident (E-mail, November 11, 1996). Another example is of a man who was accosted by a group of hooded people outside his home, dragged into a garage, and beaten. They called him a Satanist and said that they were going to do all they could to drive him out of the neighborhood. He required hospital treatment (E-mail, May 14, 1998).

When the Pagans in one southern city became involved in organizing a Pagan Pride event, one lost his job and the others were threatened with job loss and even shooting (E-mail, September 20, 2002). Another case involved an actual shooting—thankfully of property not persons. The back window of a car had several Pagan window stickers. It was in a lot of about 20 cars and was the only one damaged. In order to have done this, the gunman had to climb a barbed wire fence and gone at least two yards into the property to make the shot. The person would also have to have known the car was there, since it could not be seen from outside the property (*Carpe Diem News Alert*, September 1999).

Death threats are relatively common, but one Pagan Priestess in North Carolina was able to bring her case to court and obtain a guilty plea from the defendant. In this case the judge took it very seriously saying, "One of the foundation tenants of our County is that people are free to do what they believe, so long as they do not hurt others or infringe upon the rights of others" (*Eicher v. Andrews*, Robeson County NC District Court, November 12, 2000).

Police: Friend or Foe?

When expressions of religious prejudice involve threats, harassment, and violence, it is natural to ask questions about law enforcement. One thing that leaps out from a large number of the experiences that Pagans have had is the fact that the police and other public officials are often not on their side. In fact, one is tempted to conclude that a Pagan should be grateful if the police and other "public servants" are not part of the problem. This raises questions about the cultural and political aspects of the problem. Quite frequently, the policemen and other local officials know the violators or, at least, share the local religious culture out of which the threats, harassment, and violence emerge. Even in situations where the police and prosecutors are inclined to bring the force of the law against those who have committed crimes against Pagans, there is the possibility that this type of activity will make the police or other local officials targets of the hate groups (Cookson, 1997, 744).

Also, the United States is a democratic country. This usually has the salutary effect of making public officials responsive to the wishes of the electorate. Unfortunately, there are also instances when the sympathies of a significant segment of the electorate are not with the person targeted for abuse based on prejudice. This is particularly likely to be the case where emotionally volatile issues, such as religion, are at issue. Under current law as expressed in *Employment Division v. Smith*, followers of numerically small, nontraditional religious traditions are particularly vulnerable unless they can command sufficient numbers of followers and sympathizers to permit them to attain some political influence. This is one of a complex of reasons that religious groups with long histories of persecution tend to cluster together geographically and to pay a great deal of attention to political activism. Also, persons with nonreligious gripes against members of a minority religion are particularly well situated to abuse them, using the "unacceptable" or "weird" religion as an excuse.

A retired couple had lived for a year in a northwestern city when the Wiccan wife gave an interview to a local newspaper. It was the sort of feature on Witches that the media like to run around Halloween. After that, the couple was no longer welcome in the neighborhood. There was name calling (e.g. "Witch Bitch" and "Devil Woman"), rock throwing, tire flattening, window breaking, dog poisoning, and a pushing match that left the 70-year-old husband with an injured vertebra. Subsequently, the husband was injured by a snow blower and there was a small story in the newspaper that included his address. His estranged daughter[5] thus located them. She engaged in a campaign, aided by the neighbors, to drive his Wiccan wife from his home. Her activities included stalking and threats of physical violence toward the couple (particularly the wife), accompanied by communications that said things such as "Burn witch and die." In this case, the minister of the Baptist Church tried, but was not able, to resolve the conflict. Instead, the threats escalated to blatant death threats from the daughter against the couple. The daughter also was able to gain entry into the house and steal a large sum of money.

During this period, the police were notified and wrote reports. They, however, were hostile toward the couple and did not attempt to investigate any of the incidents. On two occasions when the couple attempted to report problems, they were asked to leave the police station. In addition, they were told by police officers that they would get no help from the police and that they should "move out of" the city. Several officers removed their badges so that they could not be identified and told the couple that they knew what the wife was and that she was not welcome in the city. When asked to identify themselves, the police officers refused (E-mail, October 26, 1996).

This is an exceptionally complex case, mixing family and religious problems. Most cases are more straightforward. For instance, a Pagan student from my university was subjected to five incidents of anti-Pagan vandalism and the police refused to act on the assumption that the victim (a college student) was doing "something" to provoke the vandalism (E-mail, November 7, 2001). Another Witch was subjected to a cross-burning in her yard. "Satan's Lesbian" was written on it. The policeman who arrived said that the police had been told that ritual abuse was going on at that location. When invited to check for evidence of such abuse, he left (without investigating the abuse charge or the cross-burning) telling the woman he did not want to be called back and saying that Wicca was not a religion in that state (E-mail, June 7, 2000). Crosses were also left on the yard of a Michigan Pagan family with "a racial slur and reference to witches" (*The Salina Journal*, August 12, 2000). For Witches, given the witch burnings of the middle ages, a burning cross is just as threatening as it would be for an African American family. The seriousness of the act was acknowledged by the Supreme Court in 2003 when in *Virginia v. Black* (123 S. Ct. 1536) it upheld a Virginia law making it a felony to burn a cross with intent to intimidate.[6]

Refusal to carry out law enforcement activities is not limited to cases where actual Pagans are involved. In a small town in Pennsylvania, the volunteer fire police voted unanimously to refuse to direct traffic at a YMCA triathlon (a service they had performed for years), because the club had been reading Harry Potter books to the children in an after-school program. When a local Pagan leader queried this incident on the basis that the police were bound to offer protection regardless of religion, an official of the Pennsylvania Office of Attorney General pointed out that the police officers were really volunteer firefighters who could choose which events to protect uncontrolled by the state government because of their volunteer status. He expressed his regret that the news reports had failed to distinguish between volunteer fire police and traditional municipal police departments. Fortunately, when the story was reported in both the local and national press, local volunteers stepped forward to help the YMCA and the event was held (*New Era*, January 25, 2002).

In a more serious case, Margie Allen, the proprietor of a shop called Magic Garden, was harassed and forced to move the location of her business twice. She, her family, and customers were regularly followed home from the store. As a 2003 press release from the Betwixt & Between Community Center in Dallas, Texas put it: "Near miss car accidents, strange cars sitting in the driveways of their homes, rumors told to her that her shop might be burnt down, an interruption of her daily business dealings with strangers screaming about her 'crimes of Satanism' have become a part of everyday life for Margie Allen and her family." Repeated appeals to local officials elicited only refusals to help and at least one police officer threatened her saying that "practicing Witchcraft" would get her run out of the town. This harassment and potential for violence was a result of the repeated assertions of a local clergyperson that she held Satanic masses in her shop.

There are instances where the police may not only refuse to provide law enforcement services to Pagans, but also actively move against Pagans. For example, a group of Pagans were arrested while holding their twenty-fourth annual Yule (winter solstice) ceremony at a beach on Staten Island (*New York Times*, December 23, 1998). No reasons for the arrest were given at the time. Evidentially the traditional religious gathering, although it had a long history of uninterrupted worship, had fallen victim to the current New York Mayor's crackdown on gatherings over 20 or 25. Eventually, a judge dismissed the charges against the Pagans, saying "There are some occasions and situations where it is appropriate for the government to step back and allow special things to happen" (*The Washington Post*, January 28, 1999).

Similarly, in 2002, park police in Tennessee interrupted a Pagan marriage ceremony, despite the fact that the groom had obtained a permit and that the Pagans had used the park without incident for both large and small rituals for more than ten years. Only eight people were present and the ceremony was just ending when, in the words of one participant: "We were stormed by 6 park rangers. They roared into the area with searchlights on, jumped out of their cars with guns raised, cocked and loaded. They screamed at us to freeze, and raise our hands. We were quickly surrounded by men with guns trained on us." The permit was produced immediately, but that did not seem to make a difference. For a period of 30 minutes, the wedding participants were questioned and verbally abused, while being required to keep their hands constantly in the air. All of their belongings were searched. The police were very interested in the Pagan business of one of the participants and asked several questions about religion, including whether the participants were Wiccan. The wedding participants were told that they were unorthodox and that this was a problem. The harassment continued for an hour, before the wedding participants were allowed to leave. No formal charges were filed. Subsequently, a participant verified with the police supervisor that the permit was adequate to legalize the event (E-mail, October 9, 2002).

The park police showed particular interest in a ritual knife (athame) and sword, both of which they confiscated. Wiccans are not the only minority religion that uses ceremonial knives. Sikh males are required to wear certain symbols of their faith, including a kirpan (a ceremonial knife). This situation came to the attention of the federal courts in 1995 in *Cheema v. Thompson* (67 F.3d 883). Three young Sikh males were forbidden to wear their kirpans to school. The court of appeals approved a set of limitations that had been developed by the federal district court to allow the children to fulfill their religious obligation to wear kirpans without unduly endangering anyone in their school, but it left an opening for the school district to make an adequately convincing case against the wearing of kirpans by school children. The school district decided not to exercise its right to continue pursuing the case. Adult Sikh males have also been charged with carrying a concealed weapon—in one case a 69-year-old Sikh priest (*Ohio Beacon Journal*, September 19, 1999). The case was dismissed as part of a negotiated settlement. Such precedents have been helpful when Pagan's rights to carry ritual knives and swords have become an issue—if the case ever gets to court.

Most of the time, however, the ritual knives and swords are used as a justification for police stops and searches, particularly when Pagans are entering or leaving the sites of Pagan gatherings. Seldom are any charges filed. It is just an excuse for harassment. As one Pagan pointed out, his grandfather, a Shriner, had paraded without incident wearing a 32" sword (E-mail, September 13, 1997). The same is true of members of the U.S. Marine Corps who participate in weddings by using their swords to form a ceremonial arch when the couple is exiting the wedding site. In fact, traditionally the bride is ritually slapped with the flat end of one of the swords at the end of this ceremonial exit. When a sword arch was used by a group of Pagan men at a wedding (without the bride being hit), the park police charged a participant with having a dangerous weapon in the park (a sword).[7] Another Pagan male was charged with carrying concealed weapons, a ceremonial knife, and three throwing knives—all clearly visible. Both were acquitted of all charges. As in many other cases, the Pagans were vindicated, but not without a great deal of hassle and the expense of a court hearing (E-mail, September 15, 1998).

Other pretexts for police harassment on such occasions include searches for forbidden animal parts. In general, Pagans open themselves to police harassment when they use Pagan-oriented bumper stickers or t-shirts. Also, owners of Pagan businesses have reported that police have stopped and questioned customers leaving their stores. In one case, a clerk overheard a policeman saying that the store was targeted to be closed. One Pagan religious rights activist, upon hearing about this practice, suggested that a camcorder recording the shop and its environs is a good, if expensive, investment against all kinds of crimes, "including the uniformed kind" (E-mail, November 15, 1997).

As a result of such experiences, Pagans have adopted two strategies, one directed to Pagans and the other directed to law enforcement. The first is to try to give all Pagans the information and resources that they need to deal with police harassment. For years, Pagans have used the Internet to share information about Pagan religious rights and to help Pagans whose religious rights were being violated. Two of the most notable among these are the Earth Religions Assistance Network and the Lady Liberty League. Another, the Alliance for Magical and Earth Religions has maintained a website containing a very accessible "Guide to Dealing with Police Harassment." It also maintains a comparable site: "Religious Harassment in the Workplace." The Internet is not, however, the only resource for Pagans. In 2003, Dana Eilers, a Pagan lawyer, published *Pagans and the Law: Understand Your Rights*. Finally, many Pagan leaders with expertise in Pagan religious rights will, from time to time, offer workshops and other educational presentations to their fellow Pagans, most commonly at large Pagan gatherings.

Some of the same people have also been able to do presentations on Paganism at local police departments, as well as larger regional and national police meetings. In general, these seem to be well received, though the fact that an invitation was extended indicates that they were speaking to people who were open to what they had to say. Another valuable resource that has been mentioned previously, is the personal contact between police (and other government officials) and persons in their profession who are Pagans or who are well informed regarding Paganism.

To date, the best known of these is Charles Ennis of the Vancouver Canada Police Department who is also a Wiccan priest. Using the magickal name, Kerr Cuhulain, he wrote *The Law Enforcement Guide to Wicca*. Since the first edition in 1989, there have been two subsequent editions. At the time of this writing, he is in the midst of organizing an e-group for Pagan emergency workers with the objective of developing an international group, Officers of Avalon. In his announcement, he expressed this vision: "Officers of Avalon wants to show the world that we follow a valid and respectable spiritual path. We want to show the people of the free world that some of the people who are defending that freedom are Pagans like us. We want to establish a support network for those Pagans within the emergency services who do not yet feel that they can safely make their Pagan beliefs public" (www.aquatabch.org/pane-gyria/officersofavalon.shtml). Other sources of information that are readily available are listed on a website, Law Enforcement Guide to Witchcraft, Wicca, and Other Earth Religions (www.tylwythteg.com/lawguide1.html).

Individual Pagans who have reached out to their local police departments or to individual police officers have generally found that their input is both respected and appreciated. It should also be noted that many of the police themselves become targets of anti-Pagan hate groups. Cookson (1997, 744) reports a case in which the police enforced the law against a group that was assaulting a Pagan woman and her young child. Subsequently, the local prosecutor's office refused to prosecute the case and the police captain got hate mail from persons who regarded him as "the devil because his police officers investigated and aided the victims of the (alleged) harassment and assault."

One of the major problems is that Pagans, being very independent and individualistic people, have no overall organization to speak on their behalf and to call the attention of the media and other interested parties to instances of hate-based attacks against Pagans. Nor is there a single, central organization to step in when help and information are needed. Help is there, but it is relatively fragmented and, for those who are not familiar with Pagan religious rights efforts, it can be elusive. Thus, when a cross is burned at a Maryland mosque and Islamic school the Council on American Islamic Relations is instantly on the spot and talking to the press and the police. There is no equivalent organization representing Pagans and this fact limits their effectiveness and makes them more vulnerable to those who would commit hostile acts against them and law enforcement responders who may have no accurate sources of information about Paganism as a religion.

In spite of their fragmentation, however, Pagans are learning to gather together and exert political pressure on violators of Pagan religious rights. For example, in February 2004, an Illinois park district cancelled a contract for a Pagan oriented craft fair. The reason given by the superintendent of the park district was that the organizing company, Crafty Crafter's Expo, was "associated with Witches and [was] promoting Witchcraft and the Park District did not want to be associated with that" (*Crafty Crafter's Press Release*, February 12, 2004). The news spread quickly via the Internet, along with contact information for the responsible officials and local news outlets. Within 24 hours, the park officials responded to the pressure being exerted and reversed their decision (*Lady Liberty League Update*, February 13, 2004). A Pagan activist who was involved made the following comment (E-mail, February 14, 2004): "The Crafty Crafters success was because of use of a method that is being developed. While many cases cannot be easily solved, those involving public figures can be. The essence of this is to expose them to the general populace as [prejudiced]. Not just [the] local but the international community."

CHAPTER 7
CHRISTIAN PRIVILEGE AND THE PERCEPTION OF ENTITLEMENT

Christianity is a religion in which the faithful are urged to proselytize others who are not Christians and, in some cases, even members of other Christian sects. There is a range of ways in which this might be done. At one extreme is what may be called the inspirational approach. By the way in which one lives one's life it is possible to persuade others of the virtue of behaving in such a praise-worthy way and, thus, to inspire them to do likewise. On the other, darker, extreme there is the fear-based approach. Those seeking to convert others may use fear tactics, such as the threat of spending eternity in Hell.

Most Christians who evangelize do not fall at these extreme ends, but behave in ways that would place them somewhere in between. Fundamentalist Christians, however, overwhelmingly tend toward the second approach and fundamentalists are also those most likely to demand religious conformity or harass the adherents of minority religions on the theory that the end justifies the means. While many, per-haps a large majority, of Christians would not approach conversion in such a harsh and punitive manner they give it tacit support when they remain silent and tacit encouragement when they permit the expression of Christian ethnocentrism that is enshrined in many governmental practices. Although most governmental religious expressions carefully restrict themselves to naming the deity "God," it is clear to all that the deity being invoked is Judeo-Christian (e.g. Sherry, 1998; *Simpson v. Chesterfield County Board of Supervisors*, 292 F. Supp. 2d 805 [2003]).

American Christian sects can be roughly divided into three cate-gories. The first is the liberal category, of which the United Church of Christ is an example. The second is the liturgical, of which the Episcopalians are an example. Finally, there is the evangelical, of which the Southern Baptists are an example. During the late colonial period, evangelical Protestantism emerged as the normative American form of

Protestantism due to the activities of iterant preachers who moved around the countryside preaching to make up for the lack of churches or settled ministers in many areas (Newsom, 2001, 242). "Pan Protestantism, largely of the revivalist, Puritan, Zwinglian evangelical sort, continues to the be normative American religion, notwithstanding the tensions that exist between various forms of Protestantism . . ." (249).

The conversion efforts of both the liberal and liturgical Protestants tend, on average, toward the inspirational end of the dimension described above, though there are exceptions, particularly among individual members. On the other hand, evangelical Protestants institutionally tend toward fear-based conversion efforts, but again there are exceptions, particularly among individual members. Since this early growth in influence, the various Protestant evangelical sects have maintained Christian hegemony to the present day (264–266).

The hegemony of Protestantism, particularly of the evangelical variety, has resulted in the use of the government's coercive power to further the agenda of particular leaders and denominations within this grouping (252–255). In fact, in the early-nineteenth-century Supreme Court Justice Story saw it as the duty of the American government to foster and encourage Christianity (i.e. Protestantism) among the American people (1833, 986). Thus was produced a body of statutes and common law that reflected a mission on the part of hegemonic pan-Protestantism to convert, not only nonbelievers, but those of other Christian traditions (most notably Roman Catholics), as well as Native Americans—the conversion of African slaves was left to their masters and mistresses. As of 2004, the Texas Republican Party had a plank in its platform that celebrated the United States as "a Christian Nation."

Over the centuries, the dominance of Protestantism as the quintessentially American religion gave its followers a sense of entitlement. The idea that being a Christian was part of the tradition of being a "real" American became firmly entrenched in the minds of most Americans. This mind set can be seen in the Hiaheah City Council deliberations that resulted in the law that kept the devotees of Santaria from building a house of worship in Hiaheah.[1] During these deliberations a councilman said that Santeria practitioners "are in violation of everything this country stands for." There was a discussion of what the Bible allows and the chaplain of the Police Department made it clear that the country stood for Christianity: "We need to be helping people and sharing with them the truth that is found in Jesus Christ. . . . I would exhort you not to permit this church to exist" (*Church of Lukumi Babalu Aye v. Hialeah*, 113 S. Ct. 2217, 2231 [1993]).

The main vehicle for this effort to create an American norm that would facilitate conversion was the public school system, as well as certain public events, displays, and traditions. Catholic Americans were not part of this movement initially. The establishment of the Catholic school system was, in part, a reaction to the Protestant domination of the public school system (Hammond, 1998, 26). In the twentieth and early twenty-first centuries, however, Catholics began to reap some benefits from Christian hegemony and, thus, gave it their tacit (and sometimes explicit) support. For example, the addition of the words "under God" to the Pledge of Allegiance was the result of an effort spearheaded by the Catholic Knights of Columbus. Also, the Catholic school system has been a primary beneficiary of government programs that funneled money into private schools. There was always the provision that the money could not be used for religious instruction. But, there was always the fact that money that did not have to be used for other school needs could supplement the money used for religious purposes.

The biggest potential bonanza of all came with the Supreme Court's approval of school vouchers, a move that promised to funnel considerable funds to Catholic schools at a time in which additional money was sorely needed. The same applied to the directing of funds to "faith-based" charitable activities. Another example of Catholicism's inclusion in this larger effort was a California initiative proposition to amend the state constitution. It would authorize the voluntary use of the Bible for public school literature classes at all levels. Two specified versions of the Bible would be purchased by the school systems, one Protestant and one Catholic (SFGate.com, January 6, 2004).

Ceremonial Deism

As was discussed earlier, Protestant Christianity functioned as a hegemonic religious orientation from the time of the colonization of the lands that eventually became part of the United States until quite recently when Catholics increasingly became included. Freedom of religion and the prohibition of the establishment of a national religion originated as a way of keeping one Protestant sect from dominating all of the others. At the same time, it was seen as preventing the government from interfering in the affairs of the dominant Christian sects. Prejudice against nondominant religions, even nontraditional Christian ones such as The Church of Jesus Christ of the Latter-Day Saints, was not regarded as a problem until the twentieth century. Thus, there is a powerful impetus for both political leaders and courts to look at that history when making decisions about what is or is not in violation of the First Amendment religion clauses. The more religiously homogeneous past is reconciled with the increasingly heterogeneous present by means of the idea that the religious and the secular can be clearly distinguished with the aid of secularization via context, as well as the related concept of ceremonial deism.

In 1962, former Yale Law School DeanWalter Rostow coined the term "ceremonial deism," using it to reconcile the Establishment Clause with public religious activities what were, in his opinion, so traditional and uncontroversial that they did not violate the Establishment Clause (Epstein, 1996, 2091). The courts have tended to reconcile these official activities, by using some version of the following syllogism (adapted from Epstein, 1996, 2087):

> Traditional Christian-based practices obviously pass constitutional muster, because they have existed for so long.
> The practice at issue in this incident does not advance religion any more than those that have already passed constitutional muster.
> Therefore, this practice must pass constitutional muster.

For Epstein (2095), the defining characteristics of ceremonial deism involve the invocation of "God" (and sometimes Jesus) in connection with governmentally sponsored practices that are "symbolic, or ritualistic." These include "prayer, invocation, benediction, supplication, appeal, reverent reference to, or embrace of, a general or particular deity." They are "created, delivered, sponsored, or encouraged by government officials . . . during governmental functions or ceremonies, in the form of patriotic expressions, or associated with holiday observances." They are, "in and of themselves . . . unlikely to indoctrinate or proselytize their audience" and are not "specifically designed to accommodate the free religious exercise of a particular group of citizens." Finally, "as of this date [they are] are deeply rooted in the nation's history and traditions."

Epstein (2095) regards core ceremonial deism as including: "(1) legislative prayers and prayer rooms; (2) prayers at presidential inaugurations; (3) presidential addresses invoking the name of God; (4) the invocation 'God save the United States and this Honorable Court' prior to judicial proceedings; (5) oaths of public officers, court witnesses, and jurors and the use of the Bible to administer such oaths; (6) the use of 'in the year of our Lord' to date public documents; (7) the Thanksgiving and Christmas holidays; (8) the National Day of Prayer; (9) the addition of the words 'under God' to the Pledge of Allegiance; and (10) the national motto 'In God We Trust.' " After careful consideration, he concludes that all but one (presidential addresses invoking the name of God) are in clear violation of the Establishment Clause as normally interpreted by the Supreme Court.

He finds presidential speeches invoking the name of God marginally constitutional because they are not performed by clergy, nor are they a formal prayer. Most significant is the fact that "when the President speaks it is very difficult to draw the line between the individual and the office," thus raising a freedom of speech issue. He adds, "presidents should refrain from wrapping their speeches in religious imagery, for in doing so they certainly can make [non-Christian] Americans feel like outsiders in their own political community" (2142–2143). The practices of ceremonial deism increased significantly during the Cold War when the American political leadership wished to emphasize the difference between the United States and "godless Communism." Thus, the words "under God" were added to the Pledge of Allegiance and a new national motto "In God We Trust" was created.

Ceremonial deism embodies certain assumptions, the most important one being that references to "God" are unobjectionable, both because the term is an all-encompassing, unifying national force and because official references to "God" have historically been considered traditional and unobjectionable. For a different point of view, try substituting the names "Brahma" or "Athena" or "Allah," in official slogans where the term "God" is currently used and considered unobjectionable: "Brahma save the United States and this Honorable Court," or "In Athena We Trust." Should the president take his oath with his hand on the Koran and end it with "so help me Allah"? Should the chaplains of one or both of the U.S. congressional houses be Sikhs or Buddhists? This is how the current practice of ceremonial deism appears to many Americans who are not Christians or Jews.

In 1996, Steven Epstein observed, "within the last six years alone, over two hundred and fifty opening prayers delivered by congressional chaplains have included supplications to Jesus Christ" (2104). Even the inclusion of Catholic congressional chaplains has not been without controversy. As of 2003, 119 Protestants and two Catholics have served as chaplains of the House or the Senate (*The Washington Post*, June 18, 2003). The single Catholic Senate chaplain served from 1832 to 1833; the single Catholic House chaplain was appointed in 2000. This latter was a controversial move, but even more controversial was the first (and, to date, only) invocation by a Hindu priest in connection with an address by the Indian prime minister to a joint meeting of Congress.

The Family Research Council (FRC), a Fundamentalist Christian organization, issued a press release that stated: "Our founders expected that Christianity—and no other religion—would receive support from the government as long as that support did not violate people's consciences and their right to worship. They would have found utterly incredible the idea that religions, including [Hinduism], be treated with equal deference." They added that the assumption that "all religions are equally valid" would result "in moral relativism and ethical chaos." Subsequently, in a clarification, FRC's executive vice president said: "It is not our position that America's Constitution forbids representatives of religions other than Christianity from praying before Congress. . . ." (www.religioustolerance.org/hinduism1.htm). Another fundamentalist Christian commentator attacked this event in an article entitled "Spiritual Adultery—A Case of Infidelity in the Public Square" and called for repentance or excommunication of any Christian who participated in the event (*World on the Web*, October 7, 2000).

Ceremonial Deism in Practice

Many Pagans have expressed the opinion that ceremonial references to a clearly Christian (or Judeo-Christian) God act to implicitly exclude them and others who are adherents of minority faiths or no faith at all. Such references make them feel like second-class citizens, but few have seen this is a battle that they have any hope of winning. Manifestations of ceremonial deism have been declared constitutional in too many cases and opposition raises powerful political passions, as could be seen when the Ninth Circuit U.S. Court of Appeals declared the phrase "under God" in the Pledge of Allegiance an unconstitutional establishment of religion (Gey, 2003, 1866–1869; *The Washington Post*, May 1, 2003, A07). The Pledge of Allegiance did not contain the words "under God" until 1954 when it was added by President Eisenhower and a Congress bent on emphasizing the difference between the "godly" United States and the "godless" Soviet Union. Significantly, immediately after the bill adding the words "under God" to the Pledge was signed by President Eisenhower, a group of members of Congress recited it as the flag was raised to the strains of "Onward, Christian Soldiers!" (Gey, 2003, 1879).

In 2003, the Supreme Court granted certiorari to the Ninth Circuit Case which it decided in June 2004 (*Elk Grove Unified School District v. Newdow*, 2004 LEXIS 4178). The majority never reached the establishment issue, but decided that Newdow did not have standing to bring the case. This raises the question of why the Supreme Court granted certiorari if it was not ready to decide the establishment clause question—as three justices urged that it should in their minority opinions. The most practical answer lies in the fact that, if the Court had not taken the case, the Pledge in its current form would have been unconstitutional in the Ninth Circuit, but not in the rest of the United States. By using the standing issue to overturn the Ninth Circuit, the Supreme Court reestablished uniformity in the recitation of the Pledge throughout the United States—and tacitly gave its support to ceremonial deism.

Given the expense, the current unlikelihood of winning and potential political fallout of pursuing a constitutional challenge to the various practices of ceremonial deism, members of minority religions have chosen to tolerate it and concentrate their attention on battles that they thought they had some hope of winning. Pagans sometimes deal with their feelings about constitutional deism's implied religious exclusion by making jokes, such as saying "In the Gods we trust." But, at least one Pagan, with the help of the ACLU, decided to give it a try.

In 2000, Mary Lou Schmidt, a Pagan living in Topeka, Kansas, objected to the fact that Shawnee County Treasurer Rita Cline had put up posters saying "In God We Trust" on the walls of offices in the courthouse and in a mall annex. The signs measured 11 by 14 inches and the word "God" was printed in red letters and was larger than the black letters in the rest of the phrase. The notation that this was the national motto was "barely visible" (*Schmidt v. Cline*, 127 F. Supp. 2d 1169, 1171). When Schmidt contacted Cline to request the removal of the posters, Cline wrote a letter to Schmidt saying: "I understand you to say you are a pagan, do not believe in God, and refuse to recognize or honor the American flag and our national motto, all while claiming to be an American citizen. Your statements surprised me and caused me to question your patriotism and wonder just how much of an American you really are" (*The Topeka Capital-Journal*, May 20, 2000). She refused to remove the posters. Subsequently, Schmidt complained to the ACLU and it took her case. The executive director of the ACLU's Kansas City office then received a letter in which Cline told him she was praying for him.

On December 6, 2000, U.S. District Judge Sam A. Crow, dismissed the case and in 2001 ordered the ACLU to pay Cline's legal fees of $8,130 (*Schmidt v. Cline*, 171 F. Supp. 2d 1178). He found that Schmidt lacked standing to obtain an injunction, because she failed to meet the burden of demonstrating that she would "face a likelihood of future harm as a result of defendant's conduct, as is necessary to warrant injunctive relief" (*Schmidt v. Cline*, 171 F. Supp. 1169, 1174). He found that "an order prohibiting defendant from referring to her personal religious beliefs may raise its own novel issues of constitutionality to the extent it would constitute a prior restraint on defendant's free speech" (171 F. Supp. 2d 1169, 1175). He also held that the case was moot. The signs at issue had been replaced with new ones that measured 16 by 20 inches, including "the bald eagle on the American $1 bill and . . . lettering similar to that on U.S. currency. It also [included] the date that Congress adopted the phrase as the country's motto, July 30, 1956" (*The Topeka Capital-Journal*, September 20, 2000). Finally, the court found the "contention that posters bearing the phrase 'In God We Trust' violates the establishment clause, patently frivolous without any basis in law" (127 F. Supp. 2d 1169, 1181).

Schmidt's reaction was: "The lawsuit had everything to do with . . . being told that I can't be a citizen of the United States because I don't believe in God. Judge Crow doesn't seem to understand that" (*The Topeka Capital Journal*, December 13, 2000). In the meantime, the ACLU was left with a debt of $8,130 plus interest for Cline's attorney fees—an amount they were hard pressed to raise. Ms. Cline went on to become a local political hero, until she left office under the cloud of an alleged misappropriation of county funds.

When one looks at the specifics of the way in which ceremonial deism operates and the way in which its various components came about historically, it is difficult to disagree with Epstein's (1996, 2174) conclusion: "If . . . the Court means what it says when it espouses the principle that government may not, consistent with the Establishment Clause, endorse religion and send messages to citizens that cause them to feel like outsiders in the political community, the Court should have the intellectual honesty and fortitude to recognize that ceremonial deism violates a core purpose of the Establishment Clause." In a concession to the political realities of our day, he adds: "Undoubtedly such a decision will be very unpopular in an America in which the religious majority has grown all too accustomed to see its practices and traditions endorsed by the government." In fact, since these words were written, the Clinton and Bush administrations supported by a Republican dominated Congress have moved even farther in the direction of making the United States a country that strongly favors, if not technically establishes, Christianity.

Ceremonial deism has led to many practices that extend its reach. For example, the Board of Supervisors in a Virginia county "decreed that 'Judeo-Christian' prayers were constitutional—apparently because they are part of something called 'American Civil Religion' " (*First*

Amendment Center, August 10, 1003). They also included Muslims on the list, because they are monotheistic. But they rejected prayers associated with religions that are not monotheistic, including Hinduism, Buddhism, and Wicca. The need to specify "constitutional" and "unconstitutional" prayers is the result of a movement to have more prayer at public functions. Since Congress opens its sessions with a prayer, local governmental legislative bodies see no reason why they cannot do likewise.

This has led to much controversy about what prayers can be said and who can say them. Those who advocate prayer at public functions do not necessarily want to include prayers from a range of religions; they primarily have in mind Christian prayers. For example, the Salt Lake County Council voted to establish regular prayers at their meeting—ten years after abandoning the practice. The supporters pointed to tradition as the basis. When an assistant county attorney pointed out the legal fact that they would have to include all religions, such as American Indian religions and Wicca, they had second thoughts. Their solution: to formally entrust the task to a police or National Guard chaplain who would, of course, be Christian (*The Salt Lake Tribune*, January 24, 2001).

Many other local governmental bodies have established the tradition of having a prayer spoken before the start of every session. The norm is to have some system under which local clergy or the legislators themselves perform this service. In Virginia, the Chesterfield County Board of Supervisors maintained a list of volunteer clergy. Cynthia Simpson, a Wiccan, tried to get on the list and was rebuffed. In a letter sent to her by the County Attorney, she was told: "Chesterfield's non-sectarian invocations are traditionally made to a divinity that is consistent with the Judeo-Christian tradition. Based on our review of Wicca, it is neo-pagan and invokes polytheistic, pre-Christian deities. Accordingly we cannot honor your request to be included on the list of religious leaders that are invited to provide invocations at the meetings of the Board of Supervisors" (Letter from Steven L. Micas, County Attorney, September 12, 2002). Cynthia Simpson, with the help of the American Civil Liberties Union and Americans United for Separation of Church and State, took the county to court.

The U.S. District Court noted that legislative prayer is not, in and of itself, unconstitutional. It, however, questioned the nonsectarian nature of the prayers given. Between January 2000 and December 2003, 76 individuals had given invocations and only three were not Christian; one was a Rabbi and two were Islamic leaders. The court stated: "The policy, as enforced, has allowed, if not encouraged, the specific mention of the Judeo-Christian deity as well as the name of Jesus Christ . . . and it precludes the expression of common themes that would still serve the same public interest even though the speaker may be the representative of a religion outside that sanctioned by the policy" (*Simpson v. Chesterfield County Board of Supervisors*, 292 F. 2003 U.S. Dist. LEXIS 20635, 37). Its conclusion was: "If the Establishment Clause means anything, it means that government is not to demonstrate any preference for one set of religious beliefs over another, or for that matter, over the lack of any religious belief." Thus, "if government establishes a forum to which it invites a class of speakers for a specific purpose, it cannot exclude some class members because of a difference in viewpoint. . . . Such a policy of exclusion cannot survive constitutional scrutiny" (2003 U.S. Dist. LEXIS 20635, 53 [2003]). Chesterfield County is appealing this decision.

In Great Falls, South Carolina, the Town Council meetings also opened with a prayer. In this case, a Council member would lead the prayer. Darla Wynne, a Wiccan, objected to the fact that there were frequent references to Jesus, Jesus Christ, or Savior in the prayers. When she arrived late to one meeting in order to avoid the prayer, she was not allowed to speak at the meeting, even though she was listed on the agenda. When she requested that the invocation of Jesus Christ be discontinued, the Council refused. Like Cynthia Simpson, she decided to take the case to the U.S. District Court. Unlike Ms. Simpson, she represented herself. The court found that while legislative prayer was constitutional, "the practice of members of Town Council invoking the name(s) specifically associated with the Christian faith at Town Council meetings violates the Establishment Clause." Ms. Wynne's request for an injunction was granted. The injunction would keep town officials "from invoking or permitting another to invoke the name of a specific deity associated with any one specific faith or belief in prayers given at Town Council meetings" (*Wynne v. Great Falls*, 2003 U.S. Dist. LEXIS 21009, 24–25).

This case was appealed to the Fourth Circuit court of Appeals by Great Falls and was affirmed in 2004. The Forth Circuit panel unanimously concluded that the Town Council's practice crossed a constitutional line established by the Supreme Court in the 1983 case *Marsh v. Chambers* (463 U.S. 783) and the 1989 case, *County of Allegheny v. ACLU* (492 U.S. 573). The Court rejected Great Fall's argument that *Marsh v. Chambers* permits a town "to engage, as part of public business and for the citizenry as a whole in prayers a that contain explicit references to a deity in whose divinity those of only one faith believe." They also found that the Great Falls Town Council prayers "embody the precise kind of 'advancement' of one particular religion that *Marsh* cautioned against" (*Wynne v. Great Falls,* 2004 U.S. App. LEXIS 15186, 22). Great Falls, with the backing of the South Carolina Attorney General, announced that they would appeal the decision to the U.S. Supreme Court

In the meantime, Darla Wynne, who had already suffered four years of harassment by both members of the public and town officials, came home to find her pet parrot "beheaded and affixed with a note reading 'You're next'." The parrot also had its heart ripped out (*Landmark News Services,* August 16, 2004; *heraldonline,* August 17, 2004). As of this writing, Pagans within reasonable traveling distance have organized to attend Great Falls Council meetings in support of Darla. Another group of Pagans have been raising money to help Darla obtain a security system. Also, a South Carolina newspaper, *The [Chester Country] News & Reporter,* ran a feature story called "What is Wicca?" (October 9, 2004). The story ended with: "Christ exhorted his followers to never cause harm, hurt others or cast judgment."

A similar case is in the court system in Florida. The Manatee County School Board had a long-standing practice of saying the Lord's Prayer at the beginning of its meetings. Recently, in order to avoid a lawsuit, they adopted a compromise that instituted nonsectarian invocations given by local ministers. Subsequently, the prayers were all Christian. When queried about this, the leader of a group of Christian ministers, Manatee Religious Services, stated, "I would simply say to someone who is uncomfortable where they are: move." The case is currently in the court system and the School Board is making the argument that having only Christian prayer is constitutional because it fits "community standards." According to the lawyer arguing for the status quo: "If a local community should have the right to determine what kind of pornography they have, why shouldn't a community be able to decide what kind of invocation they want at a public meeting?" ([Florida] *Herald Tribune,* February 29, 2004).

Sometimes the problem can be solved without recourse to the courts. In Dallas, a Wiccan priest, Bryan Lankford, was invited to give the invocation at a council meeting. When the city began receiving calls about having a Witch do the invocation, it withdrew the invitation. The reason given was that the city wanted to find out more about Wicca. In response, the Wiccans held a protest rally outside the city hall. Ultimately, the mayor apologized and promised that a new (but unspecified) date would be set for Mr. Lankford to deliver the invocation. Then a Jewish member of the

Council formally requested that the invocation be explicitly rescheduled. She had previously criticized the lack of diversity in those invited to give invocations (*The Dallas Morning News*, September 28, 2000). The invocation was given and was "a huge success" (*Betwixt & Between Press Release*, October 4, 2000). The event even made the television news. A local columnist observed: "No goats were sacrificed. The prayer was an easy segue into the Pledge of Allegiance (although I could hear some mischievous Wiccans behind me slyly amending the words to 'one nation under Goddess'). . . . You don't have to agree with everybody. You just have to be polite" (*The Dallas Morning News*, October 5, 2001).

Sometimes a legislative invocation can make a popular hero out of a minister. On January 23, 1996, Pastor Joe Wright of Central Christian Church, "A Non-Denominational Church Where Christ is Central," gave the invocation for the Kansas Senate. His prayer has been widely praised and disseminated through the Internet and other sources. It is called a "Prayer of Repentance" and includes the following words: "Heavenly Father, we come before you today to ask your forgiveness and seek your direction and guidance. . . . We confess that we have ridiculed the absolute truth of your Word and called it moral pluralism. We have worshipped other gods and called it multiculturalism."[2] On the website from which this was taken, a commentary made the following points: "With the Lord's help, may this prayer sweep over our nation. My [*sic*] our own daily prayers be fervent and faithful so that we can continue to be called 'One Nation Under God' and receive God's blessing." This legislative prayer explicitly rejects the inclusion in American society of persons who are from different cultures and religious traditions, as well as the nonreligious. The reaction of one Pagan was: "I feel one of two things, anger or the coming of tears. I cover my mouth in disgust and I blink my eyes rapidly to hold back the flow. Is this because I'm too emotional? No, I don't think so. Is this because it actually frightens me? Yes! Yes, it frightens me to my very core" (E-mail, October 20, 2000).

Ceremonial deism and fundamentalist Christian influence do not just affect the way in which national and local governments handle religious issues. They also have an impact on the electoral system. During the 2000 presidential election, the candidates were so focused on religion that the term, God-talk, was frequently used to describe parts of their speeches. And with the exception of Vice Presidential candidate Joseph Lieberman, the God talked about was Christian (Segers, 2002, 7–8). Under both the Clinton and Bush administrations, as well as the Republican ascendancy in Congress, there has been an increasing flow of public funds into church-sponsored schools and other programs.

The 2004 presidential election campaign is even more focused on religion than that of 2000. Presidential candidates who are reluctant to exploit their personal religious convictions for political gain now feel pressured to do so if they are to have any hope of winning (Andolina and Wilcox, 2002; *The Washington Post*, January 4, 2004; *The Washington Post*, January 8, 2004; *The Boston Globe*, January 20, 2004).

Even the national park system is not immune. According to a Press Release (December 22, 2003) of Public Employees for Environmental Responsibility (PEER): "In a series of recent decisions, the National Park Service has approved the display of religious symbols and Bible verses, as well as the sale of creationist books giving a non-evolutionary explanation for the Grand Canyon and other natural wonders within the national parks." "The Bush administration prevented park rangers from publishing a rebuttal to the [creationist] book for use by interpretive staff and seasonal employees who are often confronted during tours by creationist zealots" (*counterpunch*, December 22, 2003). Also, conservative groups were able to force the Park Service to edit a videotape shown at the Lincoln Memorial "to remove any image of gay and abortion rights demonstrations that occurred at the memorial." The video was changed to include rallies of the Christian Promise Keepers and pro-Gulf War demonstrations, even though these did not occur at the Lincoln Memorial. PEER director, Jeff Ruch, has observed: "The Park Service leadership now caters exclusively to conservative Christian fundamentalist groups" (*counterpunch*, December 22, 2003).

Given the increasingly diverse religious makeup of the United States, perhaps it is time to rethink the Founders' focus on insuring that no one Protestant sect be established as the official American religion. Given the fact that the proportion of Christians in the American population is shrinking and the proportion of other "exotic" (to the United States, at least) religions are growing, it is time to consider whether Christianity is *de facto* an established religion and to ponder the possible consequences of this situation.

Public School Involvement in Evangelism

Since many of our national traditions were heavily influenced by evangelical Protestantism, Christians have grown up with a feeling of rightness about how things "have always been." This leads to a sense of entitlement that emboldens people to continue that approach, even when it is becoming less and less appropriate culturally or legally. For example, the parents of an 11-year-old Muslim girl who was pressured by her principal to accept a Bible were told that he had been distributing Bibles for 35 years, had had no previous complaints, and saw no reason to stop the practice at this point. The child, harassed by the other students, began to have nightmares about burning in Hell and her younger brother started to question the family's Muslim beliefs (*ACLU News Release*, April 10, 2001). More recently, a Pagan child was pressured to accept a Bible brought into her class by the Gideons. At first the principal was resistant to the idea that this was a violation of the Constitution, observing Bibles had been distributed thus since the principal herself was in the fifth grade. The mother was referred to the Superintendent of Schools who admitted that the practice was illegal and got in touch with the principal (E-mail, December 18, 2003).

In Hawaii, the evangelists have found a way around the unconstitutionality of having staff or invited outsiders distribute religious materials in schools. At one middle school, the students passed out more than 1,000 "student survival kits" to their peers. The kits contained an MTV-style 3D video, a CD, a modern version of the New Testament, and other books. The students, of course, did not create the kits themselves. The Jesus Hawaii Project, a group of almost 200 churches did. Their goal is to distribute approximately 70,000 kits to students in grades 6–12 at both public and private schools. The cost: $335,000. Because the students are passing out the kits, it is constitutionally protected free speech (*HonoluluAdvertiser.com*, April 24, 2003).

Even in areas where the U.S. Supreme Court has spoken unequivocally, the sheer number of schools in the United States makes it impossible to assure that the law is being respected unless someone complains. When one of my children entered first grade in a public school system, she was immediately taught a prayer. The Supreme Court's 1962 holding in *Engel v. Vitale* (370 U.S. 421) that this was unconstitutional was ignored. A quiet complaint to a friend on the school board took care of the problem. In religiously homogeneous areas, complaints are not likely and those who might be inclined to complain are often mindful of the possible consequences and decide to desist.

I am old enough to remember when the public school day opened with the Lord's Prayer. During most of my school years, I lived in a community that was overwhelmingly Catholic. It did not have one Catholic Church; it had Catholic churches for every ethnic group with numbers sufficient to support one—and there were many. But, every morning at the beginning of the school day, we all recited the Lord's Prayer in its Protestant version. Since I was Protestant, this choice seemed unobjectionable. After a while, however, I learned from my Catholic friends that they were

taught a significantly different version in their homes at
the time, it puzzled me, but I did not see it as part of
Protestant domination. Many Catholics did and, cor
ever possible established their own parochial school
ple in my town were immigrant steel mill workers,
speak English, so my Catholic friends did not have
same was true of my immigrant, Catholic, maternal grandparc.
of whose descendants converted to Protestantism, thus blending int
what seemed to them to be the American norm.

To a government heavily influenced by evangelical Protestantism, my
Catholic friends and relatives were fair game. The message was clear
that, if they wanted to be full-fledged Americans, they should be
Protestants, preferably evangelical Protestants. The same message can be
heard today in the "culture wars" about such issues as prayer and Bible
study in the public schools. Those who are advocating the return of religion to schools in the form of prayer do not mean prayers of any and all
sorts. They very clearly mean Christian prayer (and, perhaps, Jewish
prayer), not Santarian, Muslim, Wiccan, or Hindu prayer.

The public schools have, thus, become a battleground in the struggle
for conversion by Christians against members of minority religions and
the nonreligious. Newsom characterizes its basis as "an ideology of
insult—a remarkable demonstration of disrespect for religious minorities" (2002, 249). And, currently, the most blatant abuses impacting
minority religions (such as those incidents discussed in previous chapters) tend to occur in communities or regions where the overwhelming
majority of the residents belong to evangelical Protestant sects.

Many of the evangelistic activities in the public schools are not specific to Pagans or to any other minority religion. As has historically been
the case, many public school officials still act as if they have the right to
impose their Protestant Christianity on all who enter their doors—
regardless of what the courts say about Constitutional requirements. For
example, there is a long history of government support for evangelizing
Native American children. Many believe that it is a tradition that has
ceased. As recently as February 2003, and contrary to the 1993 decision
in *Berger v. Rensselaer Central School Corp.* (982 F.2d 1160), a principal
of an elementary school with a mostly Native American student population accompanied representatives of the Gideon Society while they
passed out copies of the New Testament to all of the children.

In some school systems, evangelical groups distribute book covers
displaying the Ten Commandments. For example, as of 2000, the
Family Research Council claimed to have distributed over 600,000 Ten

ommandments book covers under the auspices of its "Hang Ten" program that also promotes display of the Commandments on government property and in public schools. The American Atheists organization (AA) has taken a particular interest in this project, challenging it in a number of school systems, some as large as the Chicago school system. In the latter case, the Chicago school CEO, in response to AA objections, announced that the distribution of the book covers could only take place off school property, but "enthusiastically" endorsed the program (*People for the American Way News Release*, August 17, 2000). In a similar controversy in a large school system in Texas, the American Atheists demanded the right to distribute their own book covers along with the Christian ones and were initially denied that privilege by the school district, because the AA book cover would be "derogatory toward Christianity." Subsequently, AA was given permission to distribute the book covers, because they were found to meet the criteria for non school publications, but the School Board President made a point of saying that he did not approve of them (*The Austin American-Statesman*, August 23, 2000).

As has been noted before, however, sometimes school officials can be the "good guys." One Pagan parent complained that her first-grader was being given writing exercises about Christmas, Hanukah, and Kwanzaa, but not Yule (the winter solstice). The mother offered to do sensitivity training with the school staff and got an immediate call from the principal accepting her offer. Subsequently, the mother became involved in creating classroom materials that included both Yule and Ramadan, as well as developing sensitivity classes for the school's staff and teachers (E-mail, December 20, 2000). In another case, a Pagan parent complained about her son being forced to complete assignments based on the Ten Commandments. A meeting with the vice principal who had reviewed the course assignments resulted in a commitment by the school to become more aware of religious diversity and an instruction to the teacher that if she was going to use material from one religion, she needed to use material from others as well (E-mail, February 8, 2001).

At the classroom level, not all the news is good. In a Minnesota school a self-identified Pagan child was "preached" to by one of her public high school teachers. This "sermon" was followed by a personal, hand-written letter on school stationary that said that the teacher was praying for her and that some day she would discover God and his son Jesus (E-mail, March 29, 2001). A former student from the south sympathized, talking about being "constantly bombarded by those who wished to 'save' me" (E-mail, April 19, 2001). This type of teacher activity can have more serious results. One Pagan public school student had the misfortune to be in the class of a teacher who reportedly taught in class that the Celtic deity Pan was a helper of the Devil and that anything non-Christian was wrong. This led to physical attacks on the student that the teacher did nothing to prevent (E-mail, March 9, 1997).

In neither of the cases discussed above was the teacher punished. A Michigan teacher, however, was given a three-day suspension for loaning a child a book entitled *Wicca: A Guide for the Solitary Practitioner* (*The Herald-Palladium Online*, March 2, 2000). In an Oregon case, a school administrator was suspended one day without pay for loaning a child Silver RavenWolf's *To Ride a Silver Broomstick*. The circumstances surrounding the Michigan case were never made clear in the media, but in the Oregon case, the student asked the administrator to loan her the book (E-mail, February 25, 1999). In a Texas case, a 13-year-old was told by school officials that he was not allowed to bring to school any books dealing with Wicca, Paganism, or Witchcraft or he would be expelled. When he asked if he could bring a Christian book, he was told that Christian books would be permitted (E-mail, February 27, 2001). In another case, an assistant principal called a mother when her child brought Silver RavenWolf's book to school. The mother told him that she had no objections to the book. This began a series of events during which the assistant principal created all kinds of problems for the mother and the child, culminating with a visit from Child Protective Services (E-mail, March 31, 2000).

The Bible is another frequent area of contention, as several previously mentioned situations have illustrated. Although reading the Bible as a religious exercise is clearly unconstitutional, many evangelistic school officials and politicians have come up with creative ways to get around this limitation. One is to study parts of the Bible "as literature" in English classes. At the time of this writing, the California Secretary of State has given official support to a ballot initiative that would make the study of the Bible "voluntary" in California public school literature classes. The State would buy either the King James (Protestant) or Authorized (Catholic) Bibles at an estimated cost of $200 million. A press release from the Secretary of State's office said, "the study of the Bible in public schools would be without devotional or denominational purpose" (*SFGate.com*, January 6, 2004). There are even some instances of the Bible and the story of Jesus being taught in history classes.

Such an approach, of course, makes reading the Bible and discussing it compulsory for all students. While it may be possible to "opt out," the consequences (including subsequent testing, as well as harassment) for the child may lead many non-Christian parents to decide to let their children participate.[3] Occasionally, a public school with a Christian-oriented curriculum may modify it to include some mention of other religions. But it all depends on the teachers and school officials.

In a 2004 decision, the Court of Appeals for the Sixth Circuit upheld a district court summary judgment that found bible classes in public schools unconstitutional. The Bible Education Ministry (BEM) was a program based in a fundamentalist Christian college that used college student volunteers to come into the schools and to teach the Bible to local elementary school students. The court found that the Bible was being taught as religious truth and that the curriculum was totally unsupervised by any school personnel. It was clear to the court that there was a clear message of government endorsement of religion in general and Christianity in particular. The court attached no importance to the fact that students were allowed to "opt out" (*Doe v. Porter*, 2004 U.S. App. LEXIS 11031). In a television interview, Superintendent of Schools Sue Porter observed that Bible classes had been offered for 51 years (*CNN.com*, June 8, 2004).

This is a case in which the students and their parents fought back and won. There are others. A ninth grade Pagan in the Midwest had her self-portrait rejected from the school's Wall of Fame because she drew herself wearing a pentagram with a winged pig pulling at it. The pig represented those who objected to her religious choice. She was told that the self-portrait was rejected because it had a religious theme and contained a pentagram. Another picture that was placed on the same Wall of Fame, however, had a clearly Christian theme. When her parents pointed out that the law forbids religious discrimination and indicated their willingness to pursue the matter, the school changed its decision. Her church, Ozark Avalon, used the incident to contact the school and educate school officials about Paganism as a religion (*Lady Liberty League*, Fall 2003 Report).

What is obvious in these cases and those discussed in chapter 5 is the sense of entitlement. In the eyes of the Christians involved, it is not unconstitutional for the schools to include Christianity in their curricula, either in required subjects such as English and history or as stand-alone Bible study courses. But it is unconstitutional to include even oblique references to a minority religion. It is the same mentality that leads evangelicals to object to programs such as EarthKeepers (a program focused on ecological awareness) in which there are some elements that vaguely resemble the practices of Pagans, like sitting in a circle and wearing pendants (not pentagrams). It is also the mentality that sees no problem in allowing an evangelical Christian group to offer a sex education program in several California public school districts (*American United for Separation of Church and State, Press Release*, January 22, 2003) and mandating a curriculum in Presque Isle, Maine that does not mention religions other than Christianity and only teaches the history of Christian civilizations (*The Associated Press*, December 6, 2003).

The Consequences of "Opting Out"

The truly appalling level of ostracism and bullying that takes place in the public schools generally comes to the fore when acts of extreme violence, such as the Columbine shootings, take place. Forgotten by many, including school officials and teachers, is the harm that can be done by the less spectacular acts of rejection and intimidation that take place on a regular basis. The tendency is to regard this as "normal" childhood behavior playing down its importance. The problem becomes even less likely to be properly addressed when school officials facilitate the bullying, join it (by questioning a child's religious beliefs or failure to participate in Christian-based activities) or not protect a child who might want to opt out of a religious activity. One of the notable things about *Doe v. Porter*, the "Bible study" case, is the fact that the lawyers for the school district fought to have the objecting families names made public. The court refused because of fear that the children, in particular, would be subjected to serious harassment or worse. It also noted that threats had already been made (2004 U.S. App LEXIS 11031, 5).

In considering situations where religious activities might or might not be permitted in public school settings, the courts have placed great emphasis on the right of the student to opt out. The justices have been less sensitive to the minority status issues and psychological consequences to students who choose to opt out. The ones most often mentioned are harassment and ostracism by fellow students. Seldom considered is the possibility that some students who opt out might be singled out for negative attention by school faculty or staff because of the reason they chose to opt out—or for simply opting out.

For example, at a pep rally at a high school, all the students were asked to stand for the Pledge of Allegiance and the Lord's Prayer. A ninth grader and some of his friends all of whom were studying Wicca remained seated, as did a number of other students who were not involved with Wicca. Ignoring the other seated students, the principal came to the Wiccan study group and told them they were Devil worshippers and that they would be suspended if they were seen doing anything wrong again. He also told them they could not wear pentagrams, even under their shirts (E-mail, February 16, 1998).

This is so blatantly unconstitutional it would be a "slam dunk" in any objective court. That fact, however, did not solve the problem for these students. Their school became a hostile environment because of the specifics of the religious reason that led them to exercise their constitutional right not to participate in a school activity with religious content. There is even one case in which a child attending a supposedly secular day care center chose not to say grace before eating her afternoon snacks. She was questioned about her religious beliefs and practices. When her mother complained, the mother was told that it was customary for day care centers in the community to have prayer before meals and that the teacher couldn't understand why the child didn't want to thank God for the food. The child was subsequently allowed to continue to opt out, but was intimidated enough to lie to the teacher about her family's Wiccan religious beliefs (E-mail, February 12, 1998).

The most widely publicized case of this sort involving a Pagan child (although not the only one involving children from minority religions) is the case of India Tracy. The events of this case can be traced back to a Supreme Court decision upholding released time for religious instruction. Initially this decision seemed favorable to minority religions. In the early twentieth century, Catholics and Jews who were concerned about Protestant indoctrination in America's public schools pressured school systems to allow students, with parental approval, to leave school periodically for religious instruction in their own churches and synagogues (Epstein and Walker, 1998, 181). In 1952, the Supreme Court approved this practice in *Zorach v. Clauson* (343 U.S. 306), a case that involved a New York City program allowing students, with parental consent, to attend religious instruction off school grounds. Attendance of the participating students was mandatory and reported to school officials. The court found this arrangement to be constitutional; the majority (Justice Douglas writing) noted that separation of church and state does not mean hostility to religion.

The program in the India Tracy case was set up under the auspices of this released time policy. Run by a fundamentalist Christian group called Crusade Ministries, Inc., it was a three-day revival clearly intended to encourage the students to convert to or make a stronger commitment to the Baptist religion. At the time the India Tracy case began, the crusade was in its sixth year. With parental consent, the children were excused from school two hours a day for three days. Accompanied by teachers, they were put on school buses and taken to the revival. For three years, India did not attend the revival, because her family was Pagan and did not consent. As a result, other students called her derogatory names, such as "Satan worshipper," "baby killer" and "baby eater" (*First Amendment Center*, April 27, 2003). "Teachers and her principal questioned her about her religion and why she did not want to attend the revival" (*KnoxNews*, April 29, 2003). There were also incidents in which slurs were painted on her locker and she was injured when classmates slammed her head into the locker. No disciplinary action was taken.

"After Christmas break in early 2002, India said three boys chased her down a hall at [the middle school], grabbed her by the neck and said, 'You better change your religion or we'll change it for you'. She broke free and fled into the girls' bathroom. A teacher stopped the boys from following her." She was so terrified that her parents removed her from the school and commenced to home school her eventually placing her in a private school where she became an outstanding student. They also "filed a federal lawsuit against Union County schools, claiming the crusade, prayers over the loudspeaker, a Christmas nativity play [in which Tracy refused to play the Virgin Mary], a Bible handout and other proselytizing activities . . . have become so pervasive they are a threat to safety and religious liberty" (*CNN.com*, May 12, 2003; *Tracy v. Carter*, Plaintiff's motion for Partial Summary Judgement, U.S. District Court, E.D., Tennessee, no. 3:03-CV-106). In November 2004, the school system agreed to a $50,000 settlement in order to end the case.

This is not an isolated incident. Released time programs run by fundamentalist Christian groups trying to convert as many children as possible are a problem for many minority religious families whose children attend public schools in places where evangelistic Christianity is dominant. They can have their children "opt out" with the possibility that the children may suffer ostracism at best and violence at worst. If they allow their children to participate, their children may be converted or at least acquire fundamentalist Christian ideas about abortion, sexual orientation, demonic spirits, Hell, and other topics that are not common to all Christian denominations, not to mention minority religions.

The only way in which a minority religious parent can counter this effort is by insisting that the school allow the child to come home or go to an appropriate alternate location for religious instruction while the other students are attending the evangelical Christian program. This is not a perfect solution, because of the pervasive childhood concerns about "fitting in" with their peers and the propensity of public school students to bully those who are "different." It is also not something that the average minority religious parent is necessarily in a position to do, because many parents are both at work during the relevant school hours and because many minority religious groups are not organized properly to create a released time religious instruction program. In at least one case, however, a Pagan parent was able to arrange to have her child come home for religious instruction, since the time set aside for the Christian program could be reconciled with her lunch hour (E-mail, November 6, 2000).

This is not the only situation in which opting out is a problem. It is important to remember that the twelve public school years are a period during which a child is learning to be a member of a community outside the family. It is undisputed that a major aspect of this is most students' desire to fit in, to be accepted as a full member of this community. Opting out forces the student to conspicuously disassociate from the other members of the student body. This is painfully obvious in the fact situation described in 1993 by the majority opinion in *Doe v. Duncanville Independent School District* (994 F.2d 160). The student was a member of a school basketball team that knelt to say the Lord's Prayer before (in the locker room) and after (in center court) each game, as well as prior to leaving the school for away games and upon exiting the bus when the team came home.[4] The student's father contacted the assistant superintendent who rebuffed him. Subsequent contacts with school officials and the board of education were similarly rebuffed.

When the student decided not to participate in the Lord's Prayer at away games, she was required to stand outside the circle in full view of the spectators, thus calling attention to her desire to opt out. The result was "that her fellow students asked, 'Aren't you a Christian?' and that one spectator stood up after a game and yelled, 'Well, why isn't she praying? Isn't she a Christian?' In school, Doe's history teacher called her 'a little atheist' during one class lecture" (994 F.2d 160, 162–163). This demonstrates that the choice to opt out which the Supreme Court considers adequate to protect a student's rights, actually (in the words of the *Doe* Circuit Court opinion) "fosters a climate in which [the student] is singled out and subjected to criticism on the basis of her religious beliefs" (994 F.2d 160, 162).

The necessity for some non-Christian students to opt out frequently and obviously is made clear in the dissenting opinion in the second (1995) *Doe* case (*Doe v. Duncanville Independent School District*, 70 F.3d 402, 410):

> It is undisputed that for some twenty years, DISD, through the actions of its teachers and other employees, permitted, encouraged and even

sponsored the recitation of prayers during curricular and extrac[
activities. Prayers were recited during classes. Many events wer
and closed with a prayer. Sports teams recited prayers before gam
locker rooms, after games on the field and in the busses retu
school. At award ceremonies, prayers were recited and DISD
distributed pamphlets of religious songs for the participants to [...]
prayers and songs were always Christian.

In such an atmosphere, opting out would significantly and recurrently call everyone's attention to a student's religious nonconformity and, for the average public school student, be the source of considerable embarrassment, even if some of her fellow students and teachers did not harass her because she opted out. This is too much to ask of a public school student who espouses a minority faith or no faith at all, but its essential cruelty seems to be routinely ignored by the Supreme Court and all but a few other federal courts.

In this case, the Fifth Circuit Court enjoined school employees and agents from participating in student-initiated prayers, but left untouched everything else. This means that the non-Christian students would continue to have to constantly and conspicuously opt out or participate in activities that contradicted their religious beliefs. As Steven Gey puts it: "The dark underside of judicial decisions that permit the melding of community, religion, and government is the silent message those decisions send to religious dissenters, who are told, in effect, to shut up or get out" (2003, 434).

In another case, a student opted out by leaving out the words "under God" when she recited the Pledge of Allegiance. Here is the result in her words (E-mail, January 16, 2004):

> Students and school staff endlessly questioned me over this. "Wasn't I patriotic? Why wouldn't I recite the whole pledge" Didn't I believe in God like our forefathers intended? Etcetera, etcetera. Patiently, I tried to explain first that the words "under God" were not a part of the original pledge. I was met with skepticism. Then I tried to explain my belief that God deals only with individual souls, not with nations. I was met with confusion. Finally, I resigned my argument with the phrase, "of course I believe in God; I just see Her a little differently than you do." I was met with disgust, but at least it put an end to their questioning.

Her little sister met with similar problems when she entered the same public school, but (according to this informant) at least the teachers left her alone.

Another student similarly opted out of the religious part of the Pledge of Allegiance and was punished academically by the school administration. In Tacoma, Washington, a high school student was banned from participating in TV production assignments for the duration of the year as a result of having refused to read "under God" when he was reading the Pledge of Allegiance. The charge was misuse of school equipment to deliver a personal message. His action resulted from a current events class discussion about the Pledge of Allegiance: "After one student said, 'Christians are forcing us to listen to this,' [he] vowed" that he would not force the students to listen to the words. Since the student intended to pursue a career in broadcasting, the ban on participation in broadcast assignments was a particularly harsh punishment for opting out (*The News Tribune*, April 6, 2004).

Non-Christian students can also be tricked into taking part in Christian services. Gey[5] writes of a public school in Atlanta, Georgia, in which the students were taken to a "motivational assembly" during the school day. The students (who assumed that the assembly was mandatory) found themselves in the midst of hundreds of Baptists. Those present "sang religious songs, heard religious testimonials and listened to a local minister leading the students in 'confessions of faith in Jesus.' " The highest ranking law-enforcement official in the county told the students, "Here we are, in defiance of the U.S. Supreme Court, calling the name of Jesus Christ" (Gey, 2000, 457). In this sort of situation, opting out would be difficult, if not impossible.

Schools are not the only places where people must opt out in order to avoid what Gey calls "private religious domination of a governmental forum" (2000, 444). This language harks back to a 1995 observation by Justice O'Connor (concurring) that "at some point . . . a private religious group may so dominate a public forum that a formal policy of equal access is transformed into a demonstration of approval" (*Capital Square Review and Advisory Board v. Pinette*, 515 U.S. 753, 777). In its opinions on religious displays, the Supreme Court has settled on a "reasonable observer" test to determine whether a public forum display (or, by extension, activity) would constitute a prohibited message of state endorsement. This does not give a clear standard to the lower courts for use in Establishment Clause cases. Rather, it leads to a "We Know It When We See It" jurisprudence (Marshall, 1986). Gey (2000, 445) suggests a four-prong test: (1) Is "the scale of the religious exercise. . . . such that it essentially monopolizes a significant portion of a particular forum"? (2) Is "the religious speech . . . repetitive and frequent, thus constantly reinforcing the perceived link between the government forum and the religious perspective"? (3) Does the religious display take "a form that is especially intrusive on unwilling observers"? (4) Does the display alter "the forum in a way that draws attention to the relationship between religion and government"?

Adult Pagans in such situations seem to have two typical experiences. First, they are not aware ahead of time that the event will be religious and hesitate to leave because other values are at stake. Second, they are aware that the event will be heavily Christian, but go anyway because—again—other values are at stake. An example of the first situation was shared with me by a Pagan professional employed by a state government in the Mid-Atlantic region:

> Shortly after 9/11 . . . there was a brief "memorial" held in the courtyard of the State Office Building where I work. Attendance was not mandatory but was encouraged by those in the highest positions of our organization. I attended, expecting to hear a brief introduction followed by a moment of silence. What actually took place was an entirely Christian prayer service endorsed by our local senator and led by one of the administrators from a local bible college. During the prayer, I looked around to see that most attendees had their heads bowed with eyes closed. A significant minority, however, did not. I talked to another non-Christian co-worker after the event who felt as uncomfortable as I did. We had both considered leaving in the middle of the service but didn't because we felt it would have been too rude and would have drawn negative attention to ourselves.

Complaints to the office of the senator were met with indifference. Had this person known ahead of time about the nature of the service, she would have opted out. In retrospect, she observed: "The saddest thing about this incident is that it could have been a service that brought people together, so that we could express our common sorrow over the tragedy. Instead, it drove a solid religious wedge between people that shut non-Christians out" (E-mail, January 16, 2004).

In the previous example, the Pagan did not know that she was walking into what would amount to a Christian religious service. Sometimes, however, the person knows ahead of time, but goes anyway. An assistant professor in a state university system in the Mid-Atlantic region regularly attends convocation and commencement, both of which invariably involve Christian prayer and Christian music. Being a Witch, he would like to opt out, but has not done so because he wishes to be fully a part of the university's life and, in particular, wants to be there when his students graduate. Thus, although he has the right to opt out, he has chosen not to exercise that right. The price of being a fully participating faculty member of his public university is being forced to take part in

Christian religious practices. Similar choices are exercised hundreds of times each day by persons who are not monotheist or Christian.

The Theory of Privilege

Both the attempt to impose religious conformity and the suppression of religious nonconformity are based on the idea that there is only one basic religious orientation that is right, good, and true. Drawing from the work of Robert Devlin, Robert Post (2003) reminds us that law is commonly understood as enforcing "the common sense of the community, as well as the sense of decency, propriety and morality which most people entertain" (*Commonwealth v. Randall*, 183 Pa. Super. 603, 611 [1957]). But, Post points out that in the process of enforcing historic and widely held cultural norms, the law inescapably oversimplifies culture, assuming that a society's culture can be stable, coherent, and unified. It is not adequate to say that the law merely enforces static and unproblematic social values. One of the mottos of the United States, "E Pluribus Unum" (Out of Many, One) emphasizes the fact that it is composed of people from many places, coming from many heritages to try to form a cohesive nation. It was overshadowed by "In God We Trust" just as America was about to become even more diverse than it ever had before—and that diversity is steadily increasing.

When the law is used to enforce cultural values, it often advances one side of a many-sided cultural disagreement. In the United States, when it comes to religion and the norms of morality, that side is Christianity and it continues to prevail because the legislatures make the law and the courts interpret the law in ways that allow the most politically powerful and dominant religious tradition to thrive—often at the expense of other religious traditions. This is possible, because the people in power have seldom given much weight to the extent to which they are privileged and their actions have perpetuated and reinforced their privileged status. There has always seemed to be a certain inevitability and rightness to the process, particularly given the Supreme Court's tendency to resort to arguments emphasizing history and tradition when dealing with the privileged status of Christianity. Eliminating Christian privilege would be "a politically unattractive task" (Furth, 1998, 589) for judges, as well as politicians.

Recently, however, the examination of privilege has become a component of critical legal studies and has been fueled by the work of many researchers, mainly those studying race and feminism. Joseph Duncan summarizes the theory of privilege thus: "Privilege has been largely used to describe and criticize the benefits that individuals receive by having people that reflect their ideals and their interests in power now and throughout history." He points out that, looked at from this perspective, it is clear that Christians are privileged: "Despite a constitutional guarantee that the government of the United States will be faceless when concerning religion, a system has developed that has absorbed Christian practice at every turn . . . [and] Christians, including myself, have been blind to the privilege we have experienced" (2003, 617–618). Kenneth Karst (1994, 343) calls attention to this blindness with reference to the 1990 Supreme Court decision in *Employment Division v. Smith* (110S. Ct. 1595) that established the test of facial neutrality for the interpretation of the Free Exercise Clause: "It is a strange sense of equality that ignores the racial discrimination that produced the earliest anti-peyote legislation and the racially selective unconsciousness that kept the Oregon law [outlawing the use of peyote] on the books."

This privilege has two elements: "First, the characteristics of the privileged group define the societal norm, often benefiting those in the privileged group. Second, privileged group members can rely on their privilege and avoid objecting to oppression." Equating privilege with the social norm "and the implicit choice to ignore oppression mean that privilege is rarely seen by the holder of the privilege" (Wildman, 1995, 890). Silence plays an important role in privilege. "What we do not say, what we do not talk about, maintains the status quo" (885). There is the silence of the privileged who "believe that their privileges of being in a better-treated class are actually affirmative rights guaranteed by the government and by God." There is also the silence of minority religions that can, but should not, be interpreted as consent to the sometimes oppressive acts of the majority. Rather, it can be attributed to concern about the consequences of speaking out. In fact, the system of privilege can be so deeply ingrained that those who are not privileged "may not realize that their rights are being violated or that they do not have to subjugate their rights to the interests of the majority" (Duncan, 2003, 621). My Catholic childhood friends docilely repeating the Protestant Lord's Prayer at the start of every school day come to mind.

Thus, in chapter 5 we saw privilege as "the embodiment of the majority's willingness to force its beliefs and social values on others, while denying the guaranteed rights of the Constitution to all of those that do not fall into the norm or into the majority group." And in chapter 6, we saw the privileged embracing "the belief that those creating oppression and spreading ethnocentrism have a right to mold others governed by the social contract into their view of what is normal, or else to exclude them from the social contract altogether, unwilling to recognize their rights" (Duncan, 2003, 621). The privileged status of Christianity was established at the time the United States was created and still continues. Many Christians are not willing to acknowledge that they are privileged because of their religion and that this "privileged majority [has been] able to structure the law to be responsive to their beliefs, biases, and interests." This "blindness and lack of objectivity . . . allows [the current system of Christian privilege] to continue" (622). As Anthropology Professor Sally E. Merry observes: "Law not only constructs authoritative visions of the social world, but also exerts force behind these interpretations. It not only establishes one way of construing events but silences others, thus channeling and determining the outcome of legal proceedings" (1992, 213).

Labeling plays a major role in this dynamic. Those who oppose the notion of strict separation between (Christian) church and state often refer to those with another point of view as irreligious, against religion, or worse.[6] They similarly refer to Christian accretions on the body politic as "traditional" or "secular" (Sherry, 1998, 506). In this context, the legal "secularization" of major elements of the Christian religion is paradoxical in the sense that they are treated as indisputably religious in church contexts, but legally regarded as secular when they are in the public square. The Supreme Court has allowed the transformation of religious symbols into secular objects if they are in the proper context— one that can somehow be shoehorned into the category of "secular." Thus, depictions of the birth of Jesus as well as a national holiday celebrating that birth somehow magically become "secular."

A particularly transparent example of such secularization is found in a case the Sixth Circuit Court of Appeals decided in 2001, *ACLU v. Capital Square Review and Advisory Board* (243 F.3d 289). At issue was the motto of the state of Ohio, "With God, All Things Are Possible." The court affirmed a district court decision that held that the motto did not violate the Establishment Clause as long as it did not attribute the words to their source in the New Testament book of Matthew at 19:26. In 1998, a district court had enjoined Ohio from attributing the quotation to the Bible (*ACLU v. Capital Square Review and Advisory Board*, 20 F. Supp. 2d 1176, 1185). It noted that the motto was similar to other instances of ceremonial deism (particularly the national motto, In God We Trust) and that the idea behind it was not uniquely Christian. According to the majority opinion, no well-informed observer could possibly regard this motto as a governmental endorsement of Christianity. In a long detailed argument, the court managed to find that the words of Jesus, taken from the Biblical book of Matthew, were entirely secular. It even secularized the Bible by quoting a philosophy professor[7] who testified, "[t]he Bible has become a moral as well as religious resource of insights in our Western culture" (Bell, 2001, 951). Repeatedly, the court emphasized the secular nature of the use of the quotation from the Biblical words of Jesus. Thus, in essence, the decision was based on the interpretation of the Bible as a secular document when it was used as the source for Ohio's motto. A plaintiff was a Presbyterian minister who thought that the use of the words of Jesus as a state motto trivialized his religion.

"Where a practice or symbol is perceived as integral to American culture, or where the context of a display which includes religious articles creates an impression of mere holiday celebration or religious pluralism, the symbols will be recharacterized as secular." Also secularized are religious references in national mottoes and recitations. "Cases legitimizing public displays and national invocations of religion rely, to varying degrees, on the proposition that religiousness is a contextual label" (Furth, 1998, 591–593). This argument also depends heavily on the invocation of history and tradition, of what was considered unobjectionable when the United States was more homogeneously Christian. But, can any respectful mention of God or Jesus ever be truly secular? Why would Christians want it to be? When does God stop being the central deity in their worship and become a social choice? And, if God is a social choice, is religious piety mere conformity with a social norm? (Furth, 1998, 604; Warren, 2003, 1706).

Alexandra Furth (1998, 595, 601–607) is of the opinion that "dependence on historical practice is thoroughly inadequate to address contemporary conflicts of church and state." She thinks that by its secularization interpretation "the [Supreme] Court dilutes or entirely negates religious import, simultaneously insulting religion and imposing a watered-down version of religion on the general population." Arguing that "secularization establishes religion in general, and often the Jewish and Christian traditions, as the social norm," she concludes that the "incorporation of religious icons into civic culture suggests that the government endorses the particular religion invoked." Also, "because secularized practices are most frequently those derived from Christianity, secularization privileges religion over irreligion and Christianity over all."

Her preference would be "the complete secularization of religious and civil life" because "it would be sect-neutral . . . [and] allow dissenters to maintain a distinction between their public and religious affiliations, a distinction which protesting individuals and groups are not permitted under the current scheme." What we have now is Supreme Court support of "the construction of a putatively civil religion founded in Christian symbolism and backed by the state." Along the same lines, Charles G. Warren (2003, 1693) argues that a majoritarian analysis of the Establishment Clause is "jurisprudentially unwarranted and harmful." He sees three types of social harm resulting from the incorporation into the clause of ceremonial deism and secularization. First, it harms the individual "by making full inclusion within the political community contingent upon religious belief." Second, it harms society "by discouraging religious tolerance" and renders "peaceful coexistence in a pluralistic society untenable." Finally, it harms religion by undermining "the spiritual experience through secular iconography, making God the equivalent of a public display and limiting the reality of the deity's existence to that of a mere social phenomenon."

As was discussed in chapter 1, the religion clauses of the First Amendment were the products of a fear that one Christian sect might be favored above all others. Currently, the canvas upon which the religion clauses should be interpreted is much larger. Religious orientations that were once nonexistent or obscure in the United States, such as Paganism, Islam, or Hinduism, are now very much present and growing rapidly. Much of the support for the notion of a civil religion as the underpinning of the secularization of Christian ideas and symbols has been based on the idea that American society is homogeneous religiously, economically, and socially. Now Americans are faced with something quite different from the intra-Christian sect rivalry of the founding fathers.

We are moving toward a rivalry between and among religious traditions, both imported and indigenous to the United States. It is no longer Episcopalians versus Baptists. It is Christians versus Muslims or Hindus or Pagans. At the same time, we are moving inexorably in this direction, the ceremonial deism of the United States is linked to a secularized "Christian ethnocentrism" (Furth, 1998, 607; Van Alstyne, 1984, 786) in our public institutions that feeds the kind of intolerance and persecution exemplified by the stories told in this book—and they are only a few of numerous similar stories. Many such stories can also be told about the adherents of minority religions other than Paganism (Eck, 2001, 294–332).

While the Supreme Court invokes the theoretical "reasonable observer" asserting that this hypothetical person will understand the secularization of Christian symbols such as crèches, "it seems implausible that the average citizen would interpret a government-sponsored crèche as anything but an endorsement of religion" (Furth, 1998, 609). More specifically, it would seem to be an endorsement of the religion inspired by the infant that is at the center of the display (Warren, 2003, 1704–1705). "Late arrivals to America may suppose they can take the government's religiosity or leave it, but they are stuck with the reality that clashes so clearly with the First Amendment: Ours is basically a Christian-pretending government where they will be made to feel ungrateful should they complain" (Van Alstyne, 1984, 787).

More seriously, secularization and ceremonial deism along with the increasing religiosity of contemporary political discourse and government policy may, and (as we have seen earlier) sometimes does, incite certain Americans "to view nonadherence to this new secularized religion as un-American." This, in turn, may lead to "a corresponding fracturing of the political community along religious lines and finally, a pollution and debasement of spiritual religion." The Supreme Court has tried to further civil unity and community by drawing on the majority's religious beliefs in a nebulous sort of way. Unfortunately, It may prove to be destructive of a unified cultural identity in an increasingly heterogeneous society, and potentially result in the "unraveling of the fabric of our society" (Warren, 2003, 1698–1699).

CHAPTER 8
MAJORITARIANISM AND RELIGION

The core principle of democracy is that the majority shall rule. This inexorably means that some people in a democratic polity will be forced to adhere to laws with which they disagree. Because the Founding Fathers clearly saw the potential for harm in this arrangement, they provided safeguards against a tyrannical majority. Among these safeguards is the Bill of Rights, the first ten amendments to the U.S. Constitution. These amendments are crafted to protect minorities in certain key areas of life where it was thought that special protections against majority tyranny were particularly significant (Karst, 1992, 506). One of these areas was religion and its importance is symbolically emphasized by the fact that constitutional protections both for religious freedom and against religious domination constitute the first two clauses of the First Amendment. This reflected not just abstract theory but the experience of those who first came from Europe and settled the colonies that would eventually become the United States. Many of them were fleeing countries in which there were established religions and many of the colonists who had embraced religions that were not established were forced to hide their religious convictions and practices from the authorities.

Their goal was to be able to practice their religion openly and freely. For this, they braved dangerous voyages and the settling of untamed lands. Unfortunately, once they had gained power, many of those who had histories of religious oppression by established churches made their own religion the official religion and proceeded to persecute other religious groups. It was against this background that the First Amendment was written and ratified. While some of the former colonies had established churches, it was decided that the United States would not. It was a radical idea at the time, but it was relatively easy to implement, given the basic religious and cultural homogeneity of the country.

Over the years, the principle that all should worship in their own way and that no one religion should control the national government has been a source of considerable American pride. What is being forgotten is that the early years of the United States represented a unique moment in time. While there were many sects, almost everyone in this country was Christian. They shared certain basic principles that seemed fundamentally true, such as belief in a monotheistic deity that they called "God" and a reverence for Jesus. What is being ignored is that religiously and culturally the United States is no longer that way.

While the early Americans were concerned with the power that the state might wield over religion, contemporary Americans tend to be more concerned with the use that religious groups might make of the government. This is particularly an issue, because the dominant religious orientation has always been Christian. And, Christianity, no matter the sect, has always had as its core the proselytizing imperative. Thus, it was inevitable that the overwhelming majority of those establishing the governmental apparatus and making the laws believed that they belonged to the one true religious faith with basic precepts and morality that should unquestionably guide humankind and inform the new democratic governmental experiment. Membership in a particular sect remained important, but certain overall principles remained the same and bound people together in the face of alien (non-Christian) religions. Largely ignored, however, was the proposition that "religion and religious ideas are fundamentally incompatible with the structure of democratic government" (Gey, 2000, 451). Why?

First, democracy is based on the fundamental notion that a majority of the people will rule—that they would decide what form the government would take and what laws would govern its citizens. Decisions about these matters are supposed to be made in a way that involves differences of opinion, bargaining, persuasion, logic, and the consideration of multiple theoretically acceptable options. The essential validity of holding opposing points of view is to be recognized, even when those points of view are defeated by a majority vote. That mistakes might be made is taken for granted and there is the assumption that decisions made today might be found wanting and modified, replaced or eliminated at some future point in time.

The incompatibility of democratic government with religion inheres in the notion that religion involves faith, not reason. Christian faith is the acceptance of the supreme wisdom of a superhuman being who is infallible, even though the deity's dictates are often beyond the understanding of mere humans. In some sects, the leaders are considered God's emissaries on earth and the bringers of His infallible instructions to the faithful. Objective science cannot verify the nature and requirements of the Christian God—although some fundamentalists use the word "science" to characterize matters that are essentially based on faith, not on experimentation or any other form of objective verification by those who both do and do not share faith in the Christian God.

Thus, reasonable persons may differ regarding the religious imperatives supposedly emanating from the deity, based on interpretations of the Bible (of which there is more than one version) or simply the divine inspiration of religious leaders. "The supremacy inherent in every variation of the concept of 'God' dictates that to the extent God requires individuals to behave in certain ways, His mandates must supersede the secular demands of the state" (Gey, 2000, 452). Absolute obedience is required and the beliefs and actions dictated are usually passed down to ordinary people through some authoritative religious figure or hierarchy.

Thus, when the religious leadership speaks, the faithful must obey and must base their obedience on faith, not reason. This can come into direct conflict with democratic values. For example, in 2004, a Roman Catholic bishop decreed that elected Catholic legislators who supported abortion rights should no longer receive Holy Communion, a core sacrament in the Catholic religion. His position was upheld almost unanimously by a meeting of 183 Catholic bishops (*The Washington Post*, June 25, 2004). This clashed with the idea that in a representative democracy, elected representatives must represent all of the people who elected them, regardless of religious faith (*The [Cleveland] Plain Dealer*, January 11, 2004; *Religion and Ethics Newsweekly*, June 14, 2004). The fear that the U.S. president might "take orders from" the Pope was a major issue that John F. Kennedy had to overcome in order to win his presidency. President Kennedy affirmed the democratic value that an elected official should try to follow the will of the electorate. By 2004, however, this stance was being called into question as a Roman Catholic priest delivered the following prayer to the Colorado House of Representatives: "Almighty God, please, change and convert the hearts of all the representatives in this House. May they be the antithesis of John Kennedy, may they be women and men of God, and may their faith influence and guide every vote they make" (*The Washington Post*, April 17, 2004).

Yet, these are the easy cases. They are out there in the open for all to see. The more difficult problem is that the faith of a government official or employee might in subtle ways influence their thinking about policy issues and about how they should discharge the responsibilities of their office. In chapter 3, the story of Judge Bach illustrates the inability of a government official to see beyond his own faith and to administer justice even-handedly to those whose religion is radically different. His intentions were good, but his faith made him blind to the validity of the non-Christian religious choices of those whose religious rights the U.S. Constitution instructs him to uphold.

Second, democratic government is premised upon the essential, human imperfection of the decision maker—be it a person or a deliberative body. It is assumed that laws will be amended, abolished, and interpreted in ways their originators did not anticipate. Such events are part and parcel of the ordinary business of democracy. Majorities change and, consequently, that which was wrought by an earlier majority may be undone by a subsequent majority. Democratic governments acknowledge the importance of taking into account both experience and the fact that the world is in a constant state of social and technological change. Even those who advocate using the "original intent" of the Founding Fathers as a guide to constitutional interpretation or legislative intent with regard to statutory interpretation have to deal with what the Founding Fathers or the enacting legislators would have wanted done with regard to matters they could not and did not foresee. They also have to identify a single intent that can be ascribed to groups of highly individualistic and contentious Founding Fathers or legislators.

Religion, on the other hand, lays claim to absolute and everlasting truth as articulated by contemporary religious leaders who usually have their own agendas. Change, when it comes, is difficult and highly divisive. It has the potential to tear an institution asunder, as did the rise of Protestantism within the Catholic Church. And, in the present, the selection of an openly gay Bishop in the Episcopalian Church is threatening the unity of the worldwide Episcopalian religion. When two religions, each claiming possession of the absolute truth, clash over rule of a country, the result is likely to be violence and, in extreme cases, war.

Finally, democracy is rule by human beings. The ultimate source of authority is the ordinary (often ill-informed) citizen who shows up periodically to vote for people who may only be "known" to him by party affiliation, not even by name, let alone policy positions or qualifications for the job. That is to say, democracy depends for its authority on the will of a fallible electorate that morphs into ever changing majorities, depending on the candidates, the issues and the general state of their lives. In religion, the ultimate source of authority over both individual persons and human institutions is outside the human sphere. No one can see God; no one can be sure to a certainty of what His dictates are—though many assert that they have a special relationship with Him that permits them to know. Placing the origin of governmental authority outside the human sphere means that the wishes of the deity must be articulated by humans who assert that they "know." There is no way independently to verify these claims and, thus, the governed are left with the necessity to obey on the basis of faith.

Therefore, we are left with the essential incompatibility of religion and democracy, as well as the current state of interpretation of the first two clauses of the First Amendment. The Supreme Court's interpretation of the Establishment Clause is in flux and it has changed the interpretation of the Free Exercise Clause to make the legality of minority religious practices subject to the wishes of a Christian majority. As a practical matter, this gives a great deal of power to those who would impose majority religious values and practices on others—either unintentionally through lack of information and understanding or intentionally in the name of the Christian interpretation of such principles as morality.

Also, American politics are highly pluralistic (i.e. group-based). Acts of unfairness not only impact the particular individual involved. They usually also take place in a larger context of group discrimination. Thus, "given the group-based focus of religious politics, an environment of group discrimination is especially likely to influence legislators whose business it is to follow the pulse of majority opinion—whether their legislative 'acts of unfairness' are targeted or . . . the result of indifference" (Karst, 1994, 354). In the political sphere, it has become almost mandatory for candidates to proclaim their religiosity in order to the considered for public office. The majority is Christian and, thus, so is most of the God-talk.

Many Christians maintain that a strict separation between church and state is hostile to religion. By "religion," they do not mean Santeria, Druidism, or Islam. They have in mind Christianity and, perhaps, Judaism. They are reacting to the fear that their position of privilege in the government and laws of America is being limited or threatened in ways that that they were not in the past (crosswalk.com, June 28, 2004). This creates the kind of insecurity upon which discrimination thrives. "Invoking the power of government to strike a symbolic blow against 'Them' always seems most necessary when 'We' need to bolster our own senses of self, and the need seems most urgent when 'They' make their status claims in public" (Karst, 1994, 355; Staub, 2003, 8).

As the country becomes more religiously diverse, the historical and current governmental favoritism toward Christianity is being used to stifle voices that would move the government toward a more truly neutral point of view. And the truly neutral point of view is strict separation, for as long as the government clearly favors one religious tradition, it tacitly supports intolerance toward all others. Strict separation involves the right of each religious tradition (and all sects within them) to pursue its own beliefs and practices unhindered and protected from persecution by the government—by government officials who may not share or even agree with the religious beliefs and practices they are protecting. They must also support the right to be atheistic or agnostic. As we have seen in this book, bringing a certain religious tradition and morality into the public square can encourage zealous members of the majority to try to impose religious conformity and a kind of creeping theocracy as some members of the religious majority actively, and sometimes harshly, try to convert or, at least, silence those who do not share their beliefs.

The idea that Christianity is oppressed because it is not always free to use the government apparatus and public forums to impose its theology (instrumentally secularized, of course) and morality on everyone else is absurd. It might be credible, if so many persons in positions of governmental power did not give Christian hegemony their tacit or explicit support. Explicit support, most obviously in the form of a Christian dominated ceremonial deism or (in some places) a favoritism for Christianity that goes far beyond the purposeful vagueness of most ceremonial deism, is obviously a problem. But, tacit support in such forms as police refusal to respond appropriately to acts of violence or threatened violence against members of religious minorities can, in its own way, be more insidious. It should not be up to the police to decide on a religious basis who is worthy of protection and who is not.

The idea that Christians are oppressed is not credible when the political norm seems to be the proclamation of one's Christian beliefs as a successful vote-getting ploy. Finally, it might be credible, if more and more scarce public funds were not going to the direct or, more commonly, indirect support of Christian-sponsored (now called "faith-based") programs that have at their core a proselytizing effect— sometimes tacit, but often overt. Given what history and events elsewhere in the contemporary world tell us about the horrors that can result when politics and religion become too intertwined, this situation can be viewed as frightening.

Currently, the line against blatant governmentally sponsored intolerance and persecution is holding in most places but, as we have seen in this book, there are places the line has wavered or, for all practical purposes, disappeared. As privileged Christians see the possibility that their privilege may be reduced even more in the future, than it has in the past, they have organized politically to protect and extend their privilege. There is much political pressure on politicians, particularly

Republicans who have accepted fundamentalist Christians as a key part of their political base (Rozell, 2002). Government funds and functions have increasingly been funneled to evangelical Christian organizations and it has become more necessary for political candidates and officials to ostentatiously parade their religious fervor. The stories told in this book are ultimately about places where the line is in need of mending. The good news is that, for the most part, Christian privilege has not shaded into overt persecution more often.

The divisive potential of religious fervor can be seen throughout the contemporary world. Americans may think we are immune to it and perhaps we are. But, the government continues to side with a fundamentalist Christianity that is feeling defensive and threatened in the face of the growing diversity in what Americans believe about religion and morality. Protestant evangelical Christianity is in danger of losing its historical, disproportionate influence over government and, thus, its fellow citizens of all faiths, so it mobilizes its followers and flexes its political muscle. This is working—in the short run. But the long run is a different matter. Attempts to control others' religious beliefs and behavior lead, sooner or later, to rebellion. We are not immune to religious conflict, especially where the religion clauses of the U.S. Constitution are seen to accommodate and bow before legislatively "neutral" enactments by a Christian majority under the guise of an instrumental secularization of blatantly Christian symbols, beliefs, and values.

There are (and probably will always be) endless debates about "whether religion enhances or undermines democracy" (Segers, 2002, 4). In the contemporary United States, a democratic majority dominated by a single religious tradition within which the faithful are exhorted to convert all unbelievers is currently a threat to the religious freedom and equality of which Americans are so proud (in theory, at least). At the beginning of the twenty-first century, the question might better be whether majority rule will suppress more and more non-Christian religious practices (if not beliefs) and legally impose more and more Christian norms. If majoritarianism accomplishes this, will that eventually trigger minority religious rebellion against the use of government programs and laws to further Christian interests and proselytizing?

If the religious tradition that is becoming increasingly influential with and a financial beneficiary of the government were not a proselytizing one, the risk would be less. But that is not true of any form of Christianity. Whether spoken softly over tea or shouted loudly from a pulpit or street corner, Christianity asserts its own rightness and exhorts its followers to save others by bringing them into the fold. To ask or

do otherwise would be a denial of a (if not *the*) central
ir religious calling. And the challenge to convert those
s well as atheists and agnostics, is currently on the
vangelical Christians with the Southern Baptists
The Washington Post, October 21, 1999).

.c time, minority religious groups are growing almost
vely. Muslims now top 5.5 million and have over a thousand
islamic Centers. Buddhists number over 1.9 million and Hindus number
over 1.3 million. There are now more Muslims in the United States than
there are Episcopalians. This diversity of traditions is both remarkable
and growing. "The decline of Protestant hegemony and the growing
diversity of American society pose new challenges" (Segers, 2002, 6–7).
Soon Protestants will constitute less than 50 percent of the population.
(*The Washington Post*, July 24, 2004). Thus while historical tensions
associated with the First Amendment religion clauses have centered
around the fear that one sect will gain ascendancy over governmental
policies and practices, less attention has been paid to the fact that all the
serious contenders have always been sects of one major tradition,
Christianity. As the proportion of Christians dwindles and the proportion of non-Christians grows, this way of looking at the First
Amendment will become less and less realistic.

All Christians almost surely will never unite against the interloping
non-Christians, both imported and homegrown. There are too many
doctrinal and other differences between the various sects of Christianity.
But, these Christian sects have enough in common to constitute a
unifying political force against non-Christians. Use of the government
is more practical than trying to unify all of Christianity, since the more
evangelical sects can act overtly in the political forum while the more
restrained, "mainstream" sects can just politely avert their eyes and still
reap the benefits. Given the history and traditions of the United States
both groups can tell themselves that such actions are in harmony with
the American norm. The fact that they also represent the values and
political predispositions of the blindly privileged can be ignored. In
doing so, Christian lack of knowledge or understanding of minority
religions will inexorably lead them, as a majority, to pursue policies and
pass laws that are "neutral"—at least from their point of view.

In *Lyng v. Northwest Indian Cemetery Protective Association* (485 U.S.
439 [1988]), the Supreme Court majority was so insensitive to the very
different religious practices of the protesting Indians that they saw
nothing wrong with destroying a host of sacred practices and places in
order to build a road that was only marginally necessary, if at all. It was

treated as a matter of property rights, not religion. Thus, the act of building the road through Indian sacred lands was treated as religiously neutral. But would that road have been built through the grounds of the National Cathedral? It is unlikely. The majority would have understood what was at stake and supported the Christian position that the sacred land of the Cathedral and all that was on it was too religiously important to destroy. Two streets end at the National Cathedral grounds and continue on the far side. That their uninterrupted continuation would ease the perennially difficult traffic flow in that area of Washington, D.C. has never been considered a justifiable reason for destroying the religiously important *Christian* practices and places that are tied to that land. Yet, given the serious traffic congestion in Washington, D.C., it could be argued that the building of those roads is much more needed than the building of the road that destroyed the Indian's sacred sites. Similarly, the Eighteenth Amendment forbade the use of intoxicating liquors "for beverage purposes," thus leaving intact the use of wine for Christian communions. The use of peyote for religious purposes by American Indians was not seen in the same way, originally in Oregon and subsequently by the Supreme Court.

Christians may impose "God" on the national motto and money, ignoring the polytheism and atheism of many of their fellow citizens. They may arrange to have their major holidays remain national or, at least, state[1] holidays. Because they do not have the political or governmental power to change any of this, some minority traditions have tried to counteract the pressure toward conversion among their young by raising minor holidays to major ones because they fall near the time when the Christmas or Easter frenzy takes over America's public and commercial life. The most obvious example is the Jewish elevation of Hanukkah to a holiday that tries to compete with Christmas. Pagans celebrate Yule as their version of Christmas.[2] And, as a pittance, increasing numbers of Americans now wish others a "Happy Holiday," instead of the once ubiquitous "Merry Christmas."

None of this addresses the rise of evangelical Christianity that is currently taking place in America. More and more Christians are turning to the more fundamentalist sects of Christianity. This has paralleled the rise of conservative politics. Both phenomena are complex and stem from many causes. One cause, however, seems to be the desire to keep things as they were, to hold onto a past that was familiar and is increasingly romanticized in some quarters. "Family values" is one of the code phrases for this nostalgia for past privileges. The desperate struggle to ensure that marriage can only be solemnized between *a* man and *a* woman is revealing. Yes, it is about homophobia—at least up front. Lurking in the background are faiths, such as Islam, that sanction and even encourage different marriage configurations.

The fear of change seems to be the overriding emotion; the attempt to control or prevent, using government power, the change that is inevitable is the overriding behavior. The Supreme Court has been a party to this reaction against change. Its recent decisions with regard to both religion clauses in the First Amendment constitute what Kenneth L. Karst calls "the doctrinal charter for a new politics of religious division." Karst sees in these developments, "the stimulation of a politics focused on religion [that] will entail significant costs . . . borne disproportionately by Americans who are members of historically subordinated groups—in this case, religious minorities." He also notes that the principal architects of this are the "founding strategists of the New Right" whose objective is the maintenance and expansion of Christian hegemony in America. This will, in turn, "polarize local[3] politics along religious lines, in a zero-sum game of status dominance." As for the Supreme Court, he concludes, "some justices evidently have difficulty apprehending the seriousness of this harm, perhaps because it lies outside their own experience" (Karst, 1992, 503–504).

Karst (1992, 508–509) fears a situation in which symbols, such as those found in ceremonial deism, "officially define the status of various religious views, and thus the status of cultural groups in the community. If government-sponsored symbols of religion produce reactions of strong emotion, the most important reason is that they touch the sense of identity, symbolizing the status of individual citizens as members of dominant or subordinate groups." This can lead to a situation in which there are de facto religious parties: "Politicians can garner votes by portraying their opponents as anti-religious . . . [and, thus tap into] a major strand of modern politics: the construction of enemies." In politics, "nothing works quite so well as identifying a symbol that is laden with emotion for a majority of the voters, and portraying the opponent as an enemy of the symbol and all who cherish it. To serve these electoral purposes, religious symbols are the answer to a politician's prayer."

Christians are looking for politicians who will champion their interests in the public square, because they understand (or, in some cases, may only intuitively sense) that their historical system of privilege is endangered. They are used to being part of a group-based social hierarchy that has conferred social power, status, and privilege. Individuals have simply to be members of the group "Christian" and they get social power, status, and privilege that has nothing to do with their individual abilities or characteristics. This, then, can serve as a foundation upon which a politically ambitious person can build a successful career or achieve a desired office.

Roy S. Moore, for example, achieved the highest judicial office in Alabama simply by gaining notoriety as the champion of the posting of the Ten Commandments in courtrooms and other public buildings. Even after he carried his crusade a bit too far and was forced to remove his Ten Commandments monument from the rotunda of the Alabama State Judicial Building and himself from the office of Chief Justice, his political career flourishes. At last notice, under the auspices of his organization, Foundation for Moral Law, Inc., Roy Moore is busy traveling all over the United States urging his Christian supporters to become politically active in order to protect and further the Christian hegemony that was frustrated when his Ten Commandments crusade came up against the Establishment Clause of the First Amendment. There is also an organized political movement to restore him to the post of Chief Justice in Alabama. His legal loss has been translated into political power.

Religion can be used as an instrument of social dominance. In such a setting, subordinates can be easily suppressed, for law "is often written and enforced so as to favor the interests of the dominants and 'order' is often defined as those social conditions that disproportionately protect and maintain the interests of dominants." In such systems, "it is crucial that . . . 'democratic' social systems maintain *plausible deniability*, or the ability to practice discrimination, while at the same time denying that any discrimination is actually taking place" (Sidanius and Pratto, 2004, 322; italics in the original). This seems increasingly to be a characteristic of government in the United States.

In part, at least, this situation is supported by the confluence of several major trends. First, after the excesses of the 1960s and 1970s, there has been a growing conservative trend, built largely on social and cultural nostalgia for a past that has been romanticized, along with the virtual demonization of anything or anyone that can be characterized as "liberal." Second, by both following and (in some cases) leading this trend, the Republican Party has been able to change its status from a minority party to a serious contender for long term majority status. These two political trends have characterized late-twentieth-century and early-twenty-first-century American politics.

Accompanying these developments has been a parallel trend in American religion. At the same time historical Protestant Christian dominance has been threatened by the growing religious pluralism

d both by immigration and the rise of home-grown non-Christian
us traditions, the trend toward conservatism in the larger social
has been reflected in the weakening of so-called mainstream
Christian religions and an almost explosive growth in politically conservative evangelical and fundamentalist sects.

According to a survey conducted for the television program *Religion
and Ethics NewsWeekly* in 2004 these evangelicals[4] are very serious about
proselytizing: "There is nearly universal agreement about the evangelical
religious mandate to spread the faith, and the evidence shows that in this
regard white evangelicals practice what they preach. Nine out of ten
white evangelicals agree that it is important to spread their faith, and
81 percent of white evangelicals agree that it is important to convert
others." Approximately 41 percent have tried to convert coworkers and
38 percent have tried to convert strangers. In contrast, "while there is
agreement among non-evangelicals that it is important to spread their
faith (57 percent), only 38 percent feel that it is important to convert
others" and "only a third (35 percent) have ever tried to convert someone to their faith" (Greenberg and Berktold, 2004, 8–9). This indicates
that the evangelical Christians portrayed in this book are not atypical,
although they may be somewhat more enthusiastic and less scrupulous
about how they realize their mission.

Recent decades have seen the rise of politically powerful evangelical
movements as a high stakes industry. Very large congregations, varied
and elaborate sites for worship and related activities, the growth of
religious media and the celebrity status of successful preachers have
become an obsession in many parts of the country—particularly in the
less urbanized areas where many of the events described in this book
took place. More and more, evangelical Christianity is not just about
faith, but also about power, celebrity, and theater—sometimes on a large
scale and sometimes on a smaller scale that contains the aspiration to
grow. This has led some evangelical ministers to associate themselves
with "causes" (such as fighting "devil worshipping" Pagans) that they
hope will bring them more recognition and congregants. In this way,
many evangelical ministers resemble politicians.

Thus, ambitious politicians and religious leaders have worked in
tandem to offer attractive religious "products" to the American people.
And, in an increasingly frightening world fraught with domestic problems and international terrorism, many Americans have sought solace in
the certainties of faith. Thus, the purveyors of an attractive product and
people in search of comforting certainties in an uncertain world have
come together to create a situation in which it can be difficult or even

dangerous to be "other," because the very existence of a growing "other" can be seen as calling into question the privileges and comforts thus engendered. By actively, or even passively, challenging the world thus created, those who are perceived as "other" can also be perceived as the enemy. This is encouraged by the role that the devil plays in evangelical thought (Cookson, 1997, 729–730). This potential has been further encouraged by recent anti-American violence perpetrated by a radical Islamic minority that has acted in ways that can make all Muslims seem to be the "enemy." From this, it is a small step to seeing all non-Christians as potentially violent and threatening.

What can minority religions do about this? Very little, except to try to educate the majority and organize for the defense of those who are persecuted for religious reasons. It helps to make contact with Christian leaders and pursue ecumenical movements. But, in the final analysis, there will always be persons who use their dominant religious status to force conformity or to persecute "the other" and there is little that adherents to minority religions can do about that fact. The courts have proven the most effective recourse for many, but not all problems lend themselves to litigation. Although there are some signs of an increasing acceptance of minority religions' right to exist, it will be a long time before this can be translated into electoral or legislative power. In the meantime, despite the casual good will of a majority of Christians, there will always be those who use their Christian privilege to oppress minority religious practitioners and to try to convert them and, more importantly, their children. Being Christian (or at least Jewish) will continue to be a prerequisite for higher political office. America may tout itself as a land of religious freedom, but for some people who wish to practice non-Christian religions, their attempts to reap the benefits of this ideal will thrust them into a battlefield. In the United States the majority rules and that majority is Christian.

NOTES

1   The Historical and Legal Context

1. Newsom (2001) in a carefully documented argument avers that America is a Protestant empire.
2. For example, Maryland, Massachusetts, North Carolina, Pennsylvania, South Carolina, and Tennessee.
3. The others were Carolina, Delaware, Pennsylvania, and Rhode Island.
4. Also see: *Cherokee Nation v. Georgia*, 30 U.S. 1 (1830) and *Worcester v. Georgia*, 31 U.S. 515 (1832).
5. For a dramatic presentation of the Native American point of view see: Savage (1993).
6. Justice Brennan, writing for himself, Justices Marshall, and Blackmun.
7. Anti-peyote laws had been passed as part of "the federal government's turn-of-the-century holy war against 'superstition' among the Indian tribes of the southwest." Also, peyote is seldom used recreationally, because its use makes people sick (Karst, 1994, 341, 349).
8. At the time of this writing, these include Alaska, Kansas, Massachusetts, Maine, Minnesota, Montana, Oregon, and Washington. The tests instituted by these courts vary in details, but the essential elements of all are those of the *Sherbert* test.
9. The history and religious beliefs of contemporary Pagans are greatly varied and could more than fill many entire books. Because the overwhelming majority of the illustrations to be used later in this book concern Witchcraft or Wicca, the emphasis will be on this particular segment which currently represents the most numerous segment of the contemporary Pagan movement.

2   The Emerging Pagan Movement in America

1. Because many Christians tend to refer to non-Christian religions (with the usual exception of Judaism) as "pagan," this word needs to be defined. In this book, "Pagan" will refer to a group of religions that arose in the mid-twentieth century and drew primarily (although not exclusively) on ancient European and Middle Eastern religions for their inspiration. It is capitalized in keeping with traditional usage; but also to differentiate it from the more general use of the word "pagan."

2. But, some groups do encourage certain forms of political activity by their members. Most common among Pagans is a concern about environmental policy.

3. A notable recent attempt to present a relatively sophisticated study of Wicca can be found in Fisher (2002). Another source is DiZerga (2001).

4. Many Pagans have "magical" names with particular spiritual significance to them. These names can change as their spiritual paths unfold. Since many Pagan authors write under their magical names, these changes can be a problem. Thus, Otter G'Zell, a prolific writer, has a name that has undergone several changes over the years. I use the name that was associated with him when a particular book or article was written.

5. Witchcraft can also be referred to as Wicca. The use of Wicca as a label avoids the negative connotations that Witchcraft carries. In this book, the two are used synonymously. It should be noted, however, that Pagans do not necessarily use them synonymously. Many Pagans make a distinction between Witchcraft and Wicca, but there is a considerable controversy about this distinction and the exact differences between what the two terms denote and connote.

6. Aidan Kelly's position is most extreme on this point. He asserts (1991, x): "I call all Pagan Witches Gardnerian Witches, because, as far as I can tell, all the current activity derives from widespread imitating of Gardnerian practices, and from no other source. There are a few covens around that predated Gardner, but they had an utterly different theology from what the Gardnerians propose; objectively, they are not practicing the same religion." There are those who question whether the New Forest coven ever existed (Adler, 1986, 60–66; Hutton, 1999, 205–240; Kelly, 1991, but see "Robert," 1990; Valiente, 1991, 29). Whatever its sources, however, the influence of Gerald Gardner shaped Paganism in a decisive way.

7. A list, including the most important of these, was compiled by Otter G'Zell and can be found in G'Zell (1991, 2).

8. This refers to Pagan organizations that maintained some public visibility. There is no way to identify the leadership characteristics of the many Pagan groups that avoided publicity or were too small to have much recognition beyond a local area. Also, many Pagans were secretive because they feared persecution.

9. During the 1980s and 1990s, there was a considerable growth of Pagan groups that are composed exclusively of women. Many, though far from all, are lesbian in orientation. A leading figure in the lesbian, feminist part of the movement is Zsuzsanna Budapest, who claims to be a hereditary Hungarian Witch and who practices and writes about the Dianic tradition of Witchcraft (Adler, 1986, 121–125; Budapest, 1989, 52–58).

10. It is very difficult to get a head count on people who tend to hide their religious identity because of a fear of persecution. Most counts are based on factors, such as attendance at Pagan festivals and other events, as well as subscriptions to Pagan journals (www.ReligiousTolerance.org) These sources, and others, indicate that Paganism, in its many forms, may be one of the fastest growing contemporary religious movements (American

Religious Identification Survey, 2001; Pagan Population Estimates, undated; Tifiulcrum, 2003–2004).

11. This estimate is based on the membership of several organizations, as well as attendance at various pagan festivals and other events.

12. A deity Doreen Valiente charmingly called "Old Horny" (Valiente, 1991, 30).

13. Some would place a great deal of emphasis on bloodlines and racial heritage. These, however, do not want to be identified as racist, but rather as "racialist." This distinction may be hard to grasp for those on the outside (Adler, 1986, 278).

14. This is much the same problem faced by followers of Wicca who think that the words "witch" and "witchcraft" must be cleansed of their lurid, Inquisition-defined associations and reclaimed as benign labels of followers of a harmless nature religion.

15. Recently, as scholarship on this period of history has evolved, there has been some effort among Pagans to introduce more historical accuracy (e.g. Gibbons, 1999).

16. For example, the Church of All Worlds (inspired by Robert Heinlein's *Stranger in a Strange Land*) got its 501 (c)(3) rating from the U.S. Internal Revenue Service on March 4, 1968. On this basis, it claims to be "the first of the new Pagan religions to become officially recognized in this country, if not in the world" (G'Zell, 1988a, 2). Many Witchcraft traditions, of course, trace their roots back to Gardner or, in the case of family traditional covens, even further back in history.

3   The Challenge of Christian Hegemony

1. According to the Witches Anti-Discrimination League (WADL, 1998–1999, 6), this particular wording dates back to the King James Version of the Bible. In previous translations, the passage had read: "Thou shall not suffer a poisoner to live." That translation had led to the persecution of Jews when they were blamed for outbreaks of death and disease. The Witches Anti-Discrimination League transformed into the Alternative Religions Educational Network as of January 1, 2000. In this book, citations to this organization before the transformation will be to WADL and after the transformation to AREN.

2. In the Revised Standard Version of the Bible that was issued in 1952, Exod. 22:18 is translated: "You shall not permit a Sorceress to live." Thus, it is clear that those who quote this passage tend to choose their English translations with an agenda.

3. "A written or drawn pentacle is called a pentagram" (Guiley, 1989, 265). For purposes of this discussion, the two words are treated as synonyms.

4. Now that both the Church of Satan and the Temple of Set can recruit through their websites, it is difficult to know how reliable this estimate is.

5. Here and subsequently in this book, I use information gathered via personal communications and online religious rights lists. Except where there was wide media coverage, for purposes of privacy, confidentiality, and

personal safety, I do not identify the Pagan participants or the location of the incident.

6. As of 2002, the case had concluded and Rev. Thompson was serving another congregation in a distant state.

7. Subsequently, Rev. Falwell apologized on his website. But, although he called his remarks "insensitive, uncalled for at the time, and unnecessary," he did not say that they were wrong.

8. For examples of initiation rituals in which nudity is involved see Adler (1986, 94–98) and Starhawk (1989, 172–177).

9. In re: Application of Rosemary Kooiman to Celebrate the Rites of Matrimony, Nineteenth Judicial Circuit of Virginia, May 29, 1998.

10. Also see e.g. Lash (1998).

4   Paganism as a Religion

1. Most notably, President George W. Bush who stated that Wicca was not a religion and, thus, would not be eligible for public funding of its faith-based charities (Mueller, Summer 2001, 38–39).

2. Note the unexamined assumption of monotheism that continues to dominate the public arena whenever the subject of religion is broached.

3. For a more detailed discussion of these different orientations, as well as the way they seem to blur together for some Pagans, see DiZerga (2001, 3–24).

4. There is some movement in this direction, notably Cherry Hill Seminary that offers most of its curriculum online. It currently falls far short of a fully fledged theological seminary.

5. See chapter 1, 23.

6. Subsequent to the events to be discussed below, the Sacred Well Congregation issued an extensive pamphlet discussing the philosophy and practice of Wicca in the military (Oringderff and Schaefer, 2001).

7. Currently, Muslims are a frequent target.

8. For example, *United States v. Phillips*, 42 M.J. 326 (1995).

9. Hanukkah is also implicated here, but is not discussed in order to prevent undue complexity.

5   The Other: Religious Diversity and the Social Order

1. This topic is covered in more detail in chapter 7.

2. Currently, this trend is being enthusiastically supported by most Republicans, because devout Christians, particularly fundamentalist Christians, form an important segment of their political base.

3. It is also possible for the constitutional rights of the child to become an issue (Steinberg, 1995–1996).

4. Although the Supreme Court has never explicitly rejected the *Lemon* test, its use in recent years has been overshadowed by other tests proposed by various justices in other cases. Since it has never been clearly rejected, it is used here, because it is helpful in a systematic consideration of the ways in which the courts approach custody cases.

5. Although Jews are a minority religious group and face many of the same problems as other minority religious groups, they are amply represented in the legal profession and, thus, a sympathetic and knowledgeable Jewish lawyer is much more likely to be available than is the case with most other minority religions.

6. *Neely v. Neely*, 737 S.W.2d 539 (1987); *Baker v. Baker*, 1997 Tenn. App. LEXIS 837. In both of these cases, the parents were of different Christian sects and the courts found that the children could be exposed to both sects. Also see Smith (1996).

7. Although in some states they can be made by a jury (e.g. Drobac, 1997).

8. Since this case was not widely publicized in the media, both the name of the state and the names of the people involved are not used in order to protect their privacy. The source of the information is a series of communications via E-mail during the spring of 1997. The same applies to the other cases discussed without source attribution in this book.

9. According to an Internet source, the teacher was operated on for appendicitis and recovered normally.

10. Since two of these incidents took place overtly in a class, one wonders about the presence and role of the teachers in charge of the classes.

11. Public libraries have also had problems.

12. He was apparently paraphrasing Massimo Introvigne of the Center for Studies on New Religions in Turin, Italy.

13. And, it should be noted, there are many teenagers whose families are Pagan and who have been raised in that tradition.

14. Currently some Muslim women are having problems acquiring motor vehicle licenses and other forms of official identification containing photographs, because they consider hair and/or some parts of the face to be a "private part." Thus, they maintain that removing a hair covering or a partial facial covering would be a violation of Muslim doctrine (e.g. *The Washington Post*, June 7, 2003).

15. Definitions of what constitutes a "public place" vary considerably, both in statutes and in their interpretation by state and local authorities.

16. This suggests that he would find completely private Pagan rituals and clothing-optional events sufficiently immoral to be constitutionally banned by law. The standard of morality applied would, of course, be Christian, not Pagan.

17. Beltane is one of the eight major holidays in the Pagan religious calendar. It celebrates the coming of summer and is intended to insure the fertility of the fields during the growing season.

18. There are reports of Christians traveling considerable distances to place themselves in a situation to be offended by nudity and, thus, to be able to file a complaint.

19. The previous year a large number of Christians had showed up to protest against Paganism, but there were no plans to repeat the protest for this festival.

20. Interestingly, on the same day Mrs. Eicher was suspended the County Commissioners voted to post the Ten Commandments in all public schools.

6 Threats, Intimidation, and the Strategic Use of Fear

1. This stance will be explored at more length in chapter 7.
2. The official figures on (www.eeoc.gov) indicate a somewhat smaller, but definite, increase between 2001 and 2002. Press releases at the same website also tend to support an increase in Muslim complaints.
3. This is the same school district in which Crystal Seifferly attended the high school and was suspended for wearing a pentacle.
4. At the time of this writing, this case is still pending.
5. The retired man was a widower. He and his first wife had become estranged from the daughter while the daughter's mother was still alive, an event that took place 16 years before the incidents being described here.
6. Crosses have also been burned at Muslim locations, including a mosque and Islamic school in Maryland (*The Washington Post*, July 25, 2003). In this case, the police seemed to be taking the cross-burning seriously as a hate crime.
7. The rest were spirited out by other wedding participants who saw and understood what was happening.

7 Christian Privilege and the Perception of Entitlement

1. In 1993, this city ordinance was struck down by the Supreme Court on the grounds that it was an unconstitutional targeting of a particular religion.
2. The full text can be found on numerous websites, including (www.helpsaveamerica.com/repentence.htm).
3. One of my children was taught creationism in a biology class in Columbia, MD, a community that was expressly built to encourage and nurture diversity. At the child's request, I did not make an issue of it. Eventually the teacher left, but not until she had taught creationism instead of evolution to biology students for two years.
4. For a complete list of the religious "acts and customs" of that school district, see chapter 5, 127.
5. Citing *The New Republic*, March 30, 1998, 11.
6. The use of the terms "Satanism" and "devil worshipper" can provoke fear and nightmares in children and older susceptible people. It can also make both adults and children consider that conversion to Christianity will make their lives more tolerable and bring a higher degree of safety. They will "belong"; they will be "real Americans."
7. The quote is from an affidavit by Professor Thomas P. Kasulis, the chair of the Division of Comparative Studies at The Ohio State University.

8 Majoritarianism and Religion

1. Good Friday is a holiday in many states.
2. Most Americans regard "Yule" (which falls on the winter solstice) and "Christmas" as synonyms, but Pagans do not. They are distinct holidays, except that one brings a day off from work (for most) and the other does not.

3. Here, he had in mind such issues as the diversion of local resources away from public schools and toward private schools. Since this was written, however, such religious divisiveness threatens to extend to the national level with the current political push toward such programs as government funding for services rendered by "faith-based" programs.

4. This survey was limited to white evangelicals. This is not a problem because the evangelical Christians discussed in this book were, insofar as it could be ascertained, all Caucasian.

REFERENCES

Ackerman, B. A., "Beyond *Carolene* Products." 98 *Harvard Law Review* 713 (1985).

Adams, J. E., "New Religions Creating Tax Exemption Cases," *St. Louis Post-Dispatch*, April 7, 1972, as reproduced in # 47, 5 *Green Egg* [inside front cover] (1972).

Adler, M., *Drawing Down the Moon*, rev. ed. Boston, MA: Beacon Press, 1986.

Allport, G. W., "Behavioral Science, Religion, and Mental Health." 2 *Journal of Religion and Health* 187 (1963).

——, "The Religious Context of Prejudice." 5 *Journal for the Scientific Study of Religion* 447 (1966).

Allport, G. W. and Ross, J. M., "Personal Religious Orientation and Prejudice." 5 *Journal of Personal and Social Psychology* 432 (1967).

American Religious Identification Survey (www.ge.cuny.edu/studies/key_findings.htm) 2001.

Andolina, M. W. and Wilcox, C., "Stealth Politics: Religious and Moral Issues in the 2000 Election." In Segers, M. C. (ed.). *Piety, Politics, and Pluralism: Religion and Courts, and the 2000 Election.* Lanham, MD: Rowman & Littlefield Publishers, Inc., 2002.

Avery, S., "Neo-Pagan Communal Authorship, Poetic Form, and the Charge of the Goddess." 72 *Circle Network News* 35 (1999).

Ball, M. S., "Normal Religion in America." 4 *Notre Dame Journal of Law, Ethics and Public Policy* 397 (1990).

Banner, S., "When Christianity Was Part of the Common Law." 16 *Law and History Review* 27 (1998).

Bannon, J. T., "The Legality of the Religious Use of Peyote by the Native American Church: A Commentary on the Free Exercise, Equal Protection, and Establishment Issues Raised by the Peyote Way Church of God Case." 22 *American Indian Law Review* 475 (1997).

Barrette, E., "Church of Ozark Avalon Wins Property Tax Case!" #31 *PanGaia* 44 (2002).

Bartley, S. B., "The Kenton Inquisition, Part II." *YAPN Quarterly* 19 (Lughnassadh, 1995).

Baugh, R. R., "Applying the Bill of Rights to the States: A Response to William P. Gray, Jr." 49 *Alabama Law Review* 551 (1998).

Bell, E. N. V., "Constitutional Law-Establishment Clause—Is the Ohio State Motto, 'With God, All Things Are Possible,' Compatible with the First and Fourteenth Amendments?" 68 *Tennessee Law Review* 933 (2001).

Berger, H. A., *A Community of Witches: Contemporary Neo-Paganism and Witchcraft in the United States*. Columbia, SC: University of South Carolina Press, 1999.

Berger, P., *The Goddess Obscured: Transformation of the Grain Protectress from Goddess to Saint*. Boston, MA: Beacon Press, 1985.

Berman, H. J., "Religion and Law: The First Amendment in Historical Perspective." 35 *Emory Law Journal* 777 (1986).

Binder, G. and Wisberg, R., "Cultural Criticism of Law." 49 *Stanford Law Review* 1149 (1997).

Boyles, K. L., "Saving Sacred Sites: The 1989 Proposed Amendment to the American Indian Religious Freedom Act." 76 *Cornell Law Review* 1117 (1991).

Bradley, M. Z., *The Mists of Avalon*. New York, NY: Ballantine Books, 1982.

Brant, J. C., " 'Our Shield Belongs to the Lord': Religious Employers and a Constitutional Right to Discriminate." 21 *Hastings Constitutional Law Quarterly* 275 (1994).

Brewer, M. B., "The Many Faces of Social Identity: Implications for Political Psychology." 22 *Political Psychology* 115 (2001).

Budapest, Z., *The Holy Book of Women's Mysteries*. Berkeley, CA: Wingbow Press, 1989.

Campbell, J., *The Power of Myth*. New York, NY: Doubleday, 1988.

Carter S. L., "Symposium: Michael J. Perry's *Morality, Politics, and Law*: The Dissent of the Governors." 63 *Tulane Law Review* 1325 (1989).

Chapin-Bishop, C., "Out of the Broom Closet with Quiet Dignity and Grace." 2 *Tides* 35 (1993).

"Circle of the Winter Moon, Charge of Union," 112 *Green Egg* [inside front cover] (1996).

Cohen, J. L., "Strategy or Identity: New Theoretical Paradigms and Contemporary Social Movements." 52 *Social Research* 663 (1985).

Conkle, D. O., "Different Religions, Different Politics: Evaluating the Role of Competing Religious Traditions in American Politics and Law." 10 *Journal of Law and Religion* 1 (1993–1994).

——, "Symposium: Free Exercise, Federalism, and the States as Laboratories." 21 *Cardozo Law Review* 493 (1999).

——, "The Free Exercise Clause: How Redundant and Why?" 33 *Loyola University Chicago Law Journal* 95 (2001).

Cookson, C., "Reports from the Trenches: A Case Study of Religious Freedom Issues Faced by Wiccans Practicing in the United States." 39 *Journal of Church and State* 723 (1997).

——, *Regulating Religion: The Courts and the Free Exercise Clause*. New York, NY: Oxford University Press, 2001.

Cordish, M. F., "A Proposal for the Reconciliation of Free Exercise Rights and Anti Discrimination Law." 43 *UCLA Law Review* 2113 (1996).

Crane, D. A., "Beyond RFRA: Free Exercise of Religion Comes of Age in the State Courts." 10 *St. Thomas Law Review* 235 (1998).

Cuhulain, K., *Law Enforcement Guide to Wicca*. Victoria, Canada: Horned Owl Publishing, 1992.

DiZerega, G., *Pagans and Christians: The Personal Spiritual Experience*. St. Paul, MN: Llewellyn Publications, 2001.

Donovan, J. M., "God Is as God Does: Law, Anthropology, and the Definition of 'Religion'." 6 *Constitutional Law Journal* 23 (1995).

Drobac, J. A., "Demonized Women: Accused Witches in Recent Child Custody Cases." Legal Studies Colloquium (www-leland.stanford.edu/class/law495/drobac.htm) April 4, 1997.

———, "For the Sake of the Children: Court Consideration of Religion in Child Custody Cases." 50 *Stanford Law Review* 1609 (1998).

Duckitt, J., "Prejudice and Intergroup Hostility." In Sears, D. O., Huddy, L. and Jervis, R. (eds.). *Oxford Handbook of Political Psychology*. New York, NY: Oxford University Press, 2003.

Duncan, J. R. Jr., "Commentary: Privilege, Invisibility, and Religion: A Critique of the Privilege that Christianity Has Enjoyed in the United States." 54 *Alabama Law Review* 617 (2003).

Dussias, A. M., "Ghost Dance and Holy Ghost: The Echoes of Nineteenth-Century Christianization Policy in Twentieth-Century Native American Free Exercise Cases." 49 *Stanford Law Review* 773 (1997).

Eck, D. L., *A New Religious America*. San Francisco, CA: Harper San Francisco, 2001.

Eilers, D. D., "The Crystal Siefferly Case: Anatomy of a Lawsuit." 31 *Green Egg* 20 (1999).

———, *Pagans and the Law: Understand Your Rights*. Franklin Lakes, NJ: New Page Books, 2003.

Eisler, R., *The Chalice and the Blade: Our History, Our Future*. San Francisco, CA: Harper San Francisco, 1987.

Epstein, L. and Walker, T. G., *Constitutional Law for a Changing America: Rights, Liberties, and Justice*, third ed. Washington, DC: Congressional Quarterly Press, 1998.

Epstein, S. B., "Rethinking the Constitutionality of Ceremonial Deism." 96 *Columbia Law Review* 2083 (1996).

Esser, W. L., "Religious Hybrids in the Lower Courts: Free Exercise Plus or Constitutional Smoke Screen?" 74 *Notre Dame Law School* 211 (1998).

Farrar, J. and Farrar, S., *A Witches Bible Compleat*. New York, NY: Magickal Childe Publishing, Inc., 1984.

Feagan, J. R., "Prejudice and Religious Types: A Focused Study of Southern Fundamentalists." 4 *Journal for the Scientific Study of Religion* 3 (1964).

Feldman, S., "Enforcing Social Conformity: A Theory of Authoritarianism." 24 *Political Psychology* 41 (2003).

Feldman, S. and Stenner, K., "Perceived Threat and Authoritarianism." 18 *Political Psychology* 741 (1997).

Feldman, S. M., "Principle, History, and Power: The Limits of the First Amendment Religion Clauses." 81 *Iowa Law Review* 833 (1996).

———, *Please Don't Wish Me a Merry Christmas: A Critical History of the Separation of Church and State*. New York, NY: New York University Press, 1997.

Feofanov, D. N., "Defining Religion: An Immodest Proposal." 23 *Hofstra Law Review* 309 (1994).

Fisher, A. L., *Philosophy of Wicca*. Montreal, Canada: ECW Press, 2002.

Freeman, B. A., "Trends in First Amendment Jurisprudence." 66 *Missouri Law Review* 9 (2001).

Freeman, L. D., "The Child's Best Interests vs. the Parent's Free Exercise of Religion." 32 *Columbia Journal of Law and Social Problems* 73 (1998).

Frew, D. H., "A Brief History of Satanism." In G'Zell, O. (ed.). *Witchcraft, Satanism and Occult Crime: Who's Who and What's What*, fourth ed. Ukiah, CA: Green Egg, 1991, 3–4.

Friedelbaum, S. H., "Free Exercise in the States: Belief, Conduct, and Judicial Benchmarks." 63 *Albany Law Review* 1059 (2000).

Furth, A. D., "Comment: Secular Idolatry and Sacred Traditions: A Critique of the Supreme Court's Secularization Analysis." 146 *University of Pennsylvania Law Review* 579 (1998).

Gadon, E., *The Once and Future Goddess: A Symbol for Our Time*. New York, NY: Harper and Row, 1989.

Gardner, G. B., *The Meaning of Witchcraft*. New York, NY: Samual Weiser, 1959.

Gecas, V., "The Self-Concept." 8 *Annual Review of Sociology* 1 (1982).

Gedicks, F. M., "The Normalized Free Exercise Clause: Three Abnormalities." 75 *Indiana Law Journal* 77 (2000).

Gey, S. G., "When is Religious Speech not 'Free Speech'?" 2000 *University of Illinois Law Review* 379 (2000).

——, "'Under God,' The Pledge of Allegiance, and Other Constitutional Trivia." 81 *North Carolina Law Review* 1865 (2003).

Gibbons, J., "The Great European Witch Hunt." 21 *PanGaia* 25 (1999).

Giddens, A., *Modernity and Self-Identity: Self and Society in the Late Modern Age*. Cambridge: Polity, 1991.

Gilden, G. S., "A Blessing in Disguise: Protecting Minority Faiths through Stat Religious Freedom Non-Restoration Acts." 23 *Harvard Journal of Law and Public Policy* 411 (2000).

Gimbutas, M., *The Goddesses and Gods of Old Europe: Myths and Cult Images*. Berkeley, CA: University of California Press, 1982.

Gordon, J. D., "The New Free Exercise Clause." 26 *Capital University Law Review* 65 (1997).

Goodrich, N. L., *Priestesses*. New York, NY: HarperCollins Publishers, 1990.

Gray, W. P. Jr., "The Ten Commandments and the Ten Amendments: A Case Study in Religious Freedom in Alabama." 49 *Alabama Law Review* 509 (1998a).

——, "'We the People' or 'We the Judges': A Reply to Robert R. Baugh's Response." 49 *Alabama Law Review* 607 (1998b).

Green, S. K., "Justice David Josiah Brewer and the 'Christian Nation' Maxim." 63 *Albany Law Review* 427 (1999).

Greenawalt, K., "Religion as a Concept in Constitutional Law." 72 *California Law Review* 753 (1984).

——, "Religious Convictions and Political Choice: Some Further Thoughts." 39 *DePaul Law Review* 1019 (1990).

Greenberg, A. and Berktold, J., *Re: Evangelicals in America*. Washington, DC: Greenberg, Quinlan, Rosner Research, Inc., 2004.

Griffen, W. L., "The Case for Religious Values in Judicial Decision-Making." 81 *Marquette Law Review* 513 (1998).

Guiley, R. E., *The Encyclopedia of Witches and Witchcraft*. New York, NY: Facts on File, Inc., 1989.

G'Zell, O., "An Editorial History: 'It was 20 Years Ago Today . . .' " 81 *Green Egg* 2 (1988a).

——, "Theagenesis: The Birth of the Goddess." 81 *Green Egg* 4 (1988b).

——, "Lost Legacy." 22 *Green Egg* 20 (1989).

——, "Happy New Decade!" 88 *Green Egg* 2 (1990).

——, "Men and the Goddess." 94 *Green Egg* 2 (1991).

Hammond, P. E., *Liberty for All: Freedom of Religion in the United States*. Louisville, KY: Westminster John Knox Press, 1998.

Hayes, R., "Lady Liberty League Report." 3 *Circle Network News* 7 (1996).

Hodson, T., "The Religious Employer Exception under Title VII: Should a Church Define Its Own Activities?" 1994 *Brigham Young University Law Review* 571 (1994).

Huddy, L., "From Social to Political Identity: A Critical Examination of Social Identity Theory." 22 *Political Psychology* 127 (2001).

Hunsberger, B., "Religion and Prejudice: The Role of Religious Fundamentalism, Quest, and Right-Wing Authoritarianism." 51 *Journal of Social Issues* 113 (1995).

Hutton, R., *The Triumph of the Moon: A History of Modern Pagan Witchcraft*. New York: Oxford University Press, 1999.

Idleman, S. C., "The Limits of Religious Values in Judicial Decision Making." 81 *Marquette Law Review* 537 (1998).

International Clergy Association, Monterey, CA. *Marriage Laws of the Various States* (www.tangledmoon.org/marriage-laws.htm) 1999.

Karst, K. L., "Paths to Belonging: The Constitution and Cultural Identity." 64 *North Carolina Law Review* 303 (1986).

——, "The First Amendment, the Politics of Religion and the Symbols of Government." 27 *Harvard Civil Rights-Civil Liberties Law Review* 503 (1992).

——, "Religious Freedom and Equal Citizenship: Reflections on *Lukumi*." 69 *Tulane Law Review* 335 (1994).

Kasparian, F. D., "The Constitutionality of Teaching and Performing Sacred Choral Music in Public Schools." 46 *Duke Law Journal* 1111 (1997).

Kelly, A. A., *Crafting the Art of Magic: A History of Modern Witchcraft, 1939–1964*. St. Paul, MN: Llewellyn Publications, 1991.

Killen, R., "Note: The Achilles' Heel of Dress Codes: The Definition of Proper Attire in Public Schools." 36 *Tulsa Law Journal* 459 (2000).

Kordas, A., "Note: Losing My Religion: Controlling Gang Violence Through Limitations on Freedom of Expression." 80 *Boston University Law Review* 1451 (2000).

Lash, K. T., "Power and the Subject of Religion." 59 *Ohio State Law Journal* 1069 (1998).

Laycock, D., "The Remnants of Free Exercise." 1990 *Supreme Court Review* 1 (1990).

LaVey, A. S., "The Eleven Satanic Rules of the Earth" (http://www.coscentral. net/cos/Pages/Eleven.html) 1967.

Lovelock, J. E., *Gaia: A New Look at Life on Earth*. New York, NY: Oxford University Press, 1979.

———, "Gaia: A Model for Planetary and Cellular Dynamics." In Thompson, W. I. (ed.). *Gaia: A Way of Knowing: Political Implications of the New Biology*. Great Barrington, MA: The Lindisfearne Press, 1987.

———, *The Ages of Gaia: A Biography of our Living Earth*. New York, NY: Norton, 1988.

Lurmann, T. M., *Persuasions of the Witch's Craft: Ritual Magic in Contemporary England*. Cambridge, MA: Harvard University Press, 1989.

Lupu, I. C., "The Case Against Legislative Codification of Religious Liberty." 21 *Cardozo Law Review* 565 (1999).

Manner, J., "Pastors Discuss Pagan Strategy" (www.smithfieldtimes.com/ TIMEST-1.HTM) November 1, 2000.

Marshall, W. P., " 'We Know it When We See It': The Supreme Court and Establishment." 59 *Southern California Law Review* 495 (1986).

———, "In Defense of Smith and Free Exercise Revisionism." 58 *University of Chicago Law Review* 308 (1991).

———, "Religion as Ideas: Religion as Identity." 7 *Journal of Contemporary Legal Issues* 385 (1996).

McConnell, M. W., "Free Exercise Revisionism and the *Smith* Decision." 57 *University of Chicago Law Review* 1109 (1990a).

———, "The Origins and Historical Understanding of Free Exercise of Religion." 103 *Harvard Law Review* 1410 (1990b).

Mead, G. H., *The Philosophy of the Present*. Lasalle, IL: Open Court Publishing, 1959.

Members, Spindletop CUUPS, Letter, 36 *SageWoman* 87 (1996).

Merry, S. E., "Culture, Power, and the Discourse of Law." 37 *New York Law School Law Review* 209 (1992).

Metz, K., "Book Note: Turning Religion's Shield into a Sword." 108 *Yale Law Journal* 271 (1998).

Miller, A. S., *Gaia Connections: An Introduction to Ecology, Ecoethics, and Economics*. Savage, MD: Rowman & Littlefield, 1991.

Miller, G. M., "Balancing the Welfare of Children with the Rights of Parents: Petersen v. Rogers and the Role of Religion in Custody Decisions." 73 *North Carolina Law Review* 1271 (1995).

Modak-Truran, M., "The Religious Dimension of Judicial Decision Making and the De Facto Disestablishment." 81 *Marquette Law Review* 255 (1998).

Moen, M. C., "School Prayer and the Politics of Life-Style Concern." 65 *Social Science Quarterly* 1065 (1995).

Mueller, D. F., "Paganalia: Faith-Based Outrage." 9 *Connections* 38 (Summer, 2001).

———, "Paganalia: Earth as Temple." 9 *Connections* 40 (Winter, 2001).

Mykkeltvedt, R., "*Employment Division v. Smith*: Creating Anxiety by Relieving Tension." 58 *Tennessee Law Review* 603 (1991).

Nash, R., *Wilderness and the American Mind*. New Haven, CT: Yale University Press, 1967.

Newcomb, S. T., "The Evidence of Christian Nationalism in Federal Indian Law: The Doctrine of Discovery, *Johnson v. McIntosh*, and Plenary Power." 20 *Review of Law and Social Change* 303 (1993).

Newsom, M. deH., "The American Protestant Empire: A Historical Perspective." 40 *Washburn Law Journal* 187 (2001).

———, "Common School Religion: Judicial Narratives in a Protestant Empire." 11 *Southern California Interdisciplinary Law Journal* 219 (2002).

New Member's Guide. Ár nDraíocht Féin: A Druid Fellowship, Inc., 1990.

Nimmo, D. and Combs, J. E., *Subliminal Politics: Myths and Mythmakers in America*. Englewood Cliffs, NJ: Prentice-Hall, 1980.

Note. "Reinterpreting the Religion Clauses: Constitutional Construction and Conceptions of the Self." 97 *Harvard Law Review* 1468 (1984).

Note. "Developments in the Law—Religion and the State: I. Introduction." 100 *Harvard Law Review* 1609 (1987a).

Note. "Developments in the Law—Religion and the State: The Complex Interaction between Religion and Government." 100 *Harvard Law Review* 1612 (1987b).

Note. "Developments in the Law—Religion and the State: III Accommodations of Religion in Public Institutions." 100 *Harvard Law Review* 1639 (1987c).

Oringderff, D. L. and Schaefer, R. W., *Spiritual Philosophy and Practice of Wicca in the U.S. Military*. Converse, TX: The Sacred Well Congregation, 2001.

Orion, L., *Never Again the Burning Times: Paganism Revived*. Prospect Heights, IL: Waveland Press, Inc., 1995.

Pagan Population Estimates (www.paganpride.org/lc/paganpop.html) undated.

Perry, M. J., *Religion in Politics: Constitutional and Moral Perspectives*. New York, NY: Oxford University Press, 1997.

———, "Liberal Democracy and Religious Morality." 48 *DePaul Law Review* 1 (1998).

Post, R., "Law and Cultural Conflict." U.C. Berkeley School of Law, Public Law and Legal Theory Research Paper No. 120, 2003.

Ream, J. M., "Operating With Immunity." 9 (1) *PagaNet News* 1 (2002).

Reber, A. S., *The Penguin Dictionary of Psychology*. London: Penguin Books, 1995.

Reynolds, L., "Zoning the Church: The Police Power Versus the First Amendment." 64 *Boston University Law Review* 767 (1985).

Robert, "Gerald Brosseau Gardner," 23 *Green Egg* 14 (1990).

Robinson, B. (ed.), *Religious Discrimination in U.S. State Constitutions*. Ontario, Canada: Ontario Consultants on Religious Tolerance (www.religioustolerance.org) 2000.

Rogers, J., "Witchcraft and Satanism: Are they One and the Same?" (http://forerunner.com/champion/X0044_Witchcraft_and_Satan.html) 1999a.

———, "Statements of a practicing witch?" (http://forerunner.com/champion/X0041_Statements_of_a_prac.html) 1999b.

Rosenberg, E., " 'Native Americans' Access to Religious Sites: Underprotected Under the Free Exercise Clause?" 26 *Boston College Law Review* 463 (1985).

Rowan, J., "The Horned God: Why the Wildman is not Enough." 24 *Green Egg* 4 (1991).

Rowan, J., *The Horned God: Feminism and Men as Wounding and Healing.* London: Routledge and Kegan Paul, 1987.

Rozell, M. J., "The Christian Right in the 2000 GOP Presidential Campaign." In Segers, M. C. (ed.). *Piety, Politics and Pluralism: Religion, the Courts, and the 2000 Election.* Lanham, MD: Rowman and Littlefield Publishers, Inc., 2002.

Ryan J. E., "*Smith* and the Religious Freedom Restoration Act: An Iconoclastic Assessment." 78 *Virginia Law Review* 1407 (1992).

Salmons, D. B., "Toward a Fuller Understanding of Religious Exercise: Recognizing the Identity Generative and Expressive Nature of Religious Devotion." 62 *The University of Chicago Law Review* 1243 (1995).

Sanchez, V. C., "Whose God is it Anyway?: The Supreme Court, The Orishas, and Grandfather Peyote." 28 *Suffolk University Law Review* 39 (1994).

Savage, M., "The Great Secret about Federal Indian Law—Two Hundred Years in Violation of the Constitution—And the Opinion the Supreme Court Should Have Written to Reveal It." 20 *Review of Law & Social Change* 343 (1993).

Segers, M. C., "Religion and Liberal Democracy: An American Perspective." In Segers, M. C. (ed.). *Piety, Politics, and Pluralism.* Lanham, MD: Rowman & Littlefield Publishers, Inc., 2002.

Sherry. S., "Religion and the Public Square: Making Democracy Safe for Religious Minorities." 47 *DePaul Law Review* 499 (1998).

Shieber, L., "The CAW and Tribalism." 8 *Green Egg* 5 (1975).

Sidanius, J. and Pratto, F., "Social Dominance Theory: A New Synthesis." In Jost, J. T. and Sidanius, J. (ed.). *Political Psychology.* New York, NY: Psychology Press, 2004.

Sigel, R., "An Introduction to the Symposium on Social Identity." 22 *Political Psychology* 111 (2001).

Sisk, G. C., Heise, M. and Morriss, A. P., "Searching for the Soul of Judicial Decisionmaking: An Empirical Study of Religious Freedom Decisions." 65 *Ohio State Law Journal* 491 (2004).

Smith, J. M., " 'Zoned for Residential Uses'—Like Prayer?" 2000 *Brigham Young University Law Review* 1153 (2000).

Smith, K. S., "Religious Visitation Constraints on the Noncustodial Parent." 71 *Indiana Law Journal* 815 (1996).

Smith, S. D., "Legal Discourse and the De Facto Disestablishment." 81 *Marquette Law Review* 203 (1998).

Starhawk, *Truth or Dare: Encounters with Power, Authority, and Mystery.* San Francisco, CA: Harper and Row, Publishers, 1987.

——, *The Spiral Dance: A Rebirth of the Ancient Religion of the Great Goddess*, tenth anniversary ed. San Francisco, CA: Harper and Row, Publishers, 1989.

Staub, E., "Notes on Cultures of Violence, Cultures of Caring and Peace, and the Fulfillment of Basic Human Needs." 24 *Political Psychology* 1 (2003).

Stead, L., "Oppression and Community Identification." Fall issue *Moonrise* 5 (1991).

Stein, S. J., "Religion/Religions in the United States: Changing Perspectives and Prospects." 75 *Indiana Law Journal* 37 (2000).

Steinberg, M., "Free Exercise of Religion: The Conflict Between a Parent's Rights and a Minor Child's Right in Determining the Religion of the Child." 34 *Journal of Family Law* 219 (1995–1996).

Stone, M., *When God Was a Woman*. New York, NY: Harcourt Brace Jovanovich, 1976.

Stormcrow, O., "The Worship of Ah-To San or OTTO: God of the Automobile Underhood, Patron of Mechanics." 94 *Green Egg* 22 (1991).

Story, J., *Commentaries on the Constitution of the United States*. Boston, MA: Hillard, Gray, and Co, 1833.

Stouffer, S. A., *Communism, Civil Liberties, and Conformity*. Garden City, NY: Doubleday, 1955.

Taylor, C., "The Politics of Recognition." In Gutmann, A. (ed.). *Multiculturalism: Examining the Politics of Recognition*. Princeton, NJ: Princeton University Press, 1994, 25–73.

Taylor, J. C., "A Christian Speaks on the Faith and Path of Wicca." (journey1.org/freedom/achristianspeaks.htm) 1999.

Temple of Set (http://www.xeper.org/pub/tos/infoadms.html) 1997–1999.

The Holy Bible (Revised Standard Version). New York, NY: Thomas Nelson Sons, 1952, 1946.

Thiemann, R. F., "Religion and Legal Discourse: An Indirect Relation." 81 *Marquette Law Review* 289 (1998).

Tifiulcrum, S., "Just How Many Are We, Anyway?" 37 *PanGaia* 69 (2003–2004).

Toward a Constitutional Definition of Religion. 91 *Harvard Law Review* 1056 (1978).

Trope, J. F., "Protecting Native American Religious Freedom: The Legal, Historical, and Constitutional Basis for the Proposed Native American Free Exercise of Religion Act." 20 *Review of Law and Social Change* 373 (1993).

Tudor, H., *Political Myth*. New York, NY: Praeger Publishers, 1972.

Tushnet, M., "Of Church and State and the Supreme Court: Kurland Revisited." 1989 *Supreme Court Review* 373 (1989).

———, "The Redundant Free Exercise Clause?" 33 *Loyola University Chicago Law Journal* 71 (2001).

Tuttle, R. W., "Regulating Sacred Space: Religious Institutions and Land Use Controls." 68 *George Washington Law Review* 861 (2000).

Tyner, M. A., "Religious Freedom Issues in Domestic Relations Law." 8 *BYI Journal of Public Law* 457 (1994).

Valiente, E., "Interview." 6 *Firehart* 27 (1991).

Van Alstyne, W., "Trends in the Supreme Court: Mr. Jefferson's Crumbling Wall—A Comment on *Lynch V. Donnelly*." 1984 *Duke Law Journal* 770 (1984).

Victor, J. S., *Satanic Panic: The Creation of a Contemporary Legend*. Chicago, IL: Open Court, 1993.

Volokh, E., "Intermediate Questions of Religious Exemptions—A Research Agenda with Test Suites." 21 *Cardozo Law Review* 595 (1999).

WADL (The Witches Anti-Discrimination League), "Frequently Asked Questions Regarding Wicca/Witchcraft/Paganism." (http://members.tripod.com/~Elderpaths/faq.html) 1998–1999.

Walker, B. G., *The Woman's Dictionary of Symbols and Sacred Objects*. San Francisco, CA: Harper and Row, Publishers, 1988.

Walker, W. C., "Magick n' Mail." (http://www.witchvox.com/cases/dube.html) 1997.

——, "Frequently Asked Questions about Witchcraft, Wicca and Paganism." (http://www.witchvox.com/white/wwfaq.html) 1999.

Warren, C. G., "No Need to Stand on Ceremony: The Corruptive Influence of Ceremonial Deism and the Need for a Separationist Reconfiguration of the Supreme Court's Establishment Clause Jurisprudence." 54 *Mercer Law Review* 1669 (2003).

Wehmeyer, P., "Right to Practice Witchcraft." *ABCNews.com*. October 31, 2000.

Whitaker, B. A., "Religious Music in the Public Schools: A Guide for School Districts." 2003 *Brigham Young University Education and Law Journal* 339 (2003).

Wildman, S. M. and Davis, A. D., "Language and Silence: Making Systems of Privilege Visible." 35 *Santa Clara Law Review* 881 (1995).

Woolger, J. B. and Woolger, R., *The Goddess Within: A Guide to the Eternal Myths that Shape Women's Myths*. New York, NY: Fawcett Columbine, 1989.

Worthen, K. J., "Protecting the Sacred Sites of Indigenous People in U.S. Courts: Reconciling Native American Religion and the Right to Exclude." 13 *St. Thomas Law Review* 239 (2000).

Zell-Ravenheart, O., "The First Unitarian Pagans?" 9 *Connections* 10 (2001).

Index